# The Irish in New Jersey

For Fran and Bill

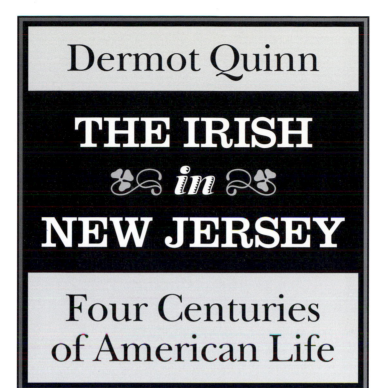

Dermot Quinn

# THE IRISH in NEW JERSEY

## Four Centuries of American Life

with the very best wishes of

*Dermot Quinn*

**RUTGERS UNIVERSITY PRESS**

*New Brunswick, New Jersey, and London*

Library of Congress Cataloging-in-Publication Data

Quinn, Dermot.

The Irish in New Jersey : four centuries of American life / Dermot Quinn.

p. cm.

Includes bibliographical references and index.

ISBN 0-8135-3421-6 (alk. paper)

1. Irish Americans—New Jersey—History. 2. Immigrants—New Jersey—History. 3. New Jersey—Emigration and immigration—History. 4. Ireland—Emigration and immigration—History. 5. New Jersey—Ethnic relations. I. Title.

F145.I6Q56 2004

974.9'0049162—dc22                                                                 2003019799


British Cataloging-in-Publication information for this book is available from the British Library.

Manufactured in the United States of America

*For Brian and Katharine Quinn—lately part of the story*

# Contents

# Acknowledgments

I am happy to acknowledge the many debts incurred in the writing of this book. Michael Glazer, editor of *An Encyclopedia of the Irish in America* (1999), first drew the subject to my attention. His initial promptings were reinforced, with good humor and extraordinary patience, by Marlie Wasserman of Rutgers University Press. Professor Maxine Lurie shared her formidable knowledge of New Jersey history. I am grateful, too, to Professors James McGlone, Joseph Mahoney, John Sweeney, and Ralph Walz, all of Seton Hall University, for their insights into the colorful world of Irish America, and to the deeply knowledgeable Father Augustine Curley of Saint Benedict's, Newark, for his many good suggestions. India Cooper copyedited the manuscript with great skill.

Exceptionally helpful were Professor Alan Delozier and Dr. Kate Dodds of the Seton Hall University archives, daily suppliers of documents and good cheer. Monsignor Francis Seymour, archivist of the Archdiocese of Newark, granted permission to reproduce many of the photographs and documentary images. Thanks are also due to Erika Gorder of Rutgers University Special Collections and Archives for permission to reproduce some of the material in her care. James Lowney allowed me to make use of his substantial private photographic collection, offering delightful (if not always publishable) details of recent New Jersey political and social history. Joe Rush, Joe Garafola, Monsignor Joseph Shenrock, Father Tom Pendrick, Father Patrick Brady, Professor Thomas Hughes, John Connolly, William Quinn, and Maura Harrington graciously granted permission for the use of photographs in their possession. Strenuous efforts were made to establish ownership of material. If by oversight a copyright has been breached, I extend a general apology.

Alneil McLeod, Ron Myzie, and Darius Woloscz helped greatly with scanning of images. The cost of tracing and reproducing photographs was defrayed in part by a grant from the New Jersey Council of the Humanities for which I am most grateful.

As ever, my labors have been greatly eased by the help of Archie and the late Timothy Thomas Quinn.

All mistakes are my own.

*West Orange, New Jersey*
*December 2003*

# The Irish in New Jersey

# Introduction

**N**EW JERSEY is a curious place with a curious history to match. Wedged between New York and Pennsylvania, its southernmost tip below the Mason-Dixon line and its long stretches of coastline opening eastward to the sea, it has always seemed geographically indeterminate as well as socially and politically divided. As a colony, then as a state, it never knew if it should look north, south, east, or west. Looking in all directions, it seemed to lack direction of its own. Early promoters made a virtue of this variety. One spoke of the colony's ideal situation "betwixt the South parts of Carolina, which is over hot, and the North parts of Pemaquitte, which are coldest,"[1] as if it combined the best of all worlds, not the worst. Later writers were unconvinced. Benjamin Franklin is supposed to have dismissed it as a "barrel tapped at both ends," the contents draining toward New York or Philadelphia, leaving dregs behind. As a matter of politics, he had a point. Between 1682 and 1703 there were *two* Jerseys, East and West, reflecting roughly a division between the northwest and southeast parts of the colony. This rule by multiple proprietors, mainly Quakers, ended with the appointment of Edward Hyde, Lord Cornbury, as royal governor in 1703, but thereafter the colony still struggled to achieve real unity. The egregious Cornbury may have had something to do with this. Although it has recently been doubted, he was long thought to have been a transvestite—the perfect personification of a place that was neither one thing nor the other. Whatever the truth of that, ambivalence has defined New Jersey for most of its history. In the Revolutionary period it tended to divide between rebels in the north and Tories in the south. During the Civil War it was frequently and erroneously held to be a Copperhead state—northern in geography, southern in sympathy. In the twentieth century its spreading suburbs suggested a state uneasily combining features of town and country. The place seems doomed to permanent in-betweenness.

This book is about one aspect of New Jersey's oddly misshapen history: the role played by Irish people in the colony and state. As its size testifies, the volume makes

*Edward Hyde, Lord Cornbury, first royal governor of New Jersey, perfect personification of New Jersey's "in-betweenness."*

❧❧

no claim to completeness or comprehensiveness. Within a limited scope, however, I propose to examine the abiding themes of the Irish experience in one part of the New World. One of these is that "Irishness" is a complex category— more complex, certainly, than the fragmentary and disaggregated story of New Jersey itself. The classification "Irish" is impermanent and fragile. It describes no fixed state or settled disposition. Who is Irish? Who is not? What is Irish? What is not? The questions are easier to ask than to answer. At one level, of course, the answer is obvious. "Irish" has to do with Ireland, its people, culture, history, and way of life. Yet deeper difficulties lurk. Ireland's history is contested ground, a bloody arena of competing "Irishnesses." Ireland is home to no single group of people but several, no unified culture but diverse cultures, no decided history but a still fought-over past. For most of its history, Ireland has had a plurality of cultures without pluralism. It has known the arts of war better than those of peace.

New Jersey has been more successful in containing, and eventually celebrating, its divergent people. Yet an ocean away from Ireland it, too, has been marked by that country's conflict. Consider an example from the late nineteenth century. On Saint Patrick's Day 1885 a priest called James McFaul mounted the pulpit of Saint Mary's Cathedral, Trenton, to preach on "Faith and Fatherland." The faith was Catholicism, the fatherland Ireland, and the two, he implied, were so intertwined as to be mutually indistinguishable. "No where in the world is there a more beautiful land or one with . . . a grander history" than Ireland, he asserted. "The Irish were . . . civilized . . . when those who form the modern nations were groveling in barbarism." It was the standard anthem: patriotism as ancient glory, as reminder of past greatness, as exhortation to future grandeur. McFaul's audience knew his song by heart. In different ways they had sung it themselves many times over. But they also knew that no hymn to Ireland was complete without a recitation of its historic woes. Pillaged by Vikings, expropriated by Normans, persecuted by Tudors, starved by all of them, the country still managed to keep alive the flame of faith and nationhood. The more miserable the trial, it seemed, the more magnificent the triumph. In Elizabethan times, Ireland "was reduced to a heap of carcasses and ashes." Under Cromwell, her manhood was butchered. (If Cromwell "hasn't a warm corner" in hell, McFaul charmingly suggested, "I'm inclined to . . . wonder . . . what's the use of it.") In the eighteenth century, the same price "was put on the head of a priest as on that of a wolf." Was it "any wonder that emigration began on such a large scale?" And so it continued. Almost parodying the Irish tradition of exaggerated lamentation, McFaul seemed to offer a funeral dirge with all appropriate accoutrements except a corpse.

Excessively maudlin, the sermon nonetheless contained clues to the Irish American personality, that strange amalgam of pride and prejudice of which the preacher himself was a notable exemplar. The first moral was that "the rising generation of Irish-Americans [should know] what their fathers endured for Faith and Fatherland that they may . . . live and act in America as becomes the children of saints and patriots." Irishness and Catholicism were thus conflated, any evidence to the contrary ignored. Other religious traditions in Ireland—Anglican, Presbyterian, and Dissenting—were less Irish, if Irish at all. Perhaps, indeed, they represented obstacles to nationhood rather than elements of it. The second lesson, not explicitly drawn but surely apparent, was that McFaul's own story shaped his patriotic imagination. Born in 1850 in the strongly Protestant village of Larne in County Antrim, his childhood stories were of sectarian hatred, the 1798 rebellion, the Liberator Daniel O'Connell. He knew what it was like to be in a minority, first in Ireland, then in America. In both countries Catholics still had to fight for social acceptance. Yet he knew, too, that America held the promise of a better life—a promise fulfilled in his own case when he became the second bishop of Trenton in 1894. As one of many Irish people who achieved prominence in New Jersey, he was grateful that his parents had put their faith in a new fatherland a half century before.

McFaul's was thus a double patriotism: for the land he left and the land he and his parents had embraced. These were complex loyalties. One reinforced the other and together they produced a third attachment: to the notion that in Irish America Ireland found its fulfillment. Somehow, he implied, a nation could achieve its destiny in dispersal. In a curious way his Irish birth made him not less but more American, as if, like thousands before him, he realized that

*Irish-born James McFaul,*
*second bishop of Trenton.*

COURTESY: MONSIGNOR JOSEPH SHENROCK

*McFaul's predecessor as bishop of Trenton, Michael O'Farrell, was also Irish. Born in Limerick in 1832, he studied in Dublin and Paris before his ordination in 1855. In 1869 he accepted appointment as a priest of the Diocese of New York. In 1881 he became bishop of the newly created Diocese of Trenton, serving until his death in 1894.*

❧

COURTESY: MONSIGNOR JOSEPH SHENROCK

Americanness itself was a matter of being an outsider made welcome in a new land. And if Irish birth made him more American, American residence, equally curiously, made him more Irish. McFaul personified the paradox that the Irish were most Irish when they left Ireland behind:

> See how the persecution of the Irish, the evictions, the famines brought about by English greed have caused a greater Ireland to grow up in America, Canada and Australia. How the faith has prospered! Where there was but a handful of Catholics a few years ago there are now thousands! The poor Celt came here without means [and] wherever he settled the Church grew up. . . . Our faith has triumphed. . . . It came forth from its mountain fastnesses stronger and more robust than ever.[2]

Long colonized by others, Ireland now colonized the rest of the world. The Irish story, in other words, would reach its climax far from Ireland.

Too much may be made of McFaul's remarks—on Saint Patrick's Day no one is on oath—but they went beyond the usual pieties. Wittingly or not, he showed the subtlety of Irishness and Irish Americanness. This book will trace some of those shifting definitions, first in Ireland, then in New Jersey. It will propose that Irishness remains a disputed idea, even in America. Read the proceedings of Ulster Scots cultural societies, for instance, and compare them with writing in the nationalist tradition: two very different views of Irish and Irish American history are on offer. It is as if the Irish crossed the ocean only to resume their conflict on a different shore. Yet the argument was fought in newspapers, periodicals, and pulpits, not in the streets. A pluralist accommodation was achieved in America that had proved impossible in Ireland. The New World took the sting from the Irish fight by speaking, almost as an endearment, of the fighting Irish.

One theme of this book, then, is that New Jersey provided an arena for different ways of being Irish. Another is that being Irish, in New Jersey and elsewhere, offered different ways of being American. The idea that an assortment of immigrants may be fashioned into a new nation is an American axiom. The adjectives will disappear—no more Irish Americans, German Americans, Italian Americans, Asian Americans—to be replaced by Americanness pure and simple. But what of the old belonging that the adjective enshrines? Must it be abandoned? Who decides? That is when controversy begins. Even the terminology of assimilation is contentious. New citizens of the United States are said to be "naturalized." "Denaturalized" might be a better term. After all, they must yield one identity to take on another. A past is abandoned, a future embraced. Yet in another sense "naturalized" has it about right. A new nature is accepted. Some cultural loss occurs, of course, but most recently minted citizens are prepared to accept it. To speak of loss of identity is to suggest a static notion of culture itself, as if "Americanness" itself were not a cultural compound, an invented idea. The Irish did not come to America and become Americans. It was they who helped to make it American in the first place.

New Jersey was and remains part of this exchange. To write the history of migration and new settlement is to tell multiple stories. Large social processes lay behind every decision to leave, every decision to come. Ireland intruded into New Jersey's history, and New Jersey into Ireland's. No single volume, of course, could capture the whole. The Irish who came to New Jersey in the seventeenth century were different, even in their Irishness, from the Irish who came a hundred years later. New Jersey, for that matter, was different. Does that invalidate the exercise? On the contrary, the very amorphousness of the categories is the point. New Jersey and Ireland are well matched—both beautiful, belligerent, striving for settled identity—and their shared history is worthy of attention. But to write that story is to recognize that the real object of exploration ought to be Irishness itself. That is this book's modest proposal.

# CHAPTER 1

# Varieties of Irishness

## WHO IS IRISH?

PEOPLE FROM Ireland who visit the United States are sometimes surprised by what they find. Much of the place is familiar, of course, and is recognized instantly as if a thousand postcards had come to life: the Statue of Liberty, the Empire State Building, the Golden Gate Bridge. This is the generic America—sunny, optimistic, welcoming—that the world wants to see. Other Americas may be less familiar, but, tutored by television, visitors still have *déjà vu* when they experience the energy of New York, the earnestness of New England, the experimentalism of California. Yet one encounter, despite expectations, always causes perplexity. Sooner or later an American will announce that he is "Irish." The surprise is heightened by the Boston or Brooklyn accent that accompanies the assertion. Our traveler has crossed an ocean only to find himself still at home. More bizarrely, if he has come from Northern Ireland, which is part of the United Kingdom, he may find his Irishness doubted by Americans who do not doubt their own. This might qualify as a joke except that no one knows what comes next: a punch line or a punch.

What, then, makes a person Irish? Birth? Parentage? A sense of belonging in Ireland or among "Irish" people? Is it possible to be both Irish and not Irish, to adopt or adapt identity as occasion demands? Does the category have any meaning at all? These are strangely difficult questions. For some scholars, the very notion of essential identity is mistaken. There is no such thing as "Irishness," a card of national belonging carried for life like a genetic code, intrinsic and ineradicable. On the contrary, it is more like an item of social clothing that may be discarded when something fancier comes along. Not an objective reality but a subjective claim, it is more a matter of boast than birth. Perhaps that is why with some people the more distant the physical connection with Ireland, the more insistent the avowals of Irishness. If national identity is a sense of place, frequently the sense becomes more important than the place itself. New York, for example, is more extravagantly Irish on Saint Patrick's Day than Dublin. Travel seems to work this way. Only by leaving home do we see it for the first time. Only in abandoning identity do we realize we possess it. The view from the departing ship is a view of the whole.

Yet this idea would have been too much for earlier writers. Most historians, certainly until the twentieth century, have taken it for granted that national characteristics *do* exist—solid facts that should not be riddled away or held to be mere inventions or conventions. It is possible, they think, to generalize about nations, to trace their development over centuries, to pass judgment. Certainly generalizations about the Irish have always been plentiful. The fourth-century Roman Ammianus noticed the belligerence and cruelty of the "Scotti [Irish] and the Picts," "wild nations" continually harassing "the Britons with . . . afflictions." Claudian, his near contemporary, spoke of "the Scot with wandering dagger" and "ice-cold Ireland [with] the heaped-up corpses of her Scots."[1] Irish uncouthness was taken for granted until the coming of Christianity, after which it was continental Europe that seemed uncivilized and Ireland peaceful. The Venerable Bede considered the Irish "a harmless people . . . ever most friendly towards the English": any wrongdoing lay with the latter, not the former.[2] But by the twelfth century Saint Bernard of Clairvaux could write of Saint Malachy that he was "born in Ireland of a barbarous people, . . . but from the barbarism of his birth he contracted no taint, any more than the fishes of the sea from their native salt."[3] In 1183 Gerald of Wales noticed that the Irish were poor farmers and worse businessmen (with "little use for the money-making of towns") and were incorrigibly lazy, their greatest pleasure being "not to work . . . [and their] greatest wealth [being] to enjoy liberty."[4] Aggressive in the fourth century, idle in the twelfth, the Irish were a puzzle to late ancient and medieval writers.

A thread seems to run through these early observations: the Irish did nothing by halves. Defined by the furthest reaches of bellicosity, piety, or laziness, they seemed to represent in pure form the characteristic that the observer wished to praise or blame. The irony is obvious: this depiction of extremes made the observer himself seem immoderate. Consider Edmund Campion—scholar, Jesuit, martyr—who visited the country in 1569. His *History of Ireland* tumbles over itself with words:

> The people are thus inclined: religious, frank, amorous, ireful, sufferable of pains infinite, very glorious, many sorcerers, excellent horsemen, delighted with wars, great almsgivers, passing in hospitality. . . . They follow the dead corpses to the grave with howlings and barbarous outcries, pitiful in appear-

ance whereof grew (as I suppose) the proverb, to weep Irish. . . . They are sharp-witted, lovers of learning capable of any study whereunto they bend themselves, constant in travail, adventurous, intractable, kind-hearted, secret in displeasure.[5]

The breathlessness conveys the meaning. The Irish, extravagant and hyperbolic, were strange, difficult, a law unto themselves.

Irish oddity is a recurring theme of Tudor and Stuart literature. Barnaby Rich, a sixteenth-century soldier, polemicist, and land-grabber, wrote a detailed *New Description of Ireland* in 1610. Rich had pretenses to anthropological objectivity but his conclusions were highly tendentious. "It cannot be denied, but that the Irish are very cruel in their executions, and no less bloody in their disposition. . . . That which is hateful to all the world . . . is . . . beloved and embraced by the Irish. I mean civil wars and domestic dissension." Again, the observer seemed to acquire the qualities of the observed, Rich's loathing of Irish deformity amounting almost to a moral deformity in himself. Fynes Moryson, Rich's contemporary, wrote a more temperate and therefore more compelling account of Ireland. Moryson's Irish were filthy and feckless, lazy, and uncivilized, badly in need of English rule. "Many of these wild Irish eat no flesh, but that which dies of disease or otherwise dies of itself. . . . It is strange and ridiculous, but most true, that some of our carriage horses, falling into their hands, when they found soap and starch, carried for the use of our laundresses, they, thinking them to be some dainty meats, did eat them greedily." Moryson tried to show pity, but contempt kept breaking through.[6]

Notice in these various attempts to capture Irishness the absence of *Irish* views of Ireland. It was left to outsiders to explain the eccentricity of the country and its people. The result was that, defined by others, the Irish came to be seen as other. Sketched by strangers, they became sketches of strangeness. Is the evidence of Rich et al. therefore flawed? On the contrary, lack of objectivity is precisely its value. With the immediacy of a prosecution brief, it conveys the temper of the time. Aggression dressed up as anthropology is a standard imperialist device. Rather than condemn, we would do better to explain it. William Carleton from County Tyrone, one of the few "mere" Irish to give an account of Ireland, thought he knew the reason for the persistent contempt. Writing after the Great Famine (1845–1851), he proposed that English people literally could not understand the Irish. Their accents were too thick, their idiomatic expressions too bizarre. Their unfamiliarity with English grammar caused the ridicule "unjustly heaped upon those who are found to use a language which they do not properly understand." The consequence was disastrous. Once Englishmen decided to laugh at the Irish, it was only a matter of time before they would despise them.[7]

These efforts to define Irishness assumed that the national character was fixed and ahistorical, transcending time and space to exist in some metaphysical empyrean of its own. But this is absurd. It is impossible to speak of a people without acknowledging how landscape and history form and shape them. Estyn Evans, Ireland's most distinguished historical geographer, has written that "geography counts for more than genes" in determining the behavior of most groups.[8] Historian J. C. Beckett argues similarly: "The history of Ireland must be based on a study of a relationship between the land and the people. It is in Ireland itself, the physical conditions inspired by life in this country and the effect on those who have lived there, that the historian will find the distinct and continuing character of Irish history."[9]

This makes sense. A purely Irish "racial" type does not exist, and attempts to find it usually look foolish. It was once believed that tall, fair-haired types predominated in Ulster and on the eastern seaboard where the Vikings settled. Not so: the tallest people in Ireland are in Kerry and Galway, the shortest on the east coast. It was also thought that the purest form of Irishness was to be found among the Aran Islanders of the west coast. Wrong again: many of those islanders are descended from Cromwellian soldiers recruited from East Anglia.[10] These stereotypes have ugly consequences, such as the quasi-eugenicist suggestion that the northern and southern parts of Ireland should be kept separate because the former is peopled by descendants of the English and the Scots, the latter by descendants of the Spanish.[11] This is tribal myth-making, not fair-minded scholarship. Evans's point surely holds. To reduce the Irish story to a clash of "races" is to remove from consideration every other determinant of human behavior—geography, climate, custom, law, age, gender—and offer instead an unsubtle determinism that leads in a circle back to itself. Race is history with the history removed, an explanation that explains nothing, a way of winning an argument by refusing to have it.

## RACE AND EMIGRATION

EVEN IF Irish racial purity is a will-o'-the-wisp, and a dangerous one at that, the literature of emigration could not exist without it. Books abound with titles such as *The Irish Race in America* (Edward O'Meagher Condon's effort to show that an Irishman, Saint Brendan, discovered the New World), *The Story of the Irish Race* (in which Seumus MacManus celebrates the "heroic records of Ireland's holy cause"), *The Irish Race in the Past and Present* (a paean to the "admirable stubbornness" with which the Irish stood against Protestantism and, by implication, the modern world), and *The Genius of the Gael* (which sees "liveliness of mind, individuality, a personal interest in other people, and courteous manners" as the national characteristics).[12] These are not merely sentimental: they aspire to scholarship. All purport to explain the immigrant experience as a triumph of ethnicity, the success story of a particular stock. Much of this is harmless. In 1911, to give a minor example, the American Irish Historical Society announced that its annual lecture would be given by Dr. Thomas Addis Emmet, "whose name is held in honor for the achievements of his long career, his noble qualities of character, his record in the field of historical research and his unselfish love of the Irish race."[13] That was, as it were, a stock description, suitable for a hundred such speakers. Or think of a biographical sketch penned early in the twentieth century of one James Carrel of Morris County, New Jersey, for the *Journal of the American Irish Historical Society*. Carrel

> came from sturdy Irish stock and inherited many of the strongest and best characteristics of that Race. His great-grandfather was born in the Emerald Isle, and braving the dangers incident to ocean voyages in those days, he crossed the Atlantic and took up residence in New Jersey as one of its first colonists. Establishing a home in what is now Randolph Township, Morris County, he bore his part in the work of development and progress, reclaiming the land from its primitive condition and making the region a habitable and pleasant district. All his descendants remained on the original lands.[14]

Here are all the features of the idiom: boosterism, heroism, progressivism, commitment to posterity. The emigrant is never weak but of "sturdy . . . stock"; never comes from Ireland but from "the Emerald Isle"; never crosses the sea but "braves" its dangers; never settles but "takes up residence"; never accepts American primitiveness but makes his new land "habitable and pleasant"; never thinks of himself, only of his descendants. He is such a paragon, in fact, that the reader must wonder why he had not transformed Ireland into a little America before he left.

In myth-making, these are forgivable failings. Yet to draw a racial picture of the migrant experience is to raise a question: which Irish race? America saw different kinds of settlers from Ireland: the "mere Irish" of whom Rich and Moryson spoke disparagingly, the hibernicized Anglo-Normans who emerged in the late Middle Ages, the Scots-Irish of the seventeenth century. All were *from* Ireland, but were they *of* Ireland? Were Ulster people, for example, actually Irish? In 1757 Edmund Burke wrote of those "who in America are generally called Scotch-Irish," the hyphen qualifying, even quashing, the Irishness. Certainly the Scots-Irish seemed different not only from other Irish settlers but from the generality of American immigrants. Theodore Roosevelt, for example, celebrated

*Glendalough, County Wicklow, in the late nineteenth century, a time when romantic pictures of Ireland as a land of saints and scholars proliferated in the Irish American imagination.*

❦

this stern and virile people. They formed the kernel of that American stock who were the pioneers of our people in the march westward. They were a bold and hardy people who pushed past the settled regions of America and plunged into the wilderness as the leaders of the white advance. The Irish Presbyterians were the first and last set of immigrants to do this: all others have merely followed in the wake of their predecessors.[15]

Not everyone agreed. William Strickland, an English farmer who visited America around 1800, was struck by its "savage backwoodsmen, chiefly of Irish descent . . . a race possessing all the vices of civilized and savage life, without the virtues of either . . . the outcasts of the world, and the disgrace of it. They are to be met with, on the western frontiers, from Pennsylvania inclusive, to the furthest south."[16] Differences notwithstanding, Strickland and Roosevelt never doubted that the Scots-Irish were a race. The only unresolved matter, controversial even today, is whether they were part of a larger Irish race or separate from it.

These varieties of Irishness are important for American history, but, as with many historical disputes, they are about more than history. A text beneath the text is easy to find. Notice how the Irish experience in America is made to reflect the disputes of Ireland itself. The politics of the old country—Ulster Presbyterian versus Irish Catholic—are echoed in disputes about achievements in the new one. Notice, too, how arguments about Irishness translated quickly into arguments about Americanness. Scots-Irish settlers deemed themselves more American for having arrived first; later Catholic immigrants were interlopers, mere Irish. Paradoxically, in other words, the Scots-Irish proved themselves American by boasting of, yet also denying, Irishness. Irish Catholics likewise proved themselves American by extolling the very Gaelic culture that the Scots-Irish disparaged. Writing in the 1920s, a certain William (W. H.) Mahony of Newark lauded the Irish achievement in his native city. "The spirit of Gaelic culture is strongly developed in the parochial schools. . . . The Irish element in Newark affords a splendid model for the many elements that make our many-peopled nation."[17] This was politically serviceable history. The point was to promote Catholic Irishness as a way of being American, to stake a claim against white Anglo-Saxon Protestants and white Ulster-Scots alike.

How are these disputes manifested in the literature of race and emigration? Three distinct arguments may be seen therein. One holds that the Irish and Scots-Irish are separate races and that their respective American experiences prove it. Another proposes that the Scots-Irish possess the best qualities of the Scottish and Irish peoples—a mongrel, as it were, that claims to have a pedigree.[18] A third claims that they are not separate races at all and that Scots-Irishness is an invention of nineteenth-century American Presbyterians who wished to distance themselves from their Irish Catholic counterparts. (Sophie Bryant typified this school, claiming that "an Irishman is Irish . . . even though his origin be England or Lowland Scotch.")[19] Whichever variation, race is still offered as the best way to interpret the Irish experience either in America or in Ireland itself.

Yet even early writers intuited the inadequacy of these explanations. In 1760 Lord Adam Gordon encountered in Virginia a "spurious race of mortals known by the appellation of Scotch-Irish." He noticed a disparity between geographic origin and ethnic identity, the hybridity of the Scots-Irish having more to do with culture and religion than mere physical attachment to Lowland Scotland or northeast Ulster. The most trenchant expression of that disparity came a generation later from the duke of Wellington. Asked if his Irish birth made him an Irishman, he snorted that to be born in a stable did not make a man a horse. His attitude was surprisingly modern: not unlike, in fact, those fiercely Irish Americans who have never seen Ireland.

These disputes have had a bearing on the writing of New Jersey history. The most assiduous early twentieth-century chronicler of the New Jersey Irish was the aforementioned William Mahony of Newark. Mahony was a nationalist who wished to see Ireland free of British rule, a fact that colored his entire historical project. Disparaging the racial argument for Ulster separatism, he scorned the notion that Scots-Irishness represented a distinctive identity in Ireland or, by extension, in New Jersey. On the contrary, centuries of settlement meant that "the Scottish element in Ulster [had been transformed] into Irishmen." When such people came to New Jersey they were Irish. "Scots-Irishness," he argued, was a creation of the nineteenth century, making its appearance in New Jersey annals only in 1835. To think otherwise was to invent an "ethnical hermaphrodite" that no eighteenth-century New Jerseyan would have recognized.

Mahony overstated his case. "Scots-Irishness" *was* known in New Jersey before 1835. In fact, the term was in use at least as early as 1766, when men described as "Scotch-Irish" murdered two Indian women in Burlington County. Indeed, it has a longer pedigree. When Donegal-born Francis Makemie enrolled in the University of Glasgow in 1676 he registered as "Franciscus Makemus Scoto-Hyburnus." Makemie, founder of American Presbyterianism, appears briefly in New Jersey history, serving a prison sentence for unlicensed preaching in Newark in 1705.[20] Lord Cornbury, first royal governor of New Jersey, described him as a "Jack of all Trades, a Preacher, a Doctor of Physick, a Merchant, Attorney . . . and worst of all, a disturber of Governments."[21] He was not the last Ulster preacher to disturb governments.

A plausible defense of Mahony's nationalism is that it was intended to counter Ulster Scots history, whose claims were even more tendentious. Consider the Scotch-Irish Society of America, a body likely to irritate even mild-mannered Irish nationalists. Its first congress was held in Tennessee in May 1899, and the published proceedings of that meeting make suffocatingly bumptious reading, with praise heaped on every Ulster Presbyterian who ever ventured to America and disparagement liberally laid upon the "famine Irish" who came a century later. The Ulstermen being "always in the foremost ranks of the pioneers," said one participant in the 1899 gathering, "the richest lands became theirs by right of discovery and first occupation, while the poorer country was left to the more timid people, who followed at a later and safer period."[22] If Mahony overstated his case, it was because the other side did likewise. Early twentieth-century Irish American historiography, as we have seen, was a continuation by other means of the ancient enmities of Ireland.

Nor should we be surprised by this. After all, the manipulation of memory, the fashioning of myth, is an important requirement of all societies. Without it, social cohesion could hardly exist. Ambrose Bierce's cynical definition—that history is "lies agreed upon"—contains an element of truth. (The explanation of Ireland's persistent trouble, perhaps, is that the Irish cannot even agree upon the lies.) Even if the past is to be trawled for socially useful parables, in other words, we must still try to get it right. That is where the national myth-maker goes wrong. Seeking to simplify a complex reality, he settles for one-dimensionality, a cartoon of ethnic virtue or vice, failing to realize that subtlety would give his story greater credibility. The Irish story *is* complex. Therein lies its power to move us. If it were simple it would be less worthy of attention. Let us therefore turn to New Jersey to see it reach another level of subtlety.

# CHAPTER 2

# Ireland and New Jersey in the Seventeenth Century

## IRELAND IN THE AGE OF EXPLORATION

**I**F GEOGRAPHY matters more than genes, the most significant fact about Ireland is that it is a Northern Atlantic island that looks west to America and east to continental Europe, never sure if one view is clearer than the other. All islands are ambiguous: they are at once isolated yet integrated, peripheral yet part of a wider whole. In the age of exploration Ireland was especially touched by this double personality. The Irish were backward—so, at any rate, the English said—but they were also part of what one historian has termed the "relatively homogenous" maritime community that stretched thousands of miles from Canada to Brazil.[1] Ireland was connected to powerful forces—new patterns of trade, government, and human settlement—that had the capacity to transform any backwater. In such a world, a country was either exploiter or exploited, colonizer or colonized, consumer or the thing consumed. The planting of colonies in the New World vividly demonstrates this. Even before they took the momentous step of traveling to the Americas and staying there, Europeans, Irish people among them, regarded the regions over the sea as treasure troves, places of potentially vast wealth. They crossed the Atlantic to find fish, timber, furs, never for a moment imagining that they needed to establish colonies to do so. "There goeth out of France commonly five hundred sail of ships yearly in March to Newfoundland," wrote one English pamphleteer in 1580, "to fish for Newlande fish, and comes home again in August."[2] The waters off Newfoundland, New England, Nova Scotia, and southern Labrador teemed with fish, which, salted and pickled, could be brought home in more or less edible condition. Anthony Pankhurst, a keen supporter of the annexation of Newfoundland, reported in 1578 that the French had 150 ships there, the Spanish 100, the English and Portuguese 50 apiece. The first Irish ship sailed to the Newfoundland fisheries by 1600.[3]

Ireland's part in this trade was small, more a "precolonization" than a conscious effort at settlement. Ireland was not in the business of founding colonies: that was England's job. On the contrary, its task, much resented, was to provide a training camp for English plantation in America, a place to test what worked and what did not when taking land from natives and granting it to outsiders. Tudor propagandists such as Andrew Trollope thought the Irish "not thrifty and civil or human creatures, but heathen or rather savage and brute beasts"—people who would have starved were it not for England and who would actually benefit from confiscation of their land.[4] Like errant schoolchildren they were expected to be grateful for their punishment. Ireland's other role, at least initially, was to provide a reason for England to postpone early colonization of America. As long as England remained at war with Spain, Ireland needed to be defended. More precisely, England needed to be defended from Spanish invasion and attack from Ireland. This meant that resources used for military purposes might otherwise have been devoted to North American settlement. But by the beginning of the seventeenth century peace of a sort had broken out among England, Spain, and Ireland. The establishment of colonies could begin in earnest, not least because redundant armies needed new occupations. The plantation of Ulster—undertaken in the years after 1609 to bring to heel once and for all a chronically rebellious place—was part of that redeployment. But Ireland was small beer compared to the riches that America offered. "There are other most convenient emploiments for all the superfluitie of every profession in this realme," Richard Hakluyt assured his readers in 1599. "For, not to meddle with the state of Ireland, nor that of Guiana, there is under our noses the great and ample countrey of Virginia."[5] Even as Ireland was brought into the world of early modern capitalism, in other words, it remained something of a backwater in English eyes. The ample country of America was suddenly a much greater prize.

Ireland's other duty was to provide some of the personnel for American and Caribbean settlement. In the 1650s, when Oliver Cromwell tried to solve the Irish problem by exporting the Irish, a thousand or so were banished to North America. Among them were four hundred children. The West Indies were also a favored destination. In 1678 the islands of St. Kitts, Nevis, Antigua, and Monserrat had a white population of 11,132: more than a quarter of them were Irish. Indeed, Monserrat was mainly Irish. Barbados had its share, too. One early eighteenth-century immigrant reported that "the first Setlers of this nation were . . . English, Welch, Scotch, Irish, Dutch, Deans [Danes] and French. The English they brought with them drunkness & swearing the Scotch Impudence & falsehood, the Welch Covetuousness & Revenge, The Irish cruelty & perjury . . . and here they have Intermarr'd & blended together."[6] This dyspepsia suggests chronic homesickness, a desire to be away from such a mongrel assemblage. Still, it is also an accurate assessment of the demographic effects of immigration. Chief among the consequences was an amalgamation of peoples and cultures. However unwillingly, the Irish were part of that blend. Nor were they the only national group to be deported. Between 1650 and 1700 the English authorities banished Scottish rebels—a hundred of them to New Jersey after 1685—and even malcontents from England itself. The New World was peopled, at least in part, by the rejects of the Old.

## THE NEW JERSEY "IRISH" IN THE AGE OF EXPLORATION

L ATE SEVENTEENTH- and early eighteenth-century Barbados was surprisingly typical of eastern North America as a whole. The blending of Europeans sourly noticed by the homesick neo-Barbadian was also a feature of the middle colonies of the Atlantic seaboard. The earliest inhabitants of the place now named New Jersey were Native Americans called Lenni Lenape, about twelve thousand strong when Europeans first made shore; fewer than two hundred of them were left by 1800.[7] Their way of life could not withstand the diseases and desires of the white man. The wilderness of mountain, shore, and river was too tempting for French, Dutch, Swedish, Spanish, and English moneymakers and for Dutch and Swedish adventurers particularly. The Dutch West Indies Company had only a few trading posts, New Amsterdam on the eastern shore of the Hudson River being more important to them; the Swedes controlled the New Sweden Company, its solitary outpost established on the Delaware in 1638. Both settlements were poor enough affairs: Dutch numbers along the whole of the Delaware were not more

*Israel Acrelius, first historian of New Sweden, wrote of Swedes living along the Delaware River in 1693, and among them "many Hollanders . . . English, Scotch, Irish and German families, all using the Swedish language." (Quoted in Thomas Purvis, "The European Origins of New Jersey's Eighteenth-Century Population," New Jersey History 100 [1902]: 19.)*

❧

COURTESY: SPECIAL COLLECTIONS AND ARCHIVES,
RUTGERS UNIVERSITY LIBRARIES

than four thousand in 1655, Swedish numbers only a tenth of that.[8] Any predator could have had them for the asking.

Wedged between New England and Virginia, New Amsterdam represented a foreign intrusion dividing England's northern and southern colonies. That it was owned by the Dutch—after 1660 England's trading and territorial rivals in Europe—made it even more objectionable. Accordingly, in 1664 Charles II granted to his brother James, duke of York, substantial lands in America including portions of New York, New Jersey, and Maine. James appointed as governor one Richard Nicholls, who immediately embarked on an expedition to secure the territory. Dutch courage living up to its proverbial reputation, the colony was yielded virtually without a fight. Almost at once James subdivided the "most improvable part" of the new possession between two supporters, George Carteret and Lord John Berkeley. Nicholls also busied himself granting parcels of land to Puritans from Connecticut (Elizabeth-town) and New England Baptists and Quakers (Monmouth). Carteret and Berkeley disputed these titles, a source of tension in later years. New Jersey thus began as it was to continue: fractious and divided. There were two Jerseys, East and West, and it would be decades before they achieved anything recognizable as unity.

Irish elements may be seen in the Jerseys from earliest days. Almost as soon as the curtain rose on the duke of York's proprietary colony—a ramshackle show, to be sure—people from Ireland took to the stage: individuals, sometimes entire communities, attracted to the economic possibilities of a place that remained largely empty save for Indians. In addition to material motivations, they were pulled across the ocean for spiritual reasons. The New World was more congenial to the practice of their faith than the Old. Settlement and salvation, worldliness and otherworldliness, went together in the seventeenth-century mind. Piety and practicality characterized these earliest New Jerseyans. That said, the first plantations were patchy and unsystematic, certainly nothing to compare with the New England experiment. True, the middle colonies were the fastest growing of England's North American possessions in the third quarter of the seventeenth century—from about five thousand people in 1664 to fifty thousand in 1700—but New Jersey's contribution to this growth was limited. The bulk of settlement occurred in Pennsylvania, a powerful magnet for immigrants, many of them Quakers. Divided into East and West Jersey, the duke of York's colony had an unfinished, provisional feel to it. For its first two decades it lacked representative institutions, a fact that may explain its comparatively slow growth. East Jersey had ten thousand people by 1700, West Jersey a paltry thirty-five hundred.[9]

The Irish presence should not be exaggerated in size or "Irishness": both were minor. Nor should we claim too much certainty when we speak of it. With few facts

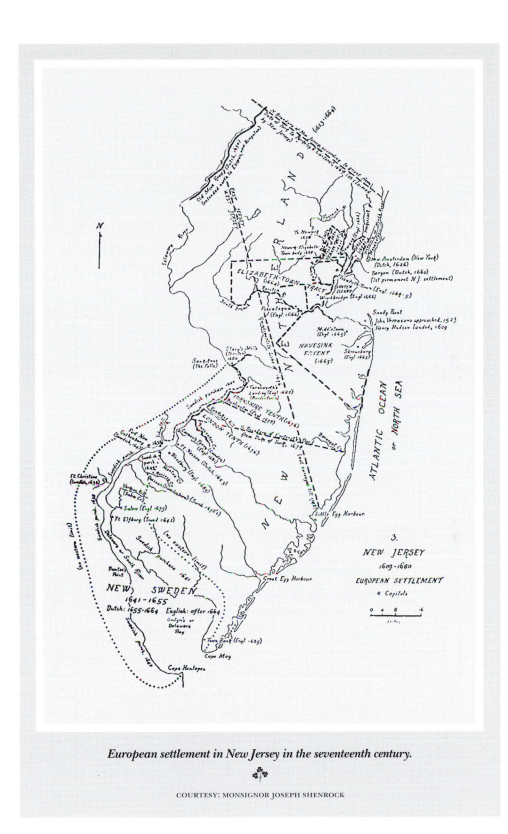

*European settlement in New Jersey in the seventeenth century.*

❧

COURTESY: MONSIGNOR JOSEPH SHENROCK

to hand, most statements about the seventeenth-century Irish immigrants—about any group, for that matter—must be speculative and inferential. Some names have survived, nonetheless. Richard Bryan, a Presbyterian from County Armagh, settled in Milford, Connecticut, in 1639, prospering there and later in New Haven as a merchant. He was one of the first residents of Newark after its foundation in 1666. Another early Newarker was Patrick Falconer, a merchant, preacher, and Irish native, who died aged thirty-three in 1692. Falconer was devout—a man "who suffered much for Christ," according to his headstone—but sufficiently worldly to marry the daughter of the deputy governor of New Haven and leave her a solid legacy after his death. W. H. Mahony, promoter of all things Irish in New Jersey, claimed him as Newark's "own Saint Patrick and patron saint."[10] This is fanciful; his cult can hardly be said to be strong today. No matter: Falconer, like Bryan, was one of those who did well in early America. Money could be made (and lost) by people willing to take a chance. Except for the banished and deported, almost everyone in the middle colonies fell into that category.

The fluidity of the colonial world helped men such as Dennis Lynch, who acquired 300 acres in Cape May County from the West Jersey Company in 1696; John De Byrne, who received a deed for 120 acres in Essex County in 1694; William Steele, a merchant from Cork, who acquired 500 acres in Gloucester County in 1685; John White, a maltster from County Carlow, who acquired joint title to 2,000 acres in Middlesex County in 1685; Thomas Atherton, a shoemaker from Dublin, who bought over 1,900 acres "on the south side of Raritan River, adjoining the Long Meadow" with three partners in 1684; Hugh Dunn, who bought and sold substantial lots in Woodbridge and "Pescataway" from 1668 until the 1690s; and Francis Buckley, a laborer, who acquired 200 acres in Salem County in 1686 and another 100 ten years later.[11]

It is easy to imagine the world of these early entrepreneurs. Armed with a skill or a trade, they moved freely along the eastern seaboard and inland, buying and selling property in Pennsylvania, New York, and New Jersey, rarely staying in one place for very long. They were mariners, merchants, weavers, maltsters, leatherworkers, builders: men of versatile and portable talent. Do their stories show seventeenth-century New Jersey to be an upwardly mobile place, especially for the Irish? Not necessarily. We know of them precisely because they succeeded. Failure is less likely to be noticed in wills and conveyances. All the same, their social ambition is striking. Some did very well indeed. Four men from various parts of Ireland—William Clark, Anthony Sharp, Roger Roberts, and Richard Hunter—jointly owned ten thousand acres of West Jersey in 1677. That was impressive by any standard. Most lots were smaller than this, but purchases of several hundred acres at a time were not unusual.

A tougher question remains. Were these people Irish by birth or simply by previous residence? Were some of them "New English" (that is, descendants of those who had come to Ireland as part of the Tudor and Stuart "plantations" of the sixteenth and seventeenth centuries) or Lowland Scots who decided they would rather be in America? It is impossible to say. Surname evidence (our best source) needs careful scrutiny. It poses three problems. Using patronyms alone, it is difficult to distinguish between Scots and Irish immigrants, to recognize Irish settlers with English surnames, and to tell the difference between an Irish-born father and his American-born son. We may be fairly confident that Thorlagh Swiney of Middletown, Thurlas Sullavan of Burlington, William Kelly of Salem, and even Joseph Royley [Reilly?], also of Salem, were not Englishmen whose journey to America had briefly included a stop in Ireland. We may be reasonably sure, too, that Thomas Atherton, the Dublin shoemaker, was more English than Irish or, at any rate, was born of English lineage. Other names fall somewhere in between: possibly English, possibly anglicized Irish, impossible to say one way or another. (The name "Steele" is a good example: it was English in origin but fairly common in northern parts of Ireland at the beginning of the seventeenth century.)[12] These difficulties did not deter one historian from overstating surname evidence as proof of extensive Irish settlement in early New Jersey. "It is just as reasonable," suggested W. H. Mahony of these seventeenth-century settlers, "to say they were Irish as to say they were English."[13] He missed the implication of his own logic: just as reasonable, it might be retorted, to say they were English as Irish. It is a silly quibble in any case. The scale of Irish settlement was not the stuff of biblical epic. To build national myths on it is foolish.

The toughest question is this: even if they were Irish, did that fact matter to them? Few mistakes are more pervasive than the assumption that national identity had meaning for early settlers. People of the seventeenth century did not possess the mental categories of the nineteenth century. Religion and language were more important to them than "national" origin. Besides, even self-consciously "Irish" settlers were unromantic types, too busy making a living to think of themselves as exiles of Erin. The idea of expatriate longing, of regretful banishment from the homeland, was the invention of the late eighteenth and early nineteenth centuries, when Irish nationalism in song and literature was mainly teary sentimentalism, nostalgia for an Eden that had never been.[14] Faced with new land to cultivate and a new life to make, the seventeenth-century Irish in New Jersey had little time to think of the world they had left behind.

## RELIGIOUS EMIGRATION:
## QUAKERS, PRESBYTERIANS, CATHOLICS

As well as individuals, entire communities traveled from Ireland to New Jersey in the seventeenth century, usually for spiritual reasons. Coming from a particular town or congregation, they were practical as well as pious, desiring to build up God's Kingdom while creating a new life away from the sanctions and discriminations of the old country. The earliest English speakers in West Jersey, now Camden County, were Quakers from Ireland. England and Ireland were uncomfortable places for religious nonconformists of any sort, even peaceable Quakers. New Jersey was more attractive: indeed, it boasted a largely Quaker proprietorship for a while.[15] "Friends that dwelt in Ireland," wrote Thomas Sharp, son of a Dublin merchant and one of the first to arrive, felt "a pressure . . . laid upon them for some years which they could not get from under the weight of." Sharp's awkward prose reflected the awkwardness of the Quaker plight. They were unable to practice their faith freely in a kingdom that remained officially Anglican. To be sure, they had only themselves to blame for some of their difficulties. Of all sects introduced to Ireland in the mid-seventeenth century, Quakers were the most radical. They defied secular authority and challenged the clergy of other denominations, naively imagining that their pertinacity would go unchecked. Quakers were repressed during the Cromwellian and Restoration periods, and it was only at the beginning of the eighteenth century that they were no longer seen a threat to the security of the realm. These legal curbs gave them no option, they thought, but "to leave their friends and relations together with a comfortable subsistence to transport themselves and familys [sic] into this wilderness part of America." The wilderness, in Thomas Sharp's case, was Newton, New Jersey.

The first Quaker agent was Robert Lane of Dublin, who arrived in 1677 to arrange passage for more than one hundred members of the Society of Friends in 1681. He was hosted by a family called Thomson, who had settled in Elsinburg, Salem County. The Thomsons were hardworking people—possibly Ulster Scots— who had transformed the wilderness "to a very good degree of living." Lane's group sailed from Ireland in September 1681, arriving in Salem two months later. To arrive in November was to experience a baptism of frost. The first winter was difficult, the chief problems being homesickness, harsh weather, and failure to find a permanent place to settle. But perseverance paid off. Eventually they established themselves in the land between the Pennsauken and Timber creeks, becoming so dominant in the area that it was soon designated the "Irish Tenth." (Years later the road between Gloucester and Salem was still the "Irish Road.") "We were at times pretty hard bestead," remembered Thomas Sharp, "having all our provisions as far as Salem to fetch by water, [and facing Indians] who put a dread upon our spirits, considering they were a savage people." Sharp offered a providential explanation for the settlement's success: it was all due to "the mercy and kindness of God" and the "zeal and fervency" of the Friends. Modesty prevented him from acknowledging his own part. Formidably energetic, he was "the first teacher in the Irish Tenth, a writer, a constable, sheriff and judge, and the surveyor who laid out the town of Gloucester." Divine purposes require human agents; Sharp seems to have been one of them.[16]

The measure of Quaker success in New Jersey, Sharp thought, was that land along Newton Creek and Gloucester, once "a wilderness," had been "planted with good seed" to provide a harvest for God and man. In purely human terms it was a bumper crop. Think of Archibald Mickle, a County Antrim Quaker, who settled in Newton Township in the early 1690s and died in 1706. The Mickles did well by New Jersey, and New Jersey did well by them. At first the family farmed about five hundred acres on the Delaware River. Subsequently they acquired land to the south, and within three generations they owned "virtually all the land between the Delaware and Cooper's Creek, from Little Newton Creek (about where Camden's Jackson Street is today) on the north to Newton Creek on the south."[17] This was impressive social mobility. Later members of the family had little time for the Irish,[18] conveniently forgetting their own origins. The Antrim connection may have been slight, but it was a connection all the same.

Perhaps the "good seed" planted by Sharp and his friends was more English than Irish, but that did not matter to West Jersey officials, who considered the area an Ireland away from Ireland. Evidence of this ethnic peculiarity came in 1682. One contribution of the Irish Tenth to West Jersey was currency. Among the first settlers was one Mark Newby, a Dublin Quaker, who arrived on the Delaware in 1680 and in Gloucester County in 1681. Newby carried with him a substantial quantity of halfpence coins that had been declared illegal in Ireland by the English government. It was a precious cargo because small-denomination coins were seriously lacking in West Jersey; known as "Newby's Irish halfpence" or "Saint Patrick's halfpence," the coins were briefly the only effective currency there. An act of May 1682 "for the more convenient payment of small sums" recognized them as legal tender and made Newby in effect the first banker in the province.[19] The coins themselves neatly symbolized the double identity of these English-Irish immigrants. One side depicted a harp-playing king, the other Saint Patrick in his familiar roles as snake banisher and evangelist. West Jerseyans unaware of Irish legends thus received a lesson in them every time they conducted small transactions.

Quakers were not the only transplanted spiritual community in West Jersey. Cohansey in Salem County was settled in 1683 by Baptists from Tipperary under the leadership of the Reverend Elias Keach. "Amidst all the inroads of heresy and fanaticism," wrote one Baptist historian, they remained "sound in the faith, respectable in size, and in a flourishing condition."[20] Their numbers were later boosted by an influx of Irish Presbyterians, who seem to have become the predominant group. Cohansey was a magnet for Irish Protestants of all sorts, who appear to have lived together fairly harmoniously. (The Presbyterian leader, the Reverend Robert Kelsey, preached for the Baptists.)[21] Fenwick's *Historical Account of the First Settlement of Salem, in West Jersey* reported that "emigrants were flocking into Cohansey from New England, Long Island, Wales and Ireland" by 1700.[22]

Other evidence confirms the Irish presence. Legal documents, especially wills, reveal Fitzgeralds, Murphys, O'Neills, and Reillys in Cohansey in the early eighteenth century. (The first Murphy in New Jersey marriage records dates to 1729; the first Fitzgerald, to a will of 1703; the first Sullivan, to a will of 1696.)[23] These names were not exclusively Baptist or Presbyterian. It is plausible to surmise that Salem and Gloucester, once established as "Irish," attracted Catholics as well as Nonconformists. In the eyes of the Established Church there was little to choose between them. Certainly we know of late seventeenth-century emigrants from Dublin, Carlow, Wexford, Waterford, and Clonmell, the last two commemorated in eponymous settlements in Gloucester and Burlington counties. Most likely there were Papists among them.

Those few and fairly wealthy Catholics who came to New Jersey could expect to find a surprisingly tolerant place. The Concessions and Agreement of 1665, drawn up by New Jersey's first proprietors, Berkeley and Carteret, was a generous instrument of government. (Proprietors of shaky colonies could not afford to put off prospective settlers.) Full freedom of conscience was guaranteed to all, "they behaving themselves quietly and not using this liberty to licentiousness."[24] This may have attracted some Catholics after the failure of the Jacobite cause in Ireland. We know of one William Golden, an officer at the Battle of the Boyne, who acquired over a thousand acres in Cape May County in 1691.[25] But such toleration was short-lived. When New Jersey became a royal colony in 1702, freedom of conscience was extended to all except Catholics. The purpose of the exclusion was to avoid the "dangers which may happen from papish recusants." Those dangers were unspecified but generally understood: Catholics had shown themselves disloyal to the established order in England, spectacularly so in Ireland. They must not be allowed to repeat the performance in New Jersey. Yet the very interdiction is suggestive. There was no point in warning against "papish recusants" unless they were coming to the colony in greater numbers than before.

## THE PENAL LAWS

**R**ELIGIOUS MIGRATION at the end of the seventeenth century thus reflected the profound consequences, for Ireland and America, of the "Glorious Revolution" of 1688–1689. For England, the defeat of James and the victory of William and Mary had important political and constitutional ramifications. It reinforced the national myth that Protestant virtue would always triumph over Catholic vice. Yet it was not a socially significant event. Most people were unaffected by it. In Ireland, on the other hand, the revolution altered the entire complexion of the country. The Catholic gentry could no longer expect the Cromwellian settlement—the laws of 1651 and 1652 by which they forfeited their lands—to be reversed. Anglicans could now rest secure in property that Catholics considered rightfully theirs. Presbyterians could now expect reward for support of the Williamite cause. In the 1690s and early 1700s the implications of this new dispensation became clear. Beginning in 1695 a series of measures known as the Popery Laws (later termed the Penal Laws) made it difficult for Catholics to maintain social standing in Ireland. They were forbidden to keep weapons, to seek education abroad, to bequeath land to children or inherit it from Protestants, to take leases for longer than thirty-one years, to practice law, to become schoolmasters, to hold office in central or local government, and to serve on grand juries and municipal corporations. Bishops, vicars-general, and regular clergy were banished from the country; secular clergy were allowed to stay but were required to register and to work in parishes singly, not in pairs or threes. No priests were allowed to enter the country after 1704. The intention was not so much to eliminate Catholicism as to crush any remaining pretensions of the Catholic aristocracy and gentry. The Catholic mercantile class (fairly small at the beginning of the eighteenth century) and the Catholic lower orders (larger but powerless) were not the first targets. (The seventeenth-century struggle in Ireland had always been between competing ruling classes, Gaelic and Old English on the one hand, New English on the other.) Still, however restricted in purpose and eventually relaxed in application, the Penal Laws succeeded. Most Catholic landowners conformed to the Church of Ireland in the course of the eighteenth century. The amount of land in Catholic hands fell from 22 percent in 1688 to 14 percent in 1703 to 5 percent in 1779. By any standards this represented social and economic obliteration.

The severity of these laws might suggest the victory of Protestantism over Catholicism, but it would be more accurate to say that the real success was of Anglicanism over all other denominations. Although Presbyterians supported the Williamite cause and were rewarded for it (they received state support called the *regium donum* for their ministers) the legal position of Presbyterianism was still inferior to that of the Church of Ireland. Under the Act to Prevent the Further Growth of Popery (1704), membership in municipal corporations and commissions in the army and navy were restricted to those who received the sacrament of the Lord's Supper "according to the usage of the Church of Ireland." As well as this, the validity of marriages conducted by Presbyterian ministers was legally doubtful until 1737. The practical effect was small. Presbyterians had far more freedom of worship than Catholics, a fact recognized in the Toleration Act of 1719, which granted to the former what it still withheld from the latter. All the same, they tended to be complainers, resenting increased rents demanded by their Anglican landlords and the payment of tithe for the support of the Established Church. These grievances were sharpened by hard times. The first quarter of the eighteenth century saw a severe recession in many parts of Ireland, especially Ulster. Presbyterians were ripe for emigration, and by the 1720s they began to leave in large numbers. This exodus, as we shall see, turned out to be highly significant for New Jersey.

# CHAPTER 3

# Ulster, Ireland, and New Jersey in the Eighteenth Century

## IRELAND IN DISTRESS

IN THE FIRST decades of the eighteenth century, commentators of all stripes agreed that the state of Ireland was unhappy. Political stagnation, economic hardship, excessive rents, restricted maritime commerce, crop failure, and frequent famine all combined to reduce much of the population to semipermanent misery. In 1718 William Nicolson, Anglican bishop of Derry, lamented the "dismal marks of hunger and want" among his people.[1] William King, archbishop of Dublin, spoke even more graphically:

> The screwing and racking of tenants has reduced the people to worse condi-
> tions than Poland. . . . [They] have already given their bread, their flesh, their
> butter, their shoes, their stockings, their beds, their house furniture and
> houses to pay their landlords and taxes. I cannot see how any more can be got
> from them, except we take away their potatoes and buttermilk, or flay them
> and sell their skins.[2]

King's assessment was not singular. The Presbyterian synod of 1720 reported that "many of our [ministers] are wanting even the necessaries of life; [some] are forced to lay down their charge, . . . others to transport themselves to America."[3] A land agent in Clones, County Monaghan, reported in 1719 that "there is a hundred families gone through this town this week past for New England . . . I believe that we shall have nothing left but Irish [i.e., Catholics]." Archbishop Hugh Boulter of Armagh warned the archbishop of Canterbury in February 1727 that the roads were "full of whole families that had left their homes to beg abroad."[4] "Abroad" meant the open countryside; soon, however, it would acquire another significance.

This penury had long- and short-term causes. Ireland's agricultural and maritime economies were in crisis at the end of the seventeenth century and the beginning of the eighteenth. The Navigation Acts (1661, 1671, 1685, 1696) banned direct exportation of most Irish goods to the colonies, requiring that they first go through English ports on English vessels. On top of this a combination of crop failures and drought between 1715 and 1720 brought many farmers to ruin. The result was starvation. Famine struck Ulster in the winter of 1728–29 and in 1741 hunger was so severe throughout the country that people spoke of *bliadhain an air,* the year of slaughter. There was, wrote the author of *The Groans of Ireland* (1741), "Want and misery in every face . . . the road spread with dead and dying bodies; mankind the colour of the [dock leaves] and nettles which they fed on; two or three, sometimes more in a car going to the grave for want of bearers to carry them."[5] The 1741 famine has been overshadowed in historical memory by the Great Hunger a century later, but it was comparably calamitous. Around three hundred thousand people perished, making it one of the worst natural disasters of the century, and the first to be caused primarily by potato failure.

The best way to survive Ireland was to leave it. That said, if emigration offered a remedy of sorts it also posed problems. Authorities in church and state worried that the country could not afford to lose its people. They also fretted, contradictorily, that the wrong people were choosing to go. These positions are less paradoxical than they may appear. The two Anglican archbishops previously mentioned, King of Dublin and Boulter of Armagh, squared the circle: too many Protestants were leaving, they said, and too many Catholics were staying. Boulter, an Englishman, warned of disaster in 1728: "The humour [of emigration] has spread like a contagious distemper, and the people will hardly hear any body that tries to cure them of their madness. The worst is that it affects only protestants, and reigns chiefly in the north, which is the seat of our linen manufacture."[6] King was equally stark. "No papists stir," he wrote as early as 1718. "The papists being already five or six to one, and being a breeding people, you may imagine in what condition we are like to be in."[7] King realized the irony of his premonition: having defeated Jacobitism, Protestants began to sense that the victory might be undone by an exodus of their own kind. A petition published in 1729 from "the noblemen and gentlemen of Ireland" warned of the "dangerous superiority of our inveterate enemies the papists, who openly and avowedly rejoice at the impending calamity and use all means and artifices to encourage and persuade the protestants to leave the nation, and cannot refrain from boasting that they shall by this means have again all the lands of this kingdom in their possession."[8]

Boulter and King were Anglicans; the majority of the emigrants were Ulster Presbyterians. Presbyterian grievances, variously social, economic, religious, and political, sharpened in the 1720s and in 1728 and 1729 reached breaking point. An *Address of Protestant Dissenting Ministers to the King* (1729) complained that the legal inferiority of Presbyterianism was "so very grievous that they have in great numbers transported themselves to the American Plantations for the sake of that liberty and ease which they are denied in their native country."[9] This was special pleading—the threat of emigration was a useful way to win political concessions—but it was also plausible. Presbyterians were excluded from full citizenship, a minor irritant compared to the legal inferiority of Catholics but still an annoyance to those who thought their support for William of Orange in 1689 should have been better rewarded. Indeed, some Anglicans justified discrimination on the grounds that Presbyterians were little better than Catholics anyway. "I held both presbyterians and Roman Catholics in the utmost abhorrence," wrote the earl of Cork and Orrery. "I esteemed presbyterians as cunning, designing, canting, ignorant hypocrites, and for Roman Catholics I thought every one of them held a knife at my throat."[10]

Those who lamented Presbyterian emigration thus had little love of Presbyterians themselves. The best to be said for them was that, concentrated in the north of Ireland, they represented a bulwark against resurgent Catholicism. But that very concentration reinforced their worst features—clannishness, exclusivity, self-regard, narrowness—and this made their going as much a relief as a regret to some members of the Established Church. Clannishness also explained the Presbyterian tendency to emigrate en masse. When they chose to leave they left in bulk, almost as if persuaded by an act of the collective will. The Scots-Irish prized individualism but did so within a highly conformist religious culture. "Just as coals burn more brightly when in contact with one another," writes the historian of eighteenth-century Ulster emigration to America, "so did resentment rise among the closely knit and numerically dominant Presbyterian congregations in north-eastern Ireland. . . . Emigration in such a community was likely to be as contagious as a fever in an insanitary town: it was liable to become an epidemic if the minister sponsored it."[11]

Whether fire or contagion, enthusiasm for emigration struck some as hysterical. Thomas Whitney described the Ulster coast in July 1728: "Here are a vast number of people shipping off for Pennsylvania and Boston, here are three ships at Larne, 5 at Derry, two at Coleraine, 3 at Belfast, and 4 at Sligo, I'm assured within these eight years there are gone above forty thousand people out of Ulster and the low part of Connacht."[12] The numbers were never that high—between eight and ten thousand would be nearer the mark for the entire 1720s—but enough people left to worry the government. Between 1731 and 1733 Prime Minister Robert Walpole urged the Irish Parliament to ease the burdens of Irish Presbyterianism. However, that parliament—an assembly of Anglican landlords with no taste for their Scripture-spouting tenants—refused to take the hint. Leniency might not have worked anyway. In truth, religion as a cause of Presbyterian emigration was somewhat puffed up. Most of the official discriminations were "legal niceties of practical concern to few people."[13] Presbyterians cared as much about their pockets as their pulpits and the one obligation that really rankled—payment of tithe to maintain the Established Church—was essentially economic. In the end, the most urgent motive for emigration in the 1720s was famine. All other considerations were secondary. "If it please God to send us a good harvest," Archbishop Boulter wrote to Walpole in March 1729, "things will gradually mend."[14] Things did mend: better harvests in 1729 and 1730 brought relief. By then, however, the damage was done. A culture of emigration had begun to form in the north of Ireland, and it was not easily eradicated.

## THE CALL OF AMERICA

WHEN ULSTER people landed in America and reported home, they had important news to impart. In 1735 a Tyrone emigrant wrote to his minister: "Here aw [all] a man works is for his ane [own]."[15] No longer a tenant but a free agent, he was typical of thousands who discovered in America a place where money could be made and spent without restriction. Where did they all go? Many found themselves in New England, then Pennsylvania. The New England migration (especially strong between 1717 and 1720) was not a success. The Scots-Irish struck some as uncouth: "Uncleanly, unwholesome and disgusting" was one New England verdict.[16] The movement to Pennsylvania was more fruitful. Connections between Ireland and the Quaker colony were long-standing, William Penn's father having had an estate in County Cork (where Penn joined the Society of Friends). Penn himself encouraged Irish Quakers to settle in Pennsylvania.

The Pennsylvanian connection with Ulster flourished after Penn's death in 1718. In 1720 the provincial secretary of the colony was James Logan, a native of Armagh. Logan thought highly of his "brave fellow-countrymen" who made a new home there. They were, he said, "a leading example to others." By 1730 he had changed his mind. They were now, he thought, "troublesome settlers to the government and hard neighbors to the Indians," forever squatting on land, squabbling about rights, and making nuisances of themselves. "If they continue to come," he feared, "they will make themselves proprietors of the province." This anxiety was tinged with a certain pacifist sanctimony. The Scots-Irish may have been "pernicious and pugnacious," but they were also good at carving out Indian land for the colony.[17] Eventually, however, they had to go. Abandoning Pennsylvania for New Jersey between 1718 and 1730, they brought to the latter colony their usual mixture of Calvinism and cantankerousness. It was a potent cocktail.

In New Jersey they made a better job of things. Their behavior was no different—if anything, it was even more rough-and-ready—but they were able to turn stubbornness and land-hunger to productive purpose. Most of them stayed in central New Jersey, hugging the Millstone, Raritan, and Passaic rivers. Many lived in Camden County, close to Philadelphia. Other Scots-Irish settlers took land in Morris, Hunterdon, and Sussex counties—cold, remote, unpromising places. They established communities that still bear their names: Hackettstown in Morris County, founded by Samuel Hackett of Tyrone in the 1720; Flemington in Hunterdon County, founded by Thomas Fleming of Tyrone in 1746. New Jersey was never the heart of Scots-Irish settlement in the American colonies—Ulster folk were far more plentiful in Pennsylvania, Virginia, the Carolinas, Tennessee, and farther west—but a strong impress was left all the same.

## THE SCOTS-IRISH LEGACY

**W**HAT WAS their achievement? The Ulster Scots in North America have suffered the peculiar fate of being praised and blamed for the wrong things. It is curious, for instance, that a "stern and virile people" should be celebrated by being sentimentalized. Think of Theodore Roosevelt, their celebrant-in-chief, who became almost weepy at the thought of these brave "pioneers of our people in the march westward."[18] The pioneers themselves would not have approved, rugged individualists being the last people to have time for self-iconography. But if Roosevelt was a friend, the Scots-Irish have had their enemies, who, motivated by ideological spleen, either find fault with them or, failing that, find that they did not exist at all. As we have seen, some writers denied the very notion of Scots-Irishness, claiming that those who came to America from Ireland were Irish pure and simple. Typical of this school was W. H. Mahony, who could see no "Scots-Irishness" in New Jersey before 1835 and could only see it after 1835 because Presbyterians invented the category to distinguish themselves from Irish Catholics.[19] Other historians, convinced that Scots-Irishness did exist, heartily disliked it. Witness Arnold Toynbee, for whom the Scots-Irish, having landed in the New World, promptly "succumbed to the barbarizing severity of their Appalachian environment . . . [becoming] no better than barbarians, the American counterpart of the Hairy Ainu."[20] The reader shudders to imagine what he would have made of Theodore Roosevelt.

Does the New Jersey experience help us assess these competing strains of praise and blame? Certainly it casts in new light the myth of the frontiersman, the quasi-racial assumption that Scots-Irish success was due to some superiority of stock. That notion needs modification. The settlers exhibited frontier virtues—resilience, hardihood, self-reliance, a degree of belligerence—precisely because they lived at the frontier. Such conditions, as Estyn Evans has remarked, "make for independence, masculine dominance, superstition, improvisation and inventiveness."[21] Geography mattered more than genes; birth and breeding had little to do with bounty. This is not to dismiss but to acknowledge the Scots-Irish achievement. Success was the more admirable for being hard won. Indeed, it was far from inevitable: witness the Scots-Irish in the Appalachian backcountry who came to a poor place and stayed poor. The prosaic conclusion that, as with most new settlements, the inventive flourished and the indolent failed is hard to resist. Only afterward was success attributed to hardiness or better stock. When George Scot promoted East Jersey in Britain, he promised prospective settlers that they could "live as comfortably" along the Raritan "as in any place in the world" but warned that success would only come to those prepared to endure loss of "friends and relations and the satisfaction of their company."[22] Frontiers rewarded the fit and punished the flabby. That was their appeal.

## EARLY SETTLEMENT: SUCCESS AND FAILURE ON THE FRONTIER

THE FIRST Scots-Irish settlers in Morris, Sussex, and Hunterdon counties were poor. Most of their neighbors despised them. They squatted on land to which they had title only in their own minds. They spoke a strange English dialect in accents even stranger. They had too many children and not enough education.[23] They were argumentative and belligerent. Their dwellings were shoddy and slapdash, their farms poorly laid out: less impressive, certainly, than the well-constructed houses and efficiently run acres of the Germans who settled nearby.[24] They were socially isolated, more likely to be found in individual homesteads in the backwoods than in towns. They were intellectually narrow—people of one book, the Bible, which some of them could not read. During the Revolutionary War the wife of a Continental officer described the Scots-Irish soldiers who had taken arms against English rule in America. They were, she wrote in 1777, "the errantist rustics you ever beheld. . . . You'd laugh to hear them talk."[25] It was a description that could have been penned anytime throughout the century.

These early Irish emigrants were mostly indentured servants, the kind of people in whom a degree of uncouthness may be pardoned. Did a few years in America confer social grace? Not necessarily. In a memoir written after the Revolution, William Dunlap, painter, author, and playwright (he is often called the father of the American theater) recalled his Perth Amboy childhood. It lacked charm and delicacy:

> I was born in the city of Perth Amboy in the province of New Jersey. My father, Samuel Dunlap, was a native of the north of Ireland and son of a merchant of Londonderry. . . . The 19th of February, 1766, is registered as the date of my birth [an important day] duly celebrated by my indulgent parents. Of education I had none, in the usual sense of the word, owing to circumstances I shall mention, and much of that which is to the child most essential was bad.
>
> Holding negroes in slavery was, in those days, the common practice. . . . Every house in my native place where any servants were to be seen swarmed with black slaves. My father's kitchen had several families of them. . . . These blacks indulged me, of course, [and] in the mirth and games of the negroes and the variety of visitors of the black race who frequented the place my desires were shaped. This may be considered my first school, and, indeed, such was the education of many a boy: The infant was taught to tyrannize, the boy was taught to despise labor, the mind of the child was contaminated by hearing and seeing [what] was not understood at the time but which remained in the memory.[26]

*William Dunlap,
"father of the American theater."*

COURTESY: SPECIAL COLLECTIONS AND ARCHIVES,
RUTGERS UNIVERSITY LIBRARIES

Dunlap, an artist, may have been sensitive to such things. It would be wrong to imagine, for example, that the Scots-Irish were untypically harsh in their treatment of slaves. Most white people behaved as they did. All the same, Dunlap conveys a sense of a group and class still rough around the edges, prosperous but not yet polished. Ulster settlers in New Jersey were not Boston Brahmins. They had all the advantages of urban life except urbanity.

Dunlap's recollection of a comfortable but strangely crude upbringing has wider application. Many eighteenth-century New Jerseyans, if asked to describe their Ulster Irish neighbors, would have offered a similarly ambivalent account. Observers were never sure if they were devout or deviant. Consider the Reverend Carl Magnus Wrangel, provost of the Swedish Lutheran congregations in America, who made a journey across New Jersey in October 1764. Traveling from Philadelphia to the Atlantic Ocean and back, 220 miles in all, he recorded his impressions of the still untamed colony. In the backwoods people could master nature or be mastered by it. The Irish, Wrangel implied, fell into both categories. He was edified by one encounter:

> We arrived late in the evening [of October 11] at the home of an Irishman named Elisha Clark, by religion a Presbyterian. We were affectionately received and well treated in this house. He lived in the middle of the forest where, by the river called Little Egg Harbor, he had built a saw and flour mill. The soil here is very poor, so that no grain will grow. Nevertheless this man had by means of these mills acquired a fine property. He buys grain at places where it is to be found, grinds it here, and then sends the flour by water on this river which has its outlet in the ocean, to the West Indian Islands. In the same way, he saws lumber and beams, which are loaded on ships here and carried to the same places. Consequently, no-one lives here except those who work for him in the woods. . . .
>
> What especially delighted me here was to find that the man with his entire household feared God. He had built a small wooden church on his property, near the house, and two or three times a year there was preaching by Presbyterian or other ministers. Between times he holds services every Sunday for his people, with talks, prayer and singing.[27]

Wrangel had stumbled on an individual but also a set of social and economic processes. Elisha Clark personified, indeed almost parodied, the self-ascribed qualities of the Scots-Irish: hardworking, God-fearing, wilderness-clearing, family-rearing. Apparently isolated, he was connected to a wider Atlantic world: economically, by his West Indian business; religiously, by his preservation of an Ulster Presbyterian heritage; culturally, by cordial relations with his Swedish Lutheran neighbors. Eighteenth-century America was made by a thousand Elisha Clarks.

Yet not all was well in the woods. The day after his stay with Clark, Wrangel saw another side of Little Egg Harbor:

> In the morning, after prayers and after we had eaten breakfast, we went out to see the place and the mills. About half a mile away we saw the loading site on the river, where more than twenty ships now lay to receive the products of the district. There was a tavern run by an Irishman by the name of Westcott, who appeared to by making money to the harm of others and with little concern about God.[28]

Richard Wescott's tavern was at a place called the Forks, near Batsto; it remained in business from 1761 to 1781, when the owner moved to May's Landing. Wrangel's experience with Clark and Wescott, or some variation of it, repeated itself time and again in New Jersey's history. Throughout the eighteenth century, and the centuries that followed, there were Irish innkeepers to satisfy the needs of New Jersey drinkers, and Irish pietists—usually clergymen—to condemn them. To complete the triangle, the drinkers themselves were often Irish. Here was a moral universe, an encounter of virtue and vice, in elegant balance and harmony.

Wrangel thought that godliness and ungodliness defined the difference between Clark and Wescott. He also realized, however, that they shared a knack for making money. The notion that infinite wealth awaited those prepared to endure wilderness was the coping stone of immigrant mythology. John Rea, a Belfast man, wrote to his brother in 1765 encouraging him to come to South Carolina. It was a place, he said, to "get land" and where there was "plenty of good eating and drinking."[29] New Jersey was also a place of land and drinking. Not every immigrant succeeded, but enough did to encourage belief in the possibilities of the limitless frontier. Think of Thomas Lowrey. Born in Ireland in 1737, he became a prominent landowner in Flemington, eventually commanding the Hunterdon County militia during the Revolutionary War and serving as a member of the Provincial Congress of New Jersey in 1775. Lowrey was typical of those mid-eighteenth-century country squires who, enriched by land and commerce, became Revolutionary patriots. In his thirties he was a member of the Hunterdon County gentry, vaguely situated on the social scale somewhere between landed "gent" and landed "gentleman." That he had prospered is evident from this offer of land for sale in 1776:

> To be Sold: A Plantation in the township of Amwell, Hunterdon County, West New-Jersey, containing three hundred acres of excellent land, twenty acres of which is good watered meadow, . . . eighty acres in wood, the rest is very fine pasture and arable, . . . capable of producing as good crops of every sort as any in the province. . . . The buildings are complete and convenient, consisting of an elegant new stone dwelling house, two stories high, the front . . . brick and handsomely finished. . . .
>
> This plantation is situated close to the village of Flemington, in a very pleasant, healthy and plentiful country at the junction of several capital roads leading from Philadelphia and New York to various parts of the country. . . . For further particulars apply to the proprietor, Thomas Lowrey.[30]

Lowrey succeeded, others failed. What never failed was the conviction that a "pleasant, healthy and plentiful country" such as New Jersey afforded opportunities for a man to thrive. When the revived British mercantilism of the 1760s threatened this expectation, the result was revolution. The likes of Lowrey left Ulster because prospects there were dim. Followed across the Atlantic by yet more restrictions on economic freedom, they chose to fight.

The success of Clark, Wescott, and Lowrey seems to confirm the immigrant ideology of upward social mobility. In some ways, though, it also belies it. Some Irishmen succeeded only because other Irishmen, in relative terms, failed. The labor that allowed estates to flourish was provided by indentured servants, many of them Irishmen (and women) who chafed at lives of poorly rewarded drudgery and occasional brutality. Most served their time, but others escaped. Those who fled their obligations were not necessarily feckless. On the contrary, escape suggests the simplest form of entrepreneurialism: a desire to become one's own master. Employers, of course, regarded runaways as unreliable. To them they were chattels, often also drunkards whose indiscipline was typical of their class and breed. For all that, the same owners wanted them back. Property remained property regardless of quality.

Throughout the eighteenth century, New Jersey newspapers were peppered with requests for the return of Irish ne'er-do-wells. It is difficult to know if these succeeded in their primary purpose of recovering lost property. In their secondary purpose of conveying the picaresque reality of runaway life, they were triumphs of verbal economy and color. In 1742 Jacob Ford of Morris County sought the whereabouts of "Richard White, an Irishman, with somewhat of the brogue on his tongue [and] very impertinent in his talk," who had absconded with "Michael Collins, an Irishman." In 1751 a reward was offered for Nicholas McDoniel "lately arrived from Ireland, said to have gone to his uncle in Amboy." In 1766 William Gilliland sought "James Ramsay, who came from County Armagh [and is] known to be in New Jersey."[31] In 1776 John Jessup of Gloucester County offered sixteen dollars reward for information about "an Irishman named Robert McFarland: he had on a felt hat almost new, two brownish jackets, the upper one with small cuffs . . . and good shoes with copper or brass buckles."[32] In March of the same year "an indented Irish servant man named John McGill" ran away from Atsion Furnace in West Jersey, "about 32 years of age . . . [with] red curled hair, sandy complexion, much pitted with the small-pox."[33] In June 1776 "an Irish servant man named Nathaniel Anster" went missing, his salient features "dark brown hair, red beard, loves strong drink, chews tobacco, and says he was five years on board a man of war."[34] The following month "an Irish servant man named Morris McQuaid" ran away from Seth Lippincott in Chester Township, Burlington County, "a well set fellow, fresh colour, black hair, grey eyes, and is very quarrelsome when in liquor. . . . It is very likely he will change his name and go towards York."[35] Even if runaways were not Irish, they might have Irish accomplices. John Eyanson ran away from Isaac Moss in February 1776, his companion "a certain Daniel McGraw . . . a black looking Irishman [who] takes a great quantity of snuff."[36] Most of the delinquents were men, but women also ran away. In February 1777 John Shields (himself Irish) offered four dollars reward for the return of "an Irish servant girl named Hester Cavanagh, about 18 years of age, 5 feet high, stout build, and looks remarkably innocent, has light brown hair, full grey eyes, and a remarkable burn, which she got lately, upon her right arm, near the elbow."[37]

Whether man or woman, the absconded servant needed a plausible new identity. Unfortunately most efforts at concealment were comically inept. One fugitive argued away his strange-sounding accent by claiming that "he was born in England but has the brogue on his tongue": that, in other words, he only *seemed* like the escaped Irishman his employer sought. Another, whose name was O'Bryan, styled himself "Bryan" to disguise his ethnic origin. Some were too colorful for their own good, larger-than-life characters quite beyond disguise. For conspicuousness few could match "an Irish servant man named James Murphey . . . kept in the station of a schoolmaster" who "sometimes ties his hair behind with a string, [is] a very proud fellow, loves drink and when drunk is very imprudent and talkative, pretends much and knows little, was in the French service and can talk French."[38] Murphy absconded in 1754. His type has never entirely disappeared.

## SCHOOLMASTERING: AN IRISH PROFESSION

**K**EPT IN THE station of a schoolmaster," the egregious James Murphey was one of a significant number of Irishmen who found employment as teachers in eighteenth-century New Jersey. Schoolmastering was a means of performing indentured service and, occasionally, of climbing a rung or two on the social ladder. In rare cases (as with those who taught for the College of New Jersey) it was a religious and professional vocation. Whether indicative of social success or failure, teaching was a calling heard disproportionately by Irishmen. "Many of our schoolteachers were Irishmen," claimed the historian of early Dutch settlement in Monmouth County. "Smart, passably educated young Irishmen" did some of the schooling in Middlesex County. The teachers of Somerset County were "generally immigrants from Ireland, England or Scotland." In Morris County, "many of those employed as teachers were of foreign birth, either Englishmen or Irishmen."[39] For better or worse, hardly any county in colonial New Jersey was untouched by Irish pedagogy.

That teaching was often left to foreigners indicates its lowly standing. Less a profession than a form of hired help, schoolmastering was work for wanderers, even for drifters. In Middlesex County, for example, it was farmed out to "men who came into the neighborhood prospecting, or without any regular employment." If they were literate, presentable, sober, and "passably educated" they would do. Francis Bazley Lee, the distinguished historian of early New Jersey, thought that "Scotch and Irish redemptioners" became teachers so that "the cause of learning and polite manners might thereby be advanced." In fact, most were not ready for the drawing room, and some were unfit even for the schoolroom itself. Consider the evidence of Casper Schaeffer, a clergyman who died in 1857 at the age of seventy-three. Schaeffer grew up in Stillwater, Sussex County, and learned his lessons in the local elementary school. Late in life he recalled the schoolmasters of his youth:

> The old school house in which I received the first elements of my English education . . . was situated close under the hill where the lime-stone rocks jut out furthest. The teachers were numerous in a long succession of years. First of all was Paddy McElvany, fresh from the green Shamrock. He gloried in teaching children to read hard names, together with the Children's and Westminster Shorter Catechism. In consequence of his too great liking for the *ardent*, his right hand refused its cunning, and he resorted to the use of copper-plates to teach his pupils chirography. The next was Hubbard, an old Revolutionary soldier from New England. He was given to inebriation also. The next was Crosby from the isle of Erin. He was generally sober, but never refused good cheer when gratuitously offered. Next came one by the name of Hand—not remarkable for any great deeds. To him succeeded Boulton, a great arithmetician, but addicted to long-continued sprees. He as well as the following, whose name I do not recollect, were both from the Emerald Isle; the last, as well as the preceding, delighted to suck the liquid poison. The next was Mr. Graham, a gentlemanly man who also came from Ireland. . . . Next came Dillingham, a Revolutionary soldier; was in the battle of Monmouth under Washington. After him succeeded Coffee, an Irish strolling play actor, who taught us something of the art of speaking dialogues etc., and gave us a taste for theatricals.[40]

Schaeffer's taste for the theatrical had plenty of material in such a troupe. Perhaps Stillwater had a bad run in the 1790s; perhaps the fact that Schaeffer became a professional moralist sharpened the memory of his uncouth boyhood; perhaps one ethnic group always tends to find fault with another. Whatever the reason, the memoir has the ring of truth. Many Irish teachers in eighteenth-century New Jersey were vagabonds and otherwise unemployable sots. Naturally a German would see little humor in the fact. Yet Schaeffer was not alone in noticing the problem. In 1760 Governor Thomas Boone issued a proclamation requiring all New Jersey schoolmasters to be licensed. Young people, he said, "ought not to be trusted but to Persons of Good Character, and loyal Principles, and professed Protestants."[41] Disloyal Catholics, many of them Irish, had infiltrated the "profession." Thus Boone's interdiction. It probably did little good.

Schaeffer's pen picture has another value: it balances those uncritical histories that offer Irish schoolmasters as selfless scholars, promoters of civility in an incorrigibly rustic world. James Snell, one of the first historians of Sussex County, noted that Patrick McIlvaney and George Matthews, both born in Ireland, were "pedagogues of much fame" who "left their impress upon the youthful minds of the vicinity."[42] This was the same McElvany who impressed Casper Schaeffer with his early morning shakes. Michael O'Brien, chronicler of eighteenth-century teachers throughout New Jersey, cites James Murphey as one "whose influence was directed in moulding the intellect and character of many a New Jersey youth."[43] This was the same long-haired, French-speaking Murphey who absconded in 1754. Examples could be multiplied. Alone, official histories tell only part of a story. Behind their dutiful lists of Flannerys and Welshes, Doughertys and Dunleavys, Finigans and Fitzpatricks, stood a parallel world altogether more rackety and uncertain.[44] The most suitable school for the majority of these characters was not Eton but Dotheboys Hall.

Not all teachers were stock characters. Some were men of genuine ability, perseverance, and scholarship. The first teacher in the "Academy" at Somerville (1801) was Lucas George, "an Irishman who proved to be a fine scholar and an efficient instructor." Edmund Barry of Trinity College, Dublin, was a "most successful" teacher of Latin in Elizabeth; later he took Episcopalian orders. John McCarter of Londonderry worked as a Sussex County schoolmaster while penning popular political journalism and later fought in the Revolutionary War. Timothy Murphy taught at Raritan before becoming a judge of the Court of Common Pleas of Monmouth County. Perhaps the most notable Irish teacher in early New Jersey was Hugh Knox, briefly of Elizabethtown, latterly of the West Indies, who "discovered" and taught Alexander Hamilton. Knox, born in Ireland in 1727 of Scots Presbyterian parents, came to America at the age of eighteen and for a time "led a life of worldly gayety, teaching for a support."[45] Abandoning this style of life, he graduated from the College of New Jersey in 1754, was ordained for the Dutch Reformed ministry in 1755, and answered a call to preach on the tiny island of Saba in the Dutch West Indies. It was then that Hamilton entered the story. Hamilton was brought up in the West Indies, and the two seem to have met on the Danish

*Gilbert Tennant, son of William Tennant, one of the founders of the College of New Jersey, later Princeton University.*

❧

island of St. Croix in early 1772. Knox was the first to recognize his talents. Although they knew each other only briefly—Hamilton left for Boston in September or October 1772—they continued to correspond. Knox's influence on Hamilton's intellect is not entirely clear, but his encouragement and moral earnestness added significantly to his political and military career.[46]

Irish teachers thus varied between the hopeless and the high-minded. Into the latter category may be placed the founders of the College of New Jersey, better known as Princeton University. The college was established as a "New Light" Presbyterian seminary in 1746, growing out of the "Log College" of Neshaminy, Pennsylvania, which was founded in 1727 by William Tennant of Armagh and his sons Gilbert, William, and John. The Reverend Samuel Finley, president in 1761, and John Blair, first professor of theology, were both Irish born. Samuel Smith, son of a Derry immigrant, became college president in 1795. In its early decades the college had solid numbers of Scots-Irish in the student body.

## CATHOLICS

**T**HE STANDARD account of Irish migration to America is that the eighteenth century was dominated by Ulster Presbyterians, the nineteenth by Roman Catholics from the rest of the country. This is largely true, but like most rules of thumb it sacrifices subtlety for simplicity. Emigration of Presbyterians continued well into the nineteenth century, only falling as a percentage of the whole when Catholic numbers became overwhelming.[47] As for Catholics themselves, their numbers in the eighteenth century seem paltry in part because in the nineteenth century they were so plentiful. When famine brought starving millions to America, everything that came before looked trivial. Of course, the eighteenth century remains the era of Presbyterian migration, but the coming of Catholics, however modest, should not be ignored.

New Jersey imitated the colonial experience as a whole. Eighteenth-century

Catholicism was small but not invisible. The historian who looks closely may see traces of it, sometimes in whole communities, more usually in scattered individuals who found employment as indentured servants. The majority of Irish Catholics in the first half of the century fell into the latter category, a fact that made life difficult for them and continues to make it difficult for their chroniclers. The great historian of eighteenth-century Ireland, W.E.H. Lecky, once wrote that "under the long discipline of the penal law Irish Catholics . . . became consummate adepts in the arts of conspiracy and disguise."[48] The same might be said of Irish Catholics in New Jersey. They seem to disappear into the woods leaving only a name, a memory, a hint of former presence. There are good reasons for this. One is that indentured service did not provide enough people to justify a priest or a parish. Unnourished, Catholicism withered. Another difficulty is that New Jersey, like Ireland, officially discriminated against Catholics. The sanctions were sharp, making it likely that at least some Catholics would abandon rather than admit their faith. A third problem is that Catholics found indentured service harder than most. They rarely worked for employers who sympathized with their religion, still less with those who shared it. This may account for the generally poor performance of Catholic bondsmen throughout the colonies. It may also explain why many of them became runaways. (Richard White and Michael Collins, noted already as absconders, were both Catholic.) It is fanciful to imagine that many Catholics left Ireland for America to escape the workings of the penal code. The evidence suggests that those who fled the country were farmers, soldiers, merchants, students, and priests—not the types to become indentured servants. Besides, most of them went to Europe, not America.[49] However, if by chance some came to New Jersey for reasons of religion, they must have been sorely disappointed in what they found.

Most Catholics, then, lived in relative isolation. They performed their service, then tried to branch out on their own. Yet there were also larger groups. In 1740 an Anglican rector reported that up to eighty Catholics had moved into his parish at Alloway's Creek, Salem County. The local legend that they had been shipwrecked seems an invention but it suggests plausibly enough that few would willingly go to such a place. These far-flung Irish found work in the Wistar glassworks (where South Jersey's first mass was celebrated in 1743), then in the iron foundries of Atsion, Batsto, and the inaptly named Pleasant Mills.[50] If they longed for home in the Pinelands it was because their work was hard and heavy, their terms of employment little more than a kind of servitude. Years later, Bishop Michael Corrigan of Newark visited Egg Harbor and Pleasant Mills. Shown a baptismal register for the 1830s, he noticed "about 100 names, chiefly Irish," and was moved by the thought of these "few Catholics lost in this wilderness of sand."[51] That was in 1879.

*Father Ferdinand Farmer, German Catholic evangelist among the early Irish of New Jersey.*

The Irish had stuck it out until the mills closed in the 1860s: a dreary exile for a lonely flock.

Elsewhere Catholics clung precariously to the faith. From 1765 until his death in 1787 a German missionary, Father Ferdinand Farmer, worked in the scattered villages and homesteads of northwestern New Jersey. His ministry was mainly to Germans, but ninety-nine families on his baptismal register had Irish or English names. Among these were ironworkers employed by the Ringwood Company, thirty-six miles north of Newark. The company provided work for nearly six hundred men, many of them Irish. Indeed, the area directly behind the foundry was known locally as "Irishtown," distinguishing it from "Germantown" in the hills above Charlottenburg and the Pequannock River. Farmer was as much an anthropologist as a pastor. He noticed, for example, how national style manifested itself in religious practice. Germans baptized their children immediately, with or without a priest; the Irish preferred to wait, sometimes bringing whole families of youngsters to be baptized at once. Farmer's suggestion, perhaps ethnically self-serving, was that the Irish tended to be casual in the faith, the Germans serious. Maybe it was simply another instance of Lecky's law: that concealment and caution, "the arts of conspiracy and disguise," had so entered Irish folk memory that it remained a strong feature of religious behavior far from the reaches of English authority. Whatever of that, Farmer was prophetic in one respect. A century after his death, differences between Irish and German Catholicism bitterly divided the New Jersey church. That was for the future. For the present, there were more pressing problems. Farmer's mission was always precarious, never guaranteed to survive from year to year. His own baptismal register contained a reminder of the difficulties. In it he carried the official notice of Governor Bernard that Catholics were specifically excluded from religious liberty. Later the state constitution (1776) granted religious freedom but continued to bar Catholics from public office and, probably, from voting. This lasted until 1844. In fact these various edicts were hardly necessary. The sheer remoteness of homesteads, Irish or German, did the work of decatholicizing New Jersey better than any formal prohibition.[52]

Alone, Farmer could do little. Most Catholics went without benefit of clergy, thereby losing any faith inherited from parents or distant memories of Ireland. At the end of the Revolution there may have been as few as two hundred of them (John Rutherford's estimate in *Notes on the State of New Jersey* in 1786) or as many as nine hundred (the more plausible guess of Barbe de Marbois, French agent-general in New York).[53] However calculated, the numbers were small. Yet if thin on the ground they were at least widespread. In the last third of the century there were Donnellys in Burlington, Duffs in New Brunswick, Colvins and Dwyers in Trenton, McDonoghs in Newark, McGlones in Salem, and Kellys and Murphys in Trenton, Gloucester, Princeton, Elizabethtown, Bound Brook, and Sussex. As with the Ulster Scots, they fell into the category of "middling folk"—merchants, farmers, carpenters, iron-workers, innkeepers. They might have remained at the lower end of the scale for longer; few made it all the way to the top. Most of them sweated for a living. In Morris County the Hibernia Furnace had a mainly Irish and Dutch workforce. To keep them sober, a law of 1767 prohibited tavernkeeping within four miles of the place. Elsewhere Catholics worked for themselves. Terence Reilly taught "book-keeping, merchant's accounts and mathematicks . . . in the best and most approved methods." Michael Kearney imported horses. Alexander McCormick was "a noted player on the Irish pipes." Garret Meade advertised "choice Irish beef."[54] Thomas Kane ran the Fox Chase Tavern in Trenton, where mass was celebrated in 1782 or 1783, mainly for Irish immigrants.[55] Far from home, some kept the faith alive.

## THE IRISH AT LARGE

**M**cCORMICK WITH his pipes and Meade with his beef were among the first to recognize that ethnicity was a marketable commodity. They were not the last. In 1778 one Thomas Moody of Princeton offered for sale, among other things, some "fine Irish linen [and] Irish sheeting" on terms "as reasonable . . . as the present times will permit."[56] In so describing his wares he was not making a political point, but many Americans were well disposed toward Ireland because of its support for the Revolution. They may have thought better of Irish goods as a result. Certainly by the end of the eighteenth century "Irishness" meant more than "belonging to Ireland." Irish linen originated in Ireland; "Irish" people could come from almost anywhere. Consider the testimony of one Jacob Stille of Gloucester County. In July 1776, the memorable month when America came of age, Stille was interested in tracing the whereabouts of "an Irish servant man named Isaac Brown . . . born near Springfield in New Jersey."[57] He made no distinction between birth in Ireland and in America. To him, Irishness was an ethnic, not a geographic, fact. Most of his contemporaries thought the same way. Historians must exercise caution in speaking of the New Jersey Irish in the eighteenth century. Some of the "Irish" never came within three thousand miles of Ireland.

Bundling together Irish born and Irish by ethnicity, how does New Jersey compare with the rest of colonial America? In 1790, when the first census was taken, New Jersey's population was 184,139. The white population was primarily English (50.6 percent) and Dutch (20.1 percent). Only 11 percent were Irish or Scots-Irish—less than 7 percent from Ulster, 4 percent from the rest of Ireland. The total population, in other words, was small, the Irish component of it even smaller. Moreover, "New Jersey's proportions of English, Scots, Scots-Irish and Irish were approximately half those of Pennsylvania."[58] Throughout the eighteenth century Pennsylvania and southern Appalachia were greater magnets, especially for Ulster Presbyterians. Yet this should not minimize the Irish contribution to colonial New Jersey: rather the opposite. As founders of towns, colleges, and businesses, people from Ireland left a mark that belied their numbers. Nowhere was this more apparent than in the Revolution itself.

## REVOLUTIONARY NEW JERSEY

SEPARATED BY an ocean, Ireland and America were rarely closer than in the middle decades of the eighteenth century. As Britain's imperial system began to unravel, observers on both sides of the Atlantic recognized important political and personal parallels between the two countries. Each had a sharp sense of constitutional inferiority, and each resented it. Ireland had a weak parliament, which met infrequently. Political power was in the hands of an absentee viceroy appointed by the Crown, and "undertakers"—political grandees—who "undertook" to navigate legislation through the Irish House of Commons in return for titles, sinecures, pensions, and powers of patronage. Under the Declaratory Act (1720), the Irish House of Commons (an assembly representing only the Protestant landed interest) was subordinate to the House of Commons at Westminster. Only the latter body could initiate legislation; the task of the Irish House of Commons was merely to approve it. Ireland's trade was regulated. Imperial and foreign affairs were in the hands of the London government.

These marks of subordination linked Ireland and America in a joint ordeal. With the accession of George III (1760) and the ending of the Seven Years' War (1763), both countries experienced the unwelcome novelty of renewed regulation by Britain. Closer control was the order of the day. "Salutary neglect" ended in America with the passage of the Sugar, Stamp, and Declaratory acts. Ireland felt the chain tighten with the ending of "government by undertakers" and its replacement by the direct political management of a resident English viceroy. This was the first sign of a major change in Ireland's constitution, and it led to the formation of a "patriot party" under the leadership of Henry Flood and Henry Grattan. Flood and Grattan were typical members of the Protestant Ascendancy: landed, well-connected Anglicans who argued that Ireland's political institutions should be strengthened within the existing imperial system. They were reluctant revolutionaries, if revolutionaries at all. Certainly they were not radicals either socially or politically. Irish independence was not on their agenda. The political arguments of the 1760s and 1770s were squabbles within a ruling class; the lower orders had little to do with them.

Political bonds between Ireland and America were reinforced by personal ties. The literate Irish classes knew of America from newspapers but also from relatives. Emigration, especially from Ulster, created a genuine transatlantic community in the mid-eighteenth century. There was, one Belfast Presbyterian remarked in 1776, "scarcely a Protestant family of the middle classes who does not reckon kindred with the inhabitants of that extensive continent."[59] For decades, letters had crossed the ocean telling of riches to be made in the New World. With prosperity now threatened, the outbreak of revolution in America was greeted enthusiastically, even enviously, by many in Ireland.

But there was a complication. When France joined the American war in 1778, Ireland's shores were unprotected against possible invasion by England's newest enemy. To remedy this, a militia known as the "Volunteers" came into being. These Volunteers were members of the rural and urban middle classes, Protestants mainly, led by the local gentry and aristocracy. Their chief enthusiasm was for dressing up and playing soldier. Grattan, Flood, and other "patriots" were prominent members. With huge numbers—forty thousand in September 1779—and with weapons supplied by the government itself, the Volunteers represented a powerful new force in Irish politics. That power was used in 1779 to win an end to restrictions on Irish trade within the Empire. Emboldened, the Volunteers demanded "Legislative Independence," which meant the right of the Irish House of Commons to initiate legislation for Ireland. With the American colonies on the brink of victory, the English administration under Lord Rockingham had little option but to concede. The Declaratory Act was repealed in June 1782, and other measures followed to secure the independence of the Irish judiciary. The "constitution of 1782" was thus achieved because revolution in America intersected with quasi-revolution in Ireland. Without the first the second could not have happened.

This, then, was Ireland's debt to America. The larger country set the stage that enabled the smaller one to arm and defend itself, then to win concessions from their mutual opponent. It also provided the political language by which the smaller country justified its actions. But America had its own debt to Ireland, and it was substantial. There was natural sympathy between the two countries, George Washington suggested in 1781, derived from shared experience of "heavy and tyrannical oppression." "It is impossible not to admire the spirit which animates the speakers in the Irish Parliament," opined the *New Jersey Journal* in March 1780, "or not to wish Ireland a similar station among nations as that we enjoy."[60] As if to personify this fellow feeling, people of Irish extraction were prominent in the American revolutionary cause. The printer of the Declaration of Independence was John Dunlap from County Tyrone. The leader of Pennsylvania radicalism, later secretary to the Continental Congress, was Charles Thomson from County Derry. The sharpest opponent in South Carolina of ratifying the federal Constitution was Aedanus Burke from County Galway. "Call this war by whatever name you may, only call it not [American]," a British officer wrote in 1778. "It is nothing more than a Scots Irish Presbyterian rebellion."[61] The rebellion was not exclusively Irish, and the Irish element not exclusively Presbyterian: even so, the soldier was not far from the truth.

Why? Part of the reason has to do with Scots-Irishness itself. The Scots-Irish myth—the story they told themselves of themselves—was replete with language of fortitude, bravery, and independence of mind. They were men of the frontier, the "stern and virile people" Theodore Roosevelt later called them: honest, egalitarian, upright, God-fearing, hardworking, and frugal. This suggests a paradox: when they were most themselves, when they exhibited most emphatically these self-ascribed virtues, they were not Scots-Irish at all but American. One myth blended naturally with the other so that it became hard to see where the first ended and the second began. The American language of liberty and equality came easily to Scots-Irish lips because they were its partial progenitors. Intellectually they inhabited a world curiously compounded of Calvinism and Lockean secularism, of righteousness and liberal rationalism. A more potent mixture has rarely been concocted. The revolutionary philosophy suited them because they imagined themselves equal to any king and equal to each other.

Few of them would have understood or cared that their principles came from very different sources. It was enough that the frontier experience, the settling of a new land, imbued them with democratic imagination, showing them how to organize politics without need of outside direction. Economics also played a part in their disengagement from Britain. Liberty of conscience and civic association were important, but so was the liberty of self-enrichment. These were not separable freedoms. "Property" to the eighteenth-century mind was a term that included all these notions.

Pennsylvania was the colony whose Scots-Irish population was most effectively mobilized in the radical cause. The Irish element was larger there, the frontier conditions more pronounced. What of New Jersey? As with other places, a rule of thumb seems to work: patriotism was strongest where New Englanders and the Scots-Irish were strong, in Morris County and lower Cumberland, and weaker where they were weak, in the southern stretches of the colony. Most of New Jersey's Irish patriots are obscure, of course: the farmers, schoolmasters, and tradesmen who fought in Washington's army; the iron-workers of Hibernia Forge who supplied its weaponry; the women who tended fields or homes or stores when menfolk were absent. Historians find it easy to ignore the anonymous many and celebrate the notable few. Naturally New Jersey had its share of the latter: William Pa-

***William Paterson.***

COURTESY: SPECIAL COLLECTIONS AND ARCHIVES, RUTGERS UNIVERSITY LIBRARIES

terson—a delegate to the Constitutional Convention, later senator, governor, and Supreme Court justice—who was born in County Antrim; John Neilson—a member of the Continental Congress—whose father was a Belfast man; the Reverend James Caldwell, the "rebel high priest," who was born in Virginia of Irish parents. Mostly, however, history was made by those whom history has forgotten. That is usually the way.

From a military perspective, New Jersey was the cockpit of the Revolution. Washington wintered his troops there on three occasions: in 1777 in Morristown, in 1778–79 in Bound Brook, and in 1779–80 in Morristown again. (His housekeeper in Morristown, by the way, was "a very worthy Irish woman" called Mrs. Thompson.)[62] The last of these encampments was especially difficult due to severe weather, poor food, and chronic boredom. By March 1780, alarmed by "mortifying proofs of inattention and relaxation of discipline," Washington feared a mutiny. To raise morale, he gave permission for a Saint Patrick's Day Ball to be held, urging that "the celebration of the day will not be attended with the least rioting or disorder." That hope seems to have been vindicated. According to a Loyalist newspaper, the festivities began "with music and the hoisting of colors, exhibiting the thirteen stripes, the favorite Harp, and an inscription declaring in capitals, The Independence of Ireland. . . . The simple-minded Teagues were charmed with the sight of the harp, forgot their sufferings, dropped their com-

*John Neilson (1745–1833), an officer in the Revolutionary army and member of the Continental Congress, was born at Raritan Landing, near New Brunswick. He was the only son of Belfast-born Dr. John Neilson. The younger Neilson later served in the New Jersey state convention that adopted the U.S. Constitution.*

plaints, and seemed perfectly happy for the moment, though not a drop of whiskey or taffie was to be seen in the camp."[63]

Not every Irishman forgot his troubles so readily. Desertion was a problem—most obviously for commanding officers but also for deserters themselves, who found that their Irishness identified them as surely as any physical mark. Scattered throughout New Jersey newspapers during the Revolutionary War were notices seeking information about a motley crew of malcontent Irishmen:

> March 30, 1776. Deserted on the 28th of March inst, from the . . . Third Battalion of New Jersey troops . . . John McBride, an Irishman, about 35 years of age, a down looking fellow, a true votary to Bacchus, very talkative and impertinent.[64]

> Princeton, April 3, 1777
> Deserted from the second Regiment of the State of New Jersey . . . the following persons, viz . . .

> Patrick McMullin, inlisted in Wood's town, Salem County . . .

> Owen Ward, a native Irishman, about 39 years of age, 5 feet 4 inches high, his fore teeth gone, knock kneed, has the letters O.W. pricked out with gun-powder on his arm . . .

> John Stephenson, . . . an Irishman, brown complexion, dark brown hair, which curls naturally on his neck.[65]

Trenton, July 10, 1777

Deserted from . . . Col. Hazen's regiment, Redmond Burk, a Sergeant, born in Ireland . . . very talkative and is a great liar, has sore legs, and a black patch on his nose.[66]

Notice again the distinction between "Irishman" and "native Irishman," the former Irish by lineage, the latter obviously by birth in Ireland itself. Whichever was the case, the story of the Irish in Revolutionary New Jersey is not one of unalloyed heroism.

If valor lies in the eyes of the beholder, so, too, does espionage. One Irishman who deserves more than a footnote in New Jersey's Revolutionary history is John Honeyman. A double agent who played an important part in Washington's decision to attack the British at the Battle of Trenton in December 1776, Honeyman was born in County Armagh of Scottish parents in 1730. His first appearance in North America may be dated to 1759, when he fought reluctantly for the British in Canada under the leadership of General James Wolfe. "He was possessed of a tolerable education," remembered his grandson, "spoke the English language correctly, but had in his speech much of the Irish brogue, which might easily have been mistaken for Scotch. . . . He was tall and commanding in stature, agile in movement, and possessing a strong and athletic frame."[67] After his conscripted service in Canada he moved south to Philadelphia and began life as a weaver, butcher, and cattle dealer. There he met his bride, Mary Henry from Coleraine, County Derry, and in early 1776 they and their young family moved to Griggstown, New Jersey, in what is now Franklin Township. During his time in Philadelphia he had met George Washington, recently appointed commander-in-chief of the Continental Army, who seems to have recognized his patriotism and potential value as an agent among the British. In a manner not entirely clear, they agreed that he would gain employment as a butcher with the British and Hessian forces stationed at Trenton, posing as a Tory while maintaining secret contact with the Revolutionary cause. His role in the Battle of Trenton was to convince the British that Washington's forces, demoralized, were in retreat to Pennsylvania, where they intended to spend the winter. This information conveyed, he then informed Washington that the British and Hessians, now off guard, planned for themselves a boisterous Christmas celebration (or so the story goes, although recent scholarship has begun to doubt it). Armed with this knowledge, Washington launched a surprise attack, which turned out to be the first major victory of the War of Independence. As for Honeyman, the fiction of his Toryism was maintained to the extent that he was subsequently captured by Washington and held briefly as a British agent. He "escaped"—that is to say, he was allowed to return to Griggstown, where

*Andrew Kirkpatrick was born in 1756 in Minebrook, New Jersey, in the homestead established by his grandfather Alexander, a strict Scots-Presbyterian who emigrated from Belfast in 1736. Alexander's values were inherited by his grandson, who was admitted to the New Jersey bar in 1785 (having trained under William Paterson) and who became chief justice of New Jersey in 1804.*

he was indicted by the Americans for treason. He was never tried. His family suffered some execration until Washington wrote to local patriots to drop the matter. The episode did his constitution no harm: he lived in Griggstown until his death at the age of ninety-two.

Honeyman was a pretend Tory. Some Irishmen were Tories by conviction or at least for purposes of self-advancement. Hugh Quigg arrived from Ireland twelve years before the outbreak of the Revolution and with his two sons supported the Loyalist cause in Morris County. Michael Kearney became a captain of the navy.[68] Robert Timpany, a Hackensack schoolmaster, was a major in the Fourth Battalion (New Jersey Loyalists), "always ready to serve his King" and receiving several wounds as a result. (The wounds were not fatal: Timpany died in Nova Scotia in 1844 at the age of 102.)[69] The list could be extended, but the point is clear. Patriotism was a complex compound of belief and necessity; so, too, was Toryism. It divided communities, churches, and even families.[70] There is no reason to imagine that it would not also divide ethnic groups. If so, it suggests a paradox: the Irish were so assimilated to America that, like many Americans, some of them remained attached to Britain. Like the larger community of which they formed a part, they were divisible along rebel and Tory lines. That renders hazardous any generalization except this: the Irish played a notable part in the Revolutionary War but "Irishness" did not. The decision to fight for king or Congress—if decision even entered the matter—was more likely to be for individual than "ethnic" reasons.

## CENTURY'S END

**A**T THE END of a century in which the histories of Ireland and New Jersey were closely intertwined, one last curious connection links the two places. As we have seen, Ireland won a constitution in 1782. America, after the failed experiment of the Articles of Confederation, fashioned her own constitution in 1789. There the parallel ended. America's revolution was over by the beginning of the 1790s; Ireland's was about to begin. Legislative independence, celebrated as a great victory in 1782, had little impact on Ireland's deeper problems—agricultural distress, rural poverty, sectarian violence, and exclusion of Catholics from public life. To these difficulties the Protestant landlord class (sole beneficiary of the constitution of 1782) had few answers. It was no surprise, then, that Irish politics, deeply influenced by the French Revolution, turned radical in the 1790s. Symbolizing this change was the formation in late 1791 of the Society of United Irishmen under the leadership of, among others, a young Dublin lawyer called Theobald Wolfe Tone. The society's aims were parliamentary reform, an end to English control of Irish affairs, and a nonsectarian politics in which all denominations would enjoy full civil and political rights. Later, the society turned to radical republicanism and insurrection.

The Dublin branch of the United Irishmen was suppressed in 1794, and the following year Wolfe Tone fled to the United States. He traveled first to Philadelphia, then to Princeton, where, somewhat improbably, he tried his hand at farming. He liked Princeton—it had "a college and some good society"—and he found New Jerseyans to be "lively and disengaged." Why, then, did he not stay? Because the Irish he met turned out to be as "boorish and ignorant as the Germans, as uncivil and uncouth as the Quakers, [with] ten times more animal spirits than both."[71] Irish republicanism was all very well; Irish republicans were another matter. In 1796 he returned to Europe, and two years later Ireland exploded in a violent uprising. Tone played a leading role in the '98 Rebellion: he was arrested while accompanying a French invasionary force and, sentenced to death, committed suicide before the authorities could execute him. Following the insurrection—the bloodiest in a century, with perhaps thirty thousand deaths—the Act of Union (1800) undid all the gains of 1782 and created the United Kingdom of Great Britain and Ireland. No moral need be drawn, but speculation is irresistible: had New Jersey shown greater charm, and its Irish population better manners, the history of Ireland might have run a different course.

CHAPTER 4

# The Nineteenth-Century Experience

## A NEW CENTURY

**N**OT EVERY Irish person who came to New Jersey came to stay. Some were simply visitors. Others were immigrants hoping to make a new life who then thought better of it, either going home or making that life elsewhere in America. A third group—not quite visitors or immigrants—were travel writers and reporters, self-appointed experts on the great American experiment. Into this last category fell Walter Cox of Dublin, who published in 1802 his *Advice to Emigrants, or Observations Made during a Nine Months' Residence in the Middle States of the American Union.* Cox was infatuated with America, thinking its freedom and prosperity an example for the rest of the world:

> Perhaps no other country besides our own, occupies so much the attention of an Irishman as does the United States of America; the rational liberty there enjoyed—the vast field for industry and enterprise—the cheapness of the necessaries of life—the easy manner of acquiring landed property—with the troubled state of Europe, makes an emigration to America a favorite topic with the artist, the husbandman, the merchant.

Rational liberty, good in itself, led to wealth that was unimaginable in Europe:

> America is the paradise of the poor man who was accustomed to the laboring life; in Europe his toil is unable to afford him one wholesome meal in the year; in America, it furnishes him with one every day. If political attachments draw him to America, he finds the cheapest and free'st government in the world—the equality so much ridiculed in Europe, as visionary theory, is no mere speculation in the western republics.

Without subtlety or understatement, Cox represented America as young and vital, Europe as stale and decadent. In this he was part of a long tradition—indeed, the longest tradition in Anglo-American cultural relations. Cox's insights were shaped by his expectations: he wanted to find an America as good as he thought it would be. Those who take his *Advice* should take it with caution.

Yet for all the boosterism, Cox was sharp in his observations and shrewd in the manner he tailored them to an Irish audience. Consider his account of New Jersey. It has the ring of truth, capturing both the pastoralism and proto-industrialism of the state at the beginning of the nineteenth century. Writing for Irish readers recently deprived of their parliament by the Act of Union, Cox was able to draw on New Jersey as a sister sufferer of British tyranny. The pamphlet was thus traveler's tale, encouragement to emigrate, and radical screed rolled into one. Everywhere he traveled, he had experiences either appealing or appalling:

> From Philadelphia we proceeded on our way to New York, arrived at the falls of the Delaware, and landed at Trenton, the capital of the Jerseys. . . . From Trenton we traveled to Brunswick, a small town, from thence to Prince-town, in which is a college, which during the war was sometime occupied by the British troops, who are accused of a Saracen atrocity, of burning a library of three thousand volumes, and destroying the celebrated Orrery, made by Dr. Rittenhouse, one of the most perfect and elegant pieces of scientific mechanism in the learned world. This college again suffered at the hands of some unknown mercenaries, who burned it to the ground, in March 1802. . . .
>
> From Prince-town we continued on our journey to Elizabeth-town; its situation is very pleasant and beautiful; it contains above two hundred houses. Then we travelled to Newark, within nine miles of New York, this town is much larger than Elizabeth-town, and very beautiful; is much resorted by the fugitives from New York, during the continuation of the yellow fever; it is inhabited by a considerable number of shoe-makers. From Newark we drove over a swamp, through which is a road made of the trunks of trees lying parallel to each other for near two miles. Arrived at the ferry on the banks of the Hudson . . . we crossed and landed in the city of New York.[1]

Cox was right to notice that by 1800 Newark was the resort of fugitives from New York. He failed to mention that it, like the state as a whole, was also increasingly the resort of fugitives from Ireland. Some locals found it hard to draw a line between honest radicals (Cox's audience) and the criminal classes for whom any lawful authority was objectionable. In 1799 William Griffith, a lawyer who advocated reform of New Jersey's constitution, complained that "our polls swarm with

*William Griffith, would-be reformer of New Jersey's electoral law, complained that the worst elements of the Irish migration threatened to overrun the state.*

❧

the very refuse of the English, Irish, Dutch and French emigrations, people whom convenience, inclination, intrigue or crimes induce to take a footing in the State."[2] Cox's paean to New Jersey, that it offered wealth and freedom, was precisely Griffith's complaint. Irishmen overwhelmed the place—"the worst sort of people from neighboring states, fugitives from justice, absconding debtors"—and were interested in democracy only insofar as it gave them opportunity to sell their votes. And elections had another attraction: rarely was there a ballot without booze. Newly democratic New Jersey had much to offer the Irishman in its early years as a state.

The delighted Cox and the dyspeptic Griffith seem to stand guard at the beginning of the nineteenth century, pointing in different ways to New Jersey's complex future. They make a paradoxical couple. Youthful enthusiasm notwithstanding, Cox was an old-fashioned writer: his celebration of American democratic prosperity could have been written a hundred years before.

Griffith was also unusual: he was a progressive who wished to preserve the past, a democrat who despised the *demos*. Yet both were right. New Jersey *was* changing—from pastoralism to industrialism, from rusticity to early urbanism. The change was gradual but, from the middle years of the century, palpable. Also altered were the people who came to the state. Immigrant farmers became factory workers, and in the transformation they discovered, often painfully, that they had entered not only a new country but a new world.

## THE PATERSON EXPERIENCE

Take a town like Paterson. Here was a place that epitomized the social and economic revolution sweeping through northern New Jersey at the end of the eighteenth century and the beginning of the nineteenth. Originally part of the township of Acquakanonk, a Dutch settlement dating from 1694, Paterson's economy and ethnic identity changed so much within a couple of generations that it had to be incorporated as a separate municipality in 1831. From its earliest days as a manufacturing town, there was "friction between the old settlers [who were Dutch] and newcomers [who were a mixture of Irish and English]." The Dutch were farmers, many of them, even in the early nineteenth century, unable to speak English; the Irish and English were industrial workers who found employment in the cotton mills and silk factories of the developing town. Tension had been high from the start. At the end of the Revolutionary War, Acquakanonk's agricultural economy was so straitened that the Society for Establishing Useful Manufactures (S.U.M.) proposed to buy up small lots to build a national cotton manufactory. The new industrial area would be called Paterson after William Paterson, New Jersey's governor. Even at this stage, farmers were divided between those who saw an opportunity to liquidate diminishing assets and those who feared that the agricultural way of life was doomed.

The latter were right to be anxious. The mill opened in 1793. At first the S.U.M. hoped to recruit local labor, but many farmers refused to allow their wives or daughters to have anything to do with it. Stymied, the S.U.M. turned to Irish immigrants in New York to make up a workforce—outsiders who served only to confirm to the locals that industrialism was indeed an alien presence in this Dutch corner of rural New Jersey. The Irish themselves were far from overjoyed at their new situation.

EDWARD FLOOD.

Edward Flood was born in Abillany, County Longford Ireland, of Thomas and Ann. He came to America in 1838, and married Miss Joanna Berry, in 1850, a circumstance of his life which he will not regret, and to which, we suspect, he can trace much of his good fortune.

With a long standing business and industrious family, life for Mr. Flood can be attended but with comfort. We can credit him with the enviable name of friend of the church. With rare and admirable zeal, and unsurpassed punctuality, does he perform any office entrusted to him in the church, even at the expense of his rest or private pursuits.

Mr. Flood was the first called on, and his ready and liberal response nerved me much for the arduous task before me, nor has he ever since forsaken the prominent position which he then assumed among the benefactors of the church, having gradually increased his donations to the sum of $425.

*Early parishioners of Saint James parish in Newark did not conceal but proclaimed their Irish roots. The effect was not merely to acknowledge origins but to suggest later success.*

❧

Catholics among them had no priest and were forced to travel to New York for mass and confession; Presbyterians (mostly of Ulster extraction) found themselves at Dutch Reformed services worshiping in a language they did not understand. Wages were poor, children went largely uninstructed, and, the *coup de grâce,* sickness swept the town in September 1794, laying up at least half the workforce.

The mill closed in 1796, but a pattern had been set. Henceforward Paterson's economy would be industrial, its population Irish and English as well as Dutch, its way of life dominated by wages and noise, not crops and silence. By 1815 the town had thirteen cotton mills, a card and wire mill, a rolling mill, and a sawmill. A generation later the change was even more pronounced:

*The Reverend William McGee, a product of the early nineteenth-century Irish migration to Paterson, was born in 1816. His parents were Patrick and Mary McGee, devout and prosperous Scots-Irish Presbyterians. McGee graduated from Princeton in 1836 and from Princeton Theological Seminary in 1841 and ministered chiefly in Sussex and Warren counties before his death in 1867.*

❧

From 1821 to 1832, the number of mills in operation went from nine to sixteen, while mill employment jumped from 663 hands to 1,597. Machine shop employment increased from 77 men in 1825 to 484 by 1838. Less mechanized, artisan crafts such as cabinet making also grew, as did the demand for the services of shoemakers, blacksmiths, millwrights, and carpenters.

Industrial expansion led to dramatic population growth. In 1822, approximately 2,200 people lived in the town; ten years later the number stood at 9,085. Unlike many other early factory towns, Paterson had a heterogeneous population comprised of English and Irish immigrants, native-born migrants from New York, New England, and New Jersey, and the descendants of the original Dutch settlers of the area.[3]

Paterson's population was so heterogeneous that even the Irish community was mixed. Most immigrants in the first two decades of the nineteenth century were Protestants from Ulster; in subsequent decades the numbers favored Catholics from the rest of the country. As early as the second decade of the century, Catholics were

*Moville, County Donegal, was the last sight of Ireland for most Ulster emigrants to the New World. Leaving from the port of Derry, they made their way up Lough Foyle and out into the unknown Atlantic.*

OOURTESY: SETON HALL UNIVERSITY SPECIAL COLLECTIONS CENTER AND UNIVERSITY ARCHIVES

sufficiently numerous to warrant their own priest. Father Philip Lariscy, a native of County Tipperary, exercised an itinerant ministry that encompassed Philadelphia and New York and places in between. Lariscy is reported to have said mass in Paterson in 1816 at the home of one Michael Gillespie on Market Street, the congregants an impressive ethnic mixture of Griffiths, Burkes, Karrs, Plunketts, Bradleys, Wades, Mahans, and Velasquezes.[4] This was the way of the future. In 1824 40 percent of the population of the town was Presbyterian, 14 percent Roman Catholic. By 1832, only eight years later, the trend was reversed: Presbyterians had declined to 28 percent; Catholics had risen to 18 percent. Regardless of religion, they all worked in the mills. In the eyes of the Dutch, who preferred to trade as blacksmiths, shoemakers, and shopkeepers, one Irishman was much the same as another.[5]

Bald numbers conceal some ironies of immigration and industrialization.

The Dutch resisted factories as alien to an agricultural way of life. They also resisted, of course, the aliens who worked in them. Yet the Irish also experienced strangeness, not simply that of a new country but also that of a new way of work. Many were weavers whose trade had languished in Ireland before and after the passage of the Act of Union in 1800. They were thus little different from the Dutch themselves: people forced to change from skilled artisanship to semiskilled industrial proletarianism. The Irish flocked to a town just as its reliance on mechanized labor tended to render their own skills redundant. In every sense, they had to cut their cloth a different way.

Apart from talent, these new workers brought with them social radicalism and a capacity for political organization. One view of the Irish in nineteenth-century America is that they came into their own as urban political operators a generation or so after the influx of the Great Famine. Not so. Their aptitude for politics was evident earlier than that. Although untutored in the ways of democracy—with no prior experience of voting in Ireland—they were able to win elections even in the first third of the century. Moreover, they brought to the ballot box a distinctly Irish American understanding of politics. In 1831, for instance, ten of thirty-eight elected officials in Paterson's local government were Irishmen. Their sympathies lay mostly with the Democratic party, and in particular with Andrew Jackson.

Sophisticated thinking lay behind this electoral achievement. Blending Irish and American themes, Patersonian Irishmen created a peculiarly Irish American iconography and in so doing fashioned a potent instrument of political progressivism. At a dinner to celebrate Jackson's election to the presidency in 1828, for instance, toasts were drunk to "the sprig of the shellah and the root of the hickory" and "the Eagle to watch and the Harp to tune the Nation till the tree of liberty be planted throughout the world." Here was a sort of transatlantic republicanism uniting both countries in freedom's cause. Certainly the Friends of Ireland, eighty-five strong in Paterson in 1828, endorsed every imaginable enlightened cause. They boosted Daniel O'Connell's campaign for Catholic Emancipation in Britain and

*Daniel O'Connell—"the Liberator"— was a powerful inspiration to Irish Catholics on both sides of the Atlantic in the first half of the nineteenth century.*

❧

COURTESY: SETON HALL UNIVERSITY
SPECIAL COLLECTIONS CENTER AND UNIVERSITY ARCHIVES

Ireland—the demand that Catholics be permitted to sit in the House of Commons at Westminster—which was an effort, they argued, to change "that system of laws by which the majority of the people of Ireland . . . have been so long oppressed"; they urged the abolition of slavery in the District of Columbia in 1828; and so on. Irishmen were thus able to blend two traditions into one, to speak the language of rights in a republic based on civic virtue, and to turn their new Americanness to good political purpose. Intellectual assimilation—acceptance of American thinking about politics and public affairs—came easily to them. The lessons of late eighteenth-century radicalism were not lost; these men became American Democrats because they had once been Irish republicans. Politically progressive, the Irish could also be industrially militant. Paterson's new prosperity came at a price: tensions with the Dutch farmers who feared for their way of life; divisions between workers and bosses on the factory floor. In 1835 two thousand textile workers went on strike in a stoppage widely attributed to Irish leadership. The strike was exceptionally bitter, producing nativist bile that had been building over several years. The Paterson *Intelligencer*, organ of the mill owners, captured the mood. The strike, it argued, was the fault of workers easily stirred by "wonderful displays of cabbage oratory."[6] This was a versatile slur, at once dividing workers from their leaders and suggesting that the latter were unsophisticated rustics. It was also ironic. Even as the Irish turned proletarian, it seemed to imply, they remained peasants at heart. In fact it was the *Intelligencer* that lacked intelligence. Its own evidence showed all too clearly that the Irish took to political and industrial activism with surprising speed. Nativists were never quick to see the obvious. All the same, this confusion in the face of new social complexity is worth noting. Within two generations two changes had occurred: Paterson was no longer a rural backwater, and the Irish who had come to live in it were no longer people of the cabbage patch but of the factory floor. For both, the growing pains were sharp, and never sharper than in 1835. The strike ended in failure: the workers had to return on the owners' terms, and the leadership and their families were permanently excluded from employment.

*The Reverend Dr. Nicholas Murray (1803–1861), an Irish American theologian, was pastor of the First Presbyterian Church of Elizabethtown and moderator of the 1849 General Assembly.*

❧

## LITTLE IRELANDS

**P**ATERSON WAS not singular. The transformed social geography of that one town—from agriculture to industry, from individualism to collectivism, from one ethnicity to another—was typical of the state, and especially its northern half, in the first decades of the nineteenth century. The Irish contributed substantially to the transformation, supplying labor to cities and industries crying out for muscle and brawn. Men took what jobs they could find: as tanners and shoemakers in Newark, carpenters and joiners in Camden, or laborers in Jersey City. They built the Morris Canal in the 1820s, the Delaware and Raritan Canal in the 1830s, and the Morris and Essex Railroad in the 1840s and 1850s. They opened shops, served in bars, became firemen and policemen, and—respectability finally beckoning in the second generation—produced a goodly number of priests and politicians. Women were employed in domestic service. They all lived in various little Irelands: the Ironbound in Newark, the Fourth Ward in Trenton ("Irishtown" in the 1850s), the "Dublin" section of Paterson, and the gerrymandered Horseshoe district in Jersey City. "New Jersey is rapidly becoming a great manufacturing state . . . a place of resort for emigrants seeking work," wrote Bishop James Roosevelt Bayley of Newark in December 1853. "The emigration is again flowing in upon us," he wrote to the rector of All Hallows Seminary in Dublin in 1860. "I was never more in want of good zealous priests."[7]

As these clusters grew, so they carried into the new country a sharp memory of the country left behind. In politics as well as culture they seemed to be curious replicas of the homeland, the preoccupations of one effortlessly, almost eerily, transplanted to the other. The great issue of Irish politics in the early 1840s, for example, was repeal of the Act of Union. This mass movement of Catholic peasants—the first such in Irish history—demanded self-government within the British imperial system. The leader of the campaign was Daniel O'Connell, "the Liberator," who had spearheaded a similar effort for Catholic Emancipation a decade before. O'Connell's efforts were followed closely throughout New Jersey. On Saint Patrick's Day 1840 the Hibernian Provident Society met in William Starr's Hotel in

*Saint John's Parish in Orange was established in 1866 to cater to the overwhelmingly Irish population of the area.*

❧

COURTESY: SETON HALL UNIVERSITY
SPECIAL COLLECTIONS CENTER
UNIVERSITY ARCHIVES

*The first parishioners of Saint John's Parish, Orange, pictured in 1886. All but one was Irish by birth or lineage.*

❦

COURTESY: SETON HALL UNIVERSITY SPECIAL COLLECTIONS CENTER AND UNIVERSITY ARCHIVES

Newark to toast Ireland's "sons and daughters: the pride and ornament of both hemispheres." Ireland itself, "the fairest of the fair: too fair to be a captive in chains," was also extolled, as was O'Connell, "who has shaken the British constitution to . . . its circumference . . . in asserting his country's rights."[8] Three years later, as the campaign for repeal reached its abortive climax (the movement failed because O'Connell, at heart a conservative figure, refused to allow it to go beyond mass meetings into defiance of the law), the Irish Association of Newark met regularly to toast O'Connell, raise morale, and generate funds. The resolutions of their meeting of November 1843 were typical. "The Irish people, as British subjects, have an undisputed . . . right to petition for the abrogation of any act of parliament," they agreed. "The act of union," they also urged, "[was] a gross fraud concocted for the purpose of annihilating [liberties]. . . . The conduct of the British government betrays a criminal recklessness . . . or a most fiendish intention." Honor satisfied, the gathering ended with three cheers for "Repeal and O'Connell," the singing of songs, and the passing of a hat to collect contributions amounting to $137.[9] Far from Ireland, these Irishmen in Newark kept it close to their hearts.

THE NINETEENTH-CENTURY EXPERIENCE **63**

*Saint Mary's Orphanage at the corner of Washington and Bleeker streets in Newark in 1859. The orphanage was refuge to many Irish children.*

❧

COURTESY: SETON HALL UNIVERSITY SPECIAL COLLECTIONS CENTER AND UNIVERSITY ARCHIVES

Nor should the southerly reaches of the state be forgotten. Little Irelands existed there, too, though hardly matching the size or political fervor of those in towns to the north. To travel south was to enter a more relaxed world. After all, the Jersey shore would soon come to be known as the "Irish Riviera," watering hole for respectable and semirespectable thirsts alike. Atlantic City was incorporated in 1854, and the following year a Catholic mission was inaugurated with masses held at Bedloe House between Atlantic and Massachusetts avenues. This was one of the first hotels of the resort; its proprietor was an Irishman called Thomas Bedloe. The first priest to minister regularly in the area was also Irish, Father Michael Francis Gallagher, born in Dromore in 1802 and ordained by Bishop Kenrick of Philadelphia in 1837.[10] Atlantic City's greatest debt, however, was to Colonel Daniel Morris, city surveyor and founder of the Morris Guards, a civilian military unit. Morris, born in Ireland in 1819, came to America as a young man. After working as surveyor of the Camden and Atlantic Railroad (under the direction of an Irish contractor, Patrick Reilly) he moved to Atlantic City and quickly recognized the possibilities of the place. It was he who laid out the streets, allowing the town to develop from less than seven hundred people in 1855 to become a major resort by the end of the century. (A division of the Ancient Order of Hibernians—with thirteen members—was established in the city in December 1890.)

Irishmen descended on New Jersey just as the national craze for canals was getting under way. As a result almost every waterway built in the state between 1825 and 1850 was largely their work. The story of the construction of the Morris Canal is well known. In 1833 a new Catholic church was opened in Paterson to cope with the overflow of Irishmen working on it. Less familiar is the contribution of Irish labor to the Delaware and Raritan Canal, begun in 1830 and completed four years later, which linked Trenton and New Brunswick. Using shovels, and sometimes bare hands, they built a waterway that became in the 1860s and 1870s one of the busiest in the country. The work was tough and, in one year, tragic. In 1832 an epidemic of Asian cholera swept the area around Princeton, killing hundreds and causing local panic. Many of the victims were Irish canalmen who were buried where they fell. Little commemorates them except the canal itself, now defunct, and a verse of contemporary doggerel:

*Irish-born Father John Fedigan ran the mission that became Our Lady Star of the Sea in Atlantic City. The picture dates from 1881.*

COURTESY: FATHER PATRICK BRADY

Ten thousand Micks
They swing their picks
To build the new canal
But the choleray
Was stronger than they
And twice it killed them all.

It was a rough-and-ready epitaph for men who deserved better.

## THE GREAT HUNGER AND THE IRISH IMAGINATION

**N**EW JERSEY changed in the nineteenth century partly because Ireland changed. The migrations of the eighteenth century were largely matters of "pull": emigrants had reasons for quitting Ireland, but mostly they had positive purposes for coming to New Jersey. Choice, not necessity, brought them across the Atlantic. The migrations of the nineteenth century were overwhelmingly matters of "push": emigrants were forced out of Ireland and would have gone almost anywhere to escape it. There were also differences of scale. Before the War of Independence Irish people came to New Jersey in hundreds, not thousands. Not wealthy, famous, or notably educated, they were mostly indentured servants who hoped to work their way to liberty and prosperity, an ambition many achieved. They became—in Governor Jonathan Belcher's words of 1748—"men of middling fortunes,"[11] builders of the towns, businesses, farms, and schools of colonial and Revolutionary New Jersey. Brought by the very "reasons of convenience and inclination" of which William Griffith complained, they formed the backbone of the place. Had such reasons not existed, America would have remained empty.

Irish immigrants of the nineteenth century were different. To begin with, there were vastly more of them. Ireland's era of mass migration began at the close of the Napoleonic Wars in 1815 and lasted until roughly 1921. During that century some eight million men, women, and children left the country to live permanently elsewhere. (One rule of thumb is worth remembering: before the Great Famine most Irish people went to Canada; between the famine and the First World War most went to the United States; after the First World War most went to Great Britain.) Between 1846 and 1850 approximately one and a half million people left the country. Postfamine emigration peaked in 1854, but Ireland's population pattern remained profoundly abnormal for another century. By 1860 two million people born in Ireland were living in the United States.

Notice, too, another feature. Almost uniquely among mass migrations, Ireland exported as many women as men; indeed, for decades more women than men left the country, seeking employment mainly as domestic servants. This was significant for Ireland and for the places where they settled. Ireland was left with no surplus female population, which meant that marriage was delayed or, for many men, did not happen at all. (The famine was partly responsible for one stock figure in Irish lore—the confirmed bachelor.) Emigration compounded the demographic disaster of famine: Ireland was left with a falling, then a stagnant, population. Only in the 1960s did emigration tail off and population trends begin to resemble European norms. As a result the country was mired in economic backwardness, political insularity, and social enervation. In America the story was different. Because women emigrated in large numbers, it was possible for Irish men to marry within their own ethnic group. The Irish could reproduce themselves abroad even as they found it difficult to do so in Ireland. In a strange way America was more "Irish" than Ireland itself. It represented a continuation of a way of life, the transplantation and preservation of communities that would otherwise have perished. America even contained a hint of what life might have been like in Ireland without the famine. It is too much to imagine that the Irish experience in America showed what could have been the Irish experience in Ireland had disaster not struck: after a century the two places remained different; besides, the famine itself was a cause of the belated modernization of Irish agriculture. It took the Irish who stayed at least a half century to discover what their emigrant cousins encountered, and partly invented, overnight— urban politics, mass industry, noisy modernity. In that sense, nineteenth-century America was Ireland speeded up; or, to invert the point, nineteenth-century Ireland was America slowed down.

*Nineteenth-century life in Ireland was based primarily on peasant agriculture. The culture shock of coming to New Jersey was sometimes overwhelming.*

❧

COURTESY: SETON HALL UNIVERSITY SPECIAL COLLECTIONS CENTER AND UNIVERSITY ARCHIVES

Dire necessity, then, not "convenience or inclination," brought Irish people to America in the middle and late nineteenth century. They saw America not as a new way of life but as life itself. Grateful for this, they also discovered that America was no paradise. At times the New World seemed little better than the one left behind. The streets were not paved with gold. Indeed, as the rueful joke had it, they were not paved at all and it was the job of the Irish to pave them. In moments of homesickness or unemployment the Irish romanticized the fields that had failed them and resented the cities that had given them a second chance.

There was another difference between these immigrant waves. Eighteenth-century migrants were mostly Presbyterians from the north of Ireland; nineteenth-century migrants were Catholics from the south and west. The distinction is important. The latter came from a premodern to a modern world and many found the adjustment difficult. Their old mental universe was one of folklore, custom, storytelling, barter, superstitious Christianity, silent landscapes, timekeeping by sun and season. Their new mental universe was one of wages, watches, rights,

*Irish rural scene of the mid-nineteenth century.*

♣

cities, noise. There was fear as well as freedom in America. New Jersey magnified these miseries: witness, as we have noticed, the Paterson story. The Irish were rural, poor, and Catholic in an urban, industrial, Protestant state. Isolated and despised, some sought escape in drinking and fighting or lapsing into petty criminality. The wonder is not that some fell but that so many did not. The Irish in nineteenth-century New Jersey behaved better than many might have predicted.

What explains the nineteenth-century exodus? The Great Famine (1845–1850) was responsible for much of it, but that was only one episode among several that prompted people to leave. Famine occurred throughout the century (the 1820s and the late 1870s were difficult times, too) and other natural disasters also sapped the will to carry on: the "Big Wind" of January 1839 uprooted trees, destroyed buildings, and killed livestock; the "Big Blizzard" of 1883 did similar damage.

The reality was that life in Ireland was chronically difficult. Indeed, there were two Irelands in the nineteenth century, both troubled. The first was the Ireland of commerce and industry, of shipping and sailing, of credit and cash. Belfast, Dublin, Galway, and Cork were maritime cities, modest by the standards of London, Liverpool, and Bristol, but still part of the Atlantic world. They were modern in a way that western Donegal, say, or Connemara was not. But there was another Ireland, almost unrecognizable as part of the same country, where primitiveness prevailed. The rural population of the west survived on barter, subsistence agriculture, and a single crop—the potato. In a world of cash, they were cashless; in a world of letters, they were illiterate; in a world of English, they spoke Irish.

Travelers to this netherworld (even those Irish people who lived in the maritime economy) were shocked by its wretchedness. Visiting Ireland in 1825, Sir Walter Scott recorded that "their poverty has not been exaggerated: it is on the extreme verge of human misery."[12] In 1835 Alexis de Tocqueville described a village of mud cabins so low and grassy that "the whole thing [has] the look of a mole-hill on which a passer-by has trod. . . . The pig in the house. The dunghill. The bare heads and feet."[13] A German visitor in 1844 concluded that "to him who has seen Ireland no mode of life in any other part of Europe, however wretched, will seem pitiable."[14] Most conscious of the misery were those who had to endure it. A small tenant farmer of the 1830s wrote to the lord lieutenant begging for relief:

> The Irish are reduced to the necessity of entirely subsisting on the lumper potato—a kind that grows something better in the poor man's impoverished land than the potatoes of good quality. The lumper is not indeed human food at all. Mix them with any other kind of potatoes and lay them before a pig, and she will not eat one of them until all the good kind are devoured. . . . People like you cannot have the least idea of our misery. The great governors

of nations ought to go in disguise through the country and enter the hovels of the peasantry to make themselves acquainted with the kind of food they have to live on and how they must labour for that food.[15]

The likelihood of the lord lieutenant's making such a visit was not high.

Famine was thus the fatal blow to a world already doomed. Yet in 1800 the Irish economy—rather, the two Irish economies—showed promise. In the maritime world, war with France offered opportunities for traders and suppliers; the price of grain rose, encouraging a shift from grazing to tillage and increasing demand for agricultural labor. In the world of agricultural subsistence, the potato—cheap, nutritious, and easy to grow—enabled rapid growth in population and division of land into smaller lots. Families reproduced knowing that a crop could be grown on otherwise unpromising ground and that remaining land could be used for cash crops to pay rent. If peasants were prepared to accept a dull diet,

*Irish peasant farmers unable to pay rent during the famine*
*faced the terrible prospect of eviction.*

☘

the potato sustained a basic but adequate life. Should the crop fail, the result would be dire.

The end of the Napoleonic Wars in 1815 brought recession in England and Ireland. Suddenly a sign of Ireland's prosperity, rising population, became a source of difficulty. There were five million people in Ireland in 1800, over six and a half million in 1821, and over eight million in 1841. The crisis was worse in the subsistence economy. Overreliance on one foodstuff meant that rural Ireland had a disaster in the making. In 1822, when the crop partially failed, the Horticultural Society of London concluded that "a general failure of the year's crop, whenever it shall have become the chief or sole support of a country, must inevitably lead to all the misery of famine."[16] After another failure in 1831 the Mansion House Relief Committee in Dublin warned that "unless a total change be effected in the condition of the Irish peasant" calls on public charity would inevitably continue. "Seasons of distress . . . must be necessarily expected," a

*A ruined cottage after an eviction.*

❧

government official noted in 1839, "so long as the [poor] subsist on that species of food."[17]

These premonitions of disaster were vindicated in 1845. On September 11 the *Freeman's Journal* reported:

> We have had communications from more than one well-informed correspondent announcing . . . "cholera" in potatoes in Ireland, especially in the north. In one instance the party had been digging potatoes—the finest he had ever seen—from a particular field . . . on Monday last; and on digging on the same ridge on Tuesday he found the tubers all blasted, and unfit for the use of man or beast.[18]

Similar stories throughout the autumn made it clear that a fine crop had been destroyed with fatal swiftness. The damage was done by a wind-borne fungus, which, once established, appeared as white spots on the underside of the leaf and caused the potato to putrefy.

Ireland was not alone in experiencing calamity. Large swathes of western Europe were also affected, France, Germany, Switzerland, and the Low Countries suffering particular privation. Yet Ireland provided the template for the rest of the continent. In Flanders, for instance, half the population was said to be living "in the Irish fashion, that is to say on potatoes, vinegar, and water."[19] They died in the Irish fashion, too: tens of thousands perished in Belgium and the Netherlands in the late 1840s, their plight partially addressed in the former country by public works and charity, in the latter by the operation of laissez-faire economics. Nowhere in Europe, however, did a disaster unfold remotely on the scale of that which awaited Ireland. Nor was any country less prepared to deal with it.

Crop loss and hunger varied from place to place. Reports from County Armagh in 1845 suggested that not all potatoes had rotted and that other foodstuffs, mainly oatmeal, were available to supplement the diet. The prosperous eastern counties of Ulster were spared the worst in the first year of the famine. In Mayo, however, the loss was calamitous. "Despondency and tears are to be seen in every face," wrote a local priest. "The country hereabouts is in a most melancholy state." Of western counties, Mayo was particularly unlucky: most escaped with partial, although still serious, potato failure in the famine's first year. They were less fortunate the following year. The worst-affected counties in 1845 were Armagh, Clare, Kilkenny, Louth, Monaghan, and Waterford, where some 40 percent of the potato crop was lost.[20]

The enormity of the disaster struck home in 1846 when the crop failed almost totally. Places partially affected in 1845 now experienced the full force of famine.

Workhouses in County Armagh were swamped; hordes of the destitute swarmed the countryside demanding "employment, money and bread."[21] In parts of Donegal, wrote James Tuke, a Quaker, "nothing can describe too strongly the dreadful condition of the people. Many families [are] living on a single meal of cabbage, and some even on a little sea-weed."[22] An additional problem was disease. Typhoid fever, dysentery, and smallpox caused as many deaths as hunger. Indeed the very means of ameliorating starvation—overcrowded workhouses, long lines at soup kitchens—spread the body lice that carried fatal sickness. The final indignity was eviction. Some landlords removed starving tenants for non-payment of rent: 3,500 families in 1846, 6,000 in 1847.[23] These owners were themselves facing ruin, but folk memory, understandably, has not forgiven them.

A disaster so severe, striking so suddenly, admitted of only one explanation: an act of God had brought Ireland low. In August 1846 Father Theobald Mathew wrote to Sir Charles Trevelyan, permanent secretary at the Treasury, that "Divine Providence, in its inscrutable ways, has again poured out upon us the vial of its wrath." How else to explain what he had seen with his own eyes?

> The food of a whole nation has perished. On the 27th of last month I passed from Cork to Dublin, and this doomed plant bloomed in all the luxuriance of an abundant harvest. Returning on the 3rd instant, I beheld, with sorrow, one wide waste of putrefying vegetation. In many places the wretched people were seated on the fences of their decaying gardens, wringing their hands and wailing bitterly the destruction that has left them foodless.[24]

Statesmen also resorted to supernatural speculation. "I am greatly troubled by this Irish calamity," wrote Sir James Graham, the home secretary, in 1846. "It is awful to observe how the Almighty humbles the pride of nations."[25] Such lamentation was a kind of prayer. More dangerously, it was also a kind of policy. Fatalism, whether from priests or politicians, encouraged a minimalist approach from government, as if God Himself, the great invisible hand, were a subscriber to the views of Adam Smith. Measures to relieve Irish hunger thus assumed that state interference would make matters worse. Any attempt to regulate food prices, thought Sir Randolph Routh, commissary general in Ireland, would "expose us to the most fatal results." Even blunter was Lord Clanricarde, postmaster general. "Ignorant people cannot see the absurdity . . . or the mischief . . . done by the attempt of government to feed the people." Sir Charles Trevelyan expected workhouses to provide food and shelter for the indigent. When the Poor Law Extension Act was passed in 1848 he thought that "too much has been done for the people . . . under such treatment [they] have grown worse instead of better." Needing little prompting from correspondents such as Father Mathew, Trevelyan typified the famine-as-providential school of thought. The catastrophe was "the judgment of God on an indolent and unself-reliant people."[26] Such were the considered views of the coordinator of Irish famine relief measures.

Ironically, 1847—"Black '47"—saw improvement in the potato crop but no amelioration in the plight of the people. With very few potatoes planted the previous year, the winter of 1847–48 saw terrible loss of life. The blight returned in 1848, wiping out the crop almost completely and causing a dire winter and spring in 1849. For example, in Ballinasloe, County Galway (population 5,000), 226 people died in the workhouse in the last week of April 1849; the following week, 490 died. These were the workhouses in which Charles Trevelyan reposed his trust.

How to enumerate death on a national scale? In 1841 the population of Ireland was 8,175,124. Had previous trends continued, it ought to have stood in 1851 at 9,018,800. In fact, the census of that year yielded a total population of only

*Collaboration between police and landlords in the eviction of Irish tenants was deeply resented and long remembered.*

❧

6,552,385. If we add to that the 1,500,000 estimated to have emigrated between 1845 and 1849 we get a figure of around 8,000,000: a shortfall, in other words, of about a million. That is the number of people who seem to have perished in the famine years. They died terribly. Here was a people, wrote the Quaker William Bennet in 1847, "not in the centre of Africa, the steppes of Asia, the backwoods of America . . . but some millions of our own Christian nation at home, living in a state and condition low and degraded to a degree unheard of before in any civilized community . . . pining away in misery and wretchedness, dying like cattle off the face of the earth."[27]

That wretchedness was not easily forgotten. The emptying of the Irish countryside embittered those who left and those who stayed behind. Both blamed the English administration. Both thought, with some reason, that starvation was looked on as a form of public policy, a way to teach a terrible lesson. If anything, the Irish in America felt this more bitterly than the Irish in Ireland, their grievance heightened by exile and the difficulties of life in a strange country. (It is no coincidence that the Fenian Brotherhood, dedicated to Irish independence through physical force, was founded in New York, not Dublin.) Ireland itself was too stunned by the famine's enormity and too preoccupied with grief to deal with politics. A woman from the Rosses in west Donegal remembered those starvation days:

> The Years of the Famine, of the bad life and of the hunger, arrived and broke the spirit and strength of the community. People simply wanted to survive. Their spirit of comradeship was lost. It didn't matter what ties or relations you had; you considered that person to be your friend who gave you food to put in your mouth. Recreation and leisure ceased. Poetry, music and dancing died. These things were lost and completely forgotten. When life improved in other ways, these pursuits never returned as they had been. The Famine killed everything.[28]

## THE FAMINE MIGRATION

EMIGRATION, THEN, was less choice than necessity in the middle of the nineteenth century. In 1854, when the worst of the famine was over, an American visitor saw "nothing unnatural in the desire of the unfortunate Irish to abandon their cheerless and damp cottages and to crawl inch by inch, while they have yet a little strength, from the graves which apparently yawn for their bodies." Seven years earlier, in 1847, mass migration occurred in earnest. One hundred and forty thousand people arrived in the United States (many by way of Liverpool), another

*Ireland seemed alarmingly empty after 1850.*

❧

110,000 in Canada. These numbers worried American officials, but, as it turned out, laws restricting Irish immigration into America were never fully enforced.[29] Yet their anxiety is easy to understand. The sheer scale of population movement staggered contemporary writers. In July 1850 the editorialist of the *Illustrated London News* could even foresee the emptying of Ireland:

> The great tide of Emigration flows steadily westward. The principal emigrants are Irish peasants and laborers. It is calculated that at least four of every five persons who leave the shores of the old country to try their fortunes in the new, are Irish. . . . The annual numbers of emigrants have gone on increasing, until they have almost become so great as to suggest the idea, and almost justify the belief, of a gradual depopulation of Ireland.[30]

As alarming as quantity was quality. Not everyone saw the Irish as huddled masses

*The cathedral in Cobh was the last view of Ireland for over a million emigrants in the second half of the nineteenth century.*

❧

yearning to breathe free. Many thought them scroungers yearning to buy drink. A report to the Massachusetts Senate in February 1848 was unsentimental: "The want of forethought in them to save their earnings for the day of sickness; the indulgence of their appetites for stimulating drinks, which are too easily obtained among us; and their strong love for their native land, which is characteristic with them, are the fruitful causes of insanity among them."[31] This anthem, sounded less elegantly from press and platform, became a nativist favorite in the years that followed.

Yet for every complaint of Irish indolence was another of Irish industry. These people came to America, the argument went, and stole American jobs, undercutting the locals by laboring for a pittance. This contradiction was never fully resolved. Indeed, it went unresolved by the Irish themselves, who embraced America as a land of plenty without always realizing that wealth demanded work. Emigrant literature warned of false optimism, frequent homesickness, and the need to lower expectations. As the Irish Emigrant Society of New York put it in 1849:

We desire . . . to caution you against entertaining any fantastic idea, such as that magnificence, ease and health are universally enjoyed in this country. . . . It is natural for persons who have adventured to leave home and to seek their fortunes in a foreign and distant country, to give highly coloured accounts of a success, which in reality, has been but the obtaining of a laborious employment; and it is equally natural for those who send you money to wish rather that you should suppose it a reckless gift from the lavishness of wealth rather than a charitable donation from the sympathy of poverty. . . . You must never forget that when you emigrate, you leave home.[32]

Hundreds of thousands crossed the Atlantic to discover this common sense for themselves.

## THE FAMINE INFLUX IN NEW JERSEY

NEW JERSEY could not remain untouched by this larger story. As the enormity of the disaster unfolded, the state struggled to come to terms with the reality of mass starvation—a challenge to its collective conscience and, soon enough, to its cities and streets. The demographic consequences were certainly dramatic. Between 1820 and 1850 New Jersey was overwhelmed with newcomers. In the 1840s the population increased by 31 percent to 489,555, of whom 56,000 were immigrants, 31,000 of them Irish. By 1870 the population was 906,096, of whom 188,943 were foreign born. Of this latter group, 86,784 were from Ireland and 54,001 from Germany. Immigration remained high at the end of the century—in 1900 94,848 residents of the state had been born in Ireland—but an influx of Germans, Italians, Hungarians, and Poles balanced the Irish numbers. In 1900 most foreigners living in the state were from southern and eastern rather than northern and western Europe.[33] By then the Irish of the middle century had moved up a rung or two—far enough to enjoy a little social superiority of their own.

These were long-term trends. The moral challenge of famine was more immediate. Even before the starving crossed the sea, news of their plight made its way to the state, evoking shock and a humanitarian impulse to help. In February 1847 the *Newark Sentinel* reported a "movement for Ireland in Elizabethtown" led by a dozen or so local philanthropists. They were not alone. The movement was part of a wider relief effort organized by Irish Quakers in cities all along the eastern seaboard. "Whereas famine prevails to an alarming extent in Ireland," resolved the Elizabethtown worthies, the result of "an afflictive dispensation of Providence," so committees ought to be formed "to solicit contributions for the [relief of] suffering" and to "correspond with other towns and villages in this state [in order that] our charity may be forwarded together as the joint offering of Jerseymen." This was more than hand-wringing. A plan was conceived and widely circulated to send a ship to Ireland:

> A small contribution from each of the men, women, and children of New Jersey, according to their means, would enable us to despatch a vessel from our own shores and laden with products of our own soil, to save those now about to perish from hunger. Is not the object worth the effort? Can anything be wanting but prompt and energetic action to ensure success?[34]

*Second-generation respectability. James Hennessy's parents, Michael and Anna, were born in Tipperary and Dublin. Coming to America as a child, Michael became a blacksmith. His son James became chief of police of Cranford.*

❧

*A Belfast Presbyterian, Hugh Burnett came to Newark to find work first as a carpenter, then as the owner of a small store selling bird foods and tonics. The business, in Mulberry Street, Newark, eventually employed over twenty people.*

❧

Other towns were similarly moved. In Newark a General Relief Committee resolved in March 1847 to engage a vessel "to carry the contributions of New Jersey to Ireland . . . at such time as . . . they may deem expedient." Led by prominent mercantile figures in the city—David Rogers, Asa Whitehead, John Darcy, and Frederick Frelinghuysen—the committee invited contributions of "money, clothing, and provisions" to be sent from throughout the state to the mayor, who would then forward them for distribution to the Central Committee of the Quakers in Dublin. The advantage of concentrating relief efforts in Newark was that they would reach Ireland "with the greatest economy and certainty, . . . and distinctly as the benevolence of [all] Jerseymen." This made sense to the people of Burlington, who responded "warmly" to the call for a Jersey ship. The mayor, recognizing local strength of feeling, appointed committees to raise contributions to the Newark appeal. Most donations, from Burlington and elsewhere, were small. Yet their very modesty made them meaningful, indeed moving: "$10 for the Irish Fund from an unknown Lady, through Col. Miller, $20 from an unknown man, through Major Knott, the postmaster, and $6 from the Hon. Silas Condit."[35] Ireland's salvation, if it were to come at all, would arrive in small packets. Little by little an impressive sum was raised. New Jersey mustered $35,000 in the winter of 1846–47. This was not the largest figure collected in the United States for Irish relief (New York sent nearly five times as much), but it was far from negligible.[36]

It is not to disparage charity to suggest that one of its consequences, intentional or not, was to keep the Irish in Ireland. It is easier to export food than

*The Newark city directory of 1870 revealed the extent of Irish settlement and its social profile.*

☘

import people. The relief of Ireland meant, in effect, the relief of America, saving the latter from a tide of indigents washing up on its shores. Nor is it insignificant that many of New Jersey's philanthropists were wealthy Episcopalians. Those were the people most likely to be affected by an influx of hungry and unsocialized Papists. Yet the influx took place all the same: a horde of the unwashed, the uneducated, and the embittered. Faced with this, the impulse to charity gave way to less generous inclinations: hostility, resentment, fear. Once objects of pity, the Irish soon became objects of scorn. Transplanted en masse to Jersey City, Newark, and Trenton, they upset the delicate balance of those towns and every other place where they settled.

One sign that the Irish had come to stay was that many wished them to go. The sudden invasion came at the price of political tension, social division, and, occasionally, physical violence. In the middle years of the century, nativism was New Jersey's besetting sin. A compound of fear, insecurity, and simple malevolence, it uglified the state's social and political arrangements for decades. Part of its staying power was its very inconsistency. New Jerseyans wanted foreign labor but not foreign laborers, and, well supplied with both, the engine of prejudice never lacked for fuel. But nativism was not confined to the lower orders. The high-minded were also guilty. All classes caricatured the Irish, using broad brushstrokes to depict a group variously drunk, aggressive, unwashed, and stupid. This was standard fare. The value of the outsider has always been to show the virtue of those who condemn him.

Distaste started early in life. Isaac Mickle—an editor, lawyer, journalist, and Democrat from Camden County —began a diary in 1837 at the age of fourteen. Precociously literate, Mickle loathed the Irish lower orders. "Many a son of the Emerald Isle will be, this night, carried out of the grog shanties, dead—dead drunk!" he wrote on Saint

*The most persistent anti-Irish image was of creatures more apelike than human. This caricature from 1884 was typical of an entire menagerie of such depictions on both sides of the Atlantic throughout the nineteenth century.*

❧

Patrick's Day 1838, when he was fifteen years old. Three years later, a similar refrain: "Had I a dollar for every Irishman that will be drunk tonight, I would have before next week the finest library in the Union. Father Mathew will have work enough in the Emerald Isle today. . . . If he can keep them sober on Saint Patrick's Day, I will stand for their sobriety for the rest of the year." This was more than priggishness. Mickle summoned prejudice at every turn, contempt for the Irish so much part of his mental furniture as to be second nature. Traveling with friends through South Jersey in July 1841, he stopped to eat at a small rooming house. The visit was not a success; "everything was so dirty that their stomachs were emptier than before the meal. For my part, the thick, disagreeable, Irish smell of the establishment was enough—I did not sit down at all." These were the reactions, strangely enough, of a political progressive. Mickle prided himself on tolerance, later condemning, for example, the nativist riots in Philadelphia in 1844. On that occasion, he wrote, the rioters behaved toward the Irish much as the Jews behaved in demanding the death of Christ.[37] (Even when professing enlightenment Mickle reached for another slur.) In the matter of prejudice, then, there was shame enough to go around. All social groups, whatever of their other beliefs, could agree that the Irish were bad news.

If anti-Irishness came easily to the educated, it bulked even larger in the lives of the working class. Philadelphia, city of brotherly love, erupted in 1844; Newark followed a few years later. That city's Irish population had been growing steadily since the 1790s. By 1826 a Catholic parish, Saint John's, was created to cater to it. From 1833 to 1866 its pastor was the indefatigable Patrick Moran of Loughrea, County Tipperary, organizer of libraries, Sunday schools, temperance societies, and literary groups; its board of trustees included men such as Patrick Murphy, John Kelly, Christopher Rourke, Maurice Fitzgerald, and John Gillespie. Such men formed the backbone of Newark's support for Daniel O'Connell in the 1840s. As the Irish presence expanded, though, so also did hostility toward it. The city held its first Saint Patrick's Day Parade in 1834: it was jeered from the sidewalks. In 1853 James Roosevelt Bayley was appointed to head the newly created Roman Catholic Diocese of Newark. His installation was marred by Protestant heckling. Worse followed. "Every week almost," Bayley later wrote to a local newspaper, "we read of some violence committed against Catholic property."[38]

The worst excess occurred in September 1854 when a procession of the American Protestant Association led to a riot in which two Irishmen died. Bayley recorded the episode in his diary:

> 6 September 1854.
> Yesterday a procession of Protestant Societies marched through Newark, and some person from amongst the crowd at the corner of Shipman and William

Street having thrown a stone at them, they immediately made an assault upon persons in the crowd, and then proceeded to attack the German Catholic Ch. which was close by, and destroyed everything they could lay their hands on. The most false statements were immediately published throwing the whole blame on the Irish Catholics—it was stated that the Priest and twenty men commenced the disturbance by firing on the procession from the Church. The examination before the Coroner Jury, tho' conducted most unfairly, tended to put an end to these lies—and the newspapers were finally obliged to acknowledge that the Catholics were not to blame.[39]

Bayley's account, written some time after the fact, captured the urgency and ugliness of the moment. Writing in its immediate aftermath, the *New York Tribune* editorialized that it brought "great discredit on Newark and belligerent Protestantism." It also revealed the sheer scale of the belligerence. Thirteen lodges of Freemasons and Orangemen came to Newark that day, about three thousand in all, many from neighboring states. From the beginning their intent was to destroy Saint Patrick's Pro-Cathedral, for which purpose they were improbably dressed in Prince Albert coats, black trousers, and round hats. They never got as far as the cathedral but had to make do instead with Saint Mary's German Church, which was seriously damaged.

In the melee, four were wounded and one, a certain McCarthy, was killed. Later another Irishman, by the name of McDermott, also died.[40] Two months after the riot, the Know-Nothing party recorded its best ever election result. The party waned thereafter, but the memory of Newark lingered for decades, a reminder of forces close to the surface in midcentury New Jersey and urban America as a whole.

The nativist stock-in-trade was anti-Catholicism. The Irish were not merely foreigners: they adhered to a foreign creed. The Protestant mind shivered at the prospect of fellow citizens taking their lead from a Roman bachelor and his obscurantist court, a medieval monarchy far from the virtuous republic of Washington or Jefferson. Compounded of exotic ritual, preposterous doctrine, and dogmatic intolerance, Catholicism was America's metaphorical opposite—unclean, dishonest, offensive to Protestants and secularists

***Bishop James Roosevelt Bayley.***

alike. Worst was its proselytism. When Americans converted to Catholicism they embraced an intellectual servitude inconceivable in a free citizen. A man such as Bishop Bayley was thus triply damned: a convert, former Episcopalian clergyman, and pastor of a largely Irish flock. "Seduced from the faith by a deluded female, his aunt," who was the "abbess of a nunnery with whom he had long held correspondence"—as a correspondent to the *Newark Sentinel* had it—he embraced with ease "the Mother of Harlots!"[41] This aunt was Elizabeth Ann Seton: mother, widow, convert, and saint.

Antagonism toward New Jersey Catholics—benighted and primitive but with a sheen of sophistication derived from their quasi-Episcopalian leadership—rarely lacked for an opportunity to express itself. One example will suffice. In June 1856 Bayley presided at an unusual ceremony, the reburial at Saint Mary's Church, Hoboken, of the bones of the obscure Christian martyr Saint Quietus. The *New York Observer* spluttered in amazement:

*The pilgrimages and penitential exercises of Irish Catholicism were not easily translated to urban America. One of the most venerated shrines was Gouganbarra, the mountain retreat of Saint Finbar, in County Cork.*

These bones, whether of man or beast it would be difficult to decide, were put into a beautiful case—were taken on a Sabbath morning, amid throngs of the poor, deluded Irish, each of whom had to pay 25 cents for a sight, and amid the ceremonies of high mass, they were solemnly inaugurated, and safely put away in a place prepared for their reception. And the chief actor in this deceptive, profane, and contemptible farce was the popish bishop Baily [*sic*] of Newark; not an imported priest from Maynooth . . . but a native American, and a pervert from the Protestant faith!![42]

This was the verbal equivalent of a Thomas Nast cartoon, the Irish crudely sketched as dupes, buffoons, scarcely human at all. (Thomas Nast, by the way, lived in New Jersey for many years.) The ceremony was a circus and a sham: more Barnum than Bayley. Many evils beset modern America, the paper continued, but none greater than that so many people should "be under the entire control of such religious charlatans" as the bishop of Newark.

## NATIVISM AND NEW JERSEY POLITICS:
## THE CASE OF JAMES P. DONNELLY

HOSTILITY TO the Irish tended to be personal and particular: the unrecorded insult, the slammed door, the anonymous sneer. Most of it is therefore lost to history and is reachable now only through urban folklore, oral tradition, and sympathetic imagination. But occasionally these private resentments merged into something larger and more public, when the populace as a whole joined unabashedly in the anti-Irishness normally hidden from view. Such a moment came in 1857 when an Irish Catholic medical student, James P. Donnelly, was hanged for the murder of one Albert Moses in Navesink, Monmouth County. The case was a *cause célèbre,* remembered and resented a generation after Moses's death and Donnelly's execution. In a curious way, it came to symbolize not only social weakness but political strength, reminding the Irish of the antipathy toward them but also of their own collective power when they cared to exercise it.

The murder itself was gruesome. It was also sufficiently peculiar to give Donnelly some hope of acquittal. The simple fact, unchallenged by any party, was that Moses had his throat cut one evening after winning fifty-five dollars from Donnelly at cards. But did Donnelly do it? Moses's wounds were not immediately fatal, so that—improbably composed and articulate for a man *in extremis*—he was able to tell one witness that "Donnelly did it. . . . He came in here and cut my throat."[43] The fact that Moses was conveniently dead and thus unavailable for cross-examination did not seem to worry the jury. They accepted his posthumous testimony without demur. To be fair, Donnelly's defense was decidedly shaky. He claimed to be the victim of mistaken identity and of perjury, the latter committed by those who knew the real killer. This might have worked had he not placed himself at the crime scene, unhelpfully suggesting that Moses properly treated would not have died. Here was an argument at best naive, at worst criminally stupid. Yet naive, innocent, or deluded, Donnelly did not behave at his trial like a man who thought he would be convicted. He was soon disabused, being easily found guilty and equally easily condemned to death.

The trial confirmed nativist stereotypes about dangerous Irishmen, even those, like Donnelly, not from Ireland. (He was born in New York of Irish parents.) Yet it also gave the Irish an opportunity to act in concert. Donnelly's troubles stood as a metaphor for those of an entire community. Accused, convicted, and executed, he became for the Irish of New Jersey their victim-in-chief, the public face of a thousand private discriminations. This role was enhanced by Donnelly's efforts after the trial to escape the noose. Protesting innocence to the last, he appealed his conviction through the state courts until finally he asked the Court of Pardons to commute his sentence to life imprisonment. At every turn he failed. Moreover, his fate lay in the hands of Protestant jurors, Protestant judges, and eventually a Protestant governor, William Newell, whose career had been an extended exercise in anti-Catholicism. (Newell began as a Know-Nothing in the mid-1850s, was elected governor in 1856 on a Republican-American ticket, and "in each of his annual addresses to the legislature . . . urged legislation increasing the time required for naturalization, limiting the voting rights of foreign-born citizens, and enforcing Protestant definitions of education and morality.")[44]

Casting himself as martyr, Donnelly thus politicized the case. It was a role he knew well and one his supports were eager to applaud. (They gathered over three thousand signatures from New Jersey, New York, Buffalo, and Washington, D.C., asking for clemency.) All the same, he probably was guilty. As Douglas Shaw has written, it is "difficult to read" the evidence in a way that exonerates him.[45] Still, the persistent refusal of appeals did reinforce a sense that nonjudicial considerations played a part in the case. Donnelly claimed that Newell had cast the deciding vote against him in the Court of Pardons. In fact, there was no deciding vote: although Newell did vote for execution, the numbers were six to two against commutation. But the story had a final twist. With fine timing, Donnelly escaped from jail five days before his appointed execution and, in the dead of night, made his way toward the coast and an awaiting boat. He never arrived. Recaptured the following morning, he was returned to prison to meet his fate.

The hanging itself was pure theater: Victorian melodrama, Passion play, and morality tale rolled into one. Armed constables guarded the cell; final visits were made by family and friends; fellow prisoners were urged by the condemned man "to seek the paths of virtue and to take warning from his untimely end"; the last rites were received; a fortifying glass of brandy was consumed.[46] The principals knew their parts and played them to perfection, as if in dispatching Donnelly they recognized a need to fashion some posthumous legend that would lend some deeper meaning to his death. Donnelly himself obliged with a speech from the scaffold, time-honored device of would-be martyrs, an attempt to write his own history at its point of consummation. Two hours long and lachrymose in the extreme, it once again proclaimed innocence, blamed accusers, and condemned Newell for his vote in denying a pardon. In his last moments he was more exercised by the latter's bigotry than by anything else. Yet he drew from it a crucial lesson:

> O cherish my name. Remember my dying declarations, made at this solemn moment without preparation. O, be satisfied with this horrible butchery! Remember the importance of one vote—vote whenever you can. Remember one vote took the life of your poor friend Donnelly.[47]

The homily delivered, he was done to death. The last indignity was that, due to an incompetent hangman, it took him fifteen minutes to expire.

Donnelly's importance did not end with his execution. He himself seemed to realize his electoral value as a corpse—not the last cadaver, indeed, to play a role in deciding the outcome of a ballot in New Jersey. "O, Governor Newell!" he orated. "In your wild schemes of political ambition, you have crushed the hopes of poor Donnelly; but you have sealed your own political fate, you have driven the last nail in your political coffin."[48] The Irish took the hint. Newell ran successfully for Congress in 1860 but was defeated for reelection in 1866, his nativist past used against him. He also lost the race for governor in 1877 to General George McClellan; Donnelly's death was again an issue in the campaign. (McClellan issued the speech from the gallows as an election pamphlet.) The *Jersey City Argus* editorialized:

> A man whose Know-Nothing and secret oath-bound political associations shut his heart to cries of humanity, of mercy, of justice, is not fit to rule the honest and manly people of a free state. That Newell's action toward poor Donnelly was prompted by his intense hatred of foreigners no honest man . . . can question.[49]

Newell protested this characterization, claiming that, if anything, he was the victim of Irish hatred, having been "threatened, hounded, and hunted" merely because of a refusal to "contravene the decision of the highest courts." He also noted—a desperate admission at the end of a nativist career—that his own grandfather had been Irish. Neither argument worked. Donnelly, twenty years dead, continued to exercise a hold on the Irish. Newell lost his bid for election with 45 percent of the vote; "in heavily Irish Hudson County he received only 38 percent."[50] That ended his career in New Jersey, although in 1880 he was appointed territorial governor of Washington, serving four years.

The murder of Moses and death of Donnelly were human tragedies but political opportunities. They offered something for everyone, the only losers being the deceased and, eventually, Newell. Nativists had prejudices confirmed; the Irish were given a martyr; law-and-order types got a hanging and newspapers a story; the public was entertained or appalled, depending on mood. Pamphlets were still being penned about the case in 1886, almost thirty years on, as if to reveal the abiding "importance of ethnic and religious conflict" in shaping the politics of nineteenth-century New Jersey.[51] It also suggests that the Irish reached instinctively for a politics of grievance long after the grievance was gone. Rightly or wrongly they wrapped themselves in victimhood. They did not lack grievances, to be sure, but had so tutored themselves in a culture of complaint that it was difficult to unlearn the lesson. The choice for succeeding years—a test of political maturity they did not always pass—was to know when to embrace victimhood and when to abandon it. In different ways and at different times, that has always been the immigrant's dilemma.


## WOMEN IN IRISH NEW JERSEY:
## THE CASE OF MOTHER MARY XAVIER MEHEGAN

THE DONNELLY story, gruesome from start to finish, spoke of the seeming masculinity of Irish New Jersey. It started with men playing poker and ended with men playing politics. In between, the grim rituals of an essentially male world were enacted: a murder, a prison break, a hanging. Women played little part, even as casual bystanders, Garden State equivalents of the French Revolution's *tricoteuses*. For good or ill, the episode epitomized a larger whole: men tended to dominate the conjoined worlds of politics, trades unionism, the law, and the Church, women scarcely rating a mention. Yet women did play an important role in shaping Irish New Jersey, appearances to the contrary notwithstanding. After all, in the midnineteenth century more women than men left Ireland for America—precisely the reason that Irish America was able to reproduce itself and become self-sustaining as a social and cultural reality. The irony is obvious. Irish women in

America allowed an ethnic community to preserve a sense of self, to remain intact, and to seize the opportunity of modernity. Lack of women in Ireland sent that country in the opposite direction. Declining population meant diminished self-confidence, economic backwardness, and political frustration: all the elements that led ultimately to nationalist agitation by the end of the nineteenth century. America showed Ireland the benefit of demographic balance, a lesson the latter was incapable of learning. Ireland showed America a more sobering, if not altogether sober, truth: a country of too many bachelors is a country without a future.

For all their centrality, however, Irish women in America have been often overlooked. The reason is not hard to grasp. Once arrived, women seemed to disappear from general sight. Domestic service claimed them, then marriage, then motherhood: the unsung tasks of private life. To be sure, the disappearance was never complete. Private life then—as now—had a public dimension and its own social distinctions and hierarchies. Even behind closed doors a pecking order prevailed. Better to be a priest's housekeeper than a washerwoman, for example, a lady who took in sewing than a factory girl, a woman who made a good marriage than a slattern. Other signs of success included the mothering of future businessmen, lawyers, doctors, or priests. There would have been no social advance for first-generation Irish Americans without women to do the generating in the first place. For all that, some women preferred to make good on their own. Teaching was a possibility, especially for the unmarried—another kind of vicariousness, perhaps, the childless woman finding fulfillment in the lives of a thousand children. Likewise, toward the end of the nineteenth century, women in greater numbers began to aspire to higher education; some wished to enter professions other than teaching, in particular medicine and the law. Finally, and most significant, one way of independent life was always available, and many embraced it: the convent. Here was not social withdrawal or misguided mimicry of male patterns of authority. Still less was it submissiveness, a denial of self. On the contrary, religious life offered a rich sphere of autonomous action. Many Irish women wanted an indoor life—to be wives and mothers. Many others wanted an interior life—to be consecrated virgins of Christ. Paradoxically, it was the latter, those who seemed to shun the public gaze, who had the greatest impact on public life. It was they who founded schools, built hospitals, and taught the rising generation (boys and girls alike) to be both Catholic and American.

Individual lives reveal these wider trends. Consider two sisters, Catherine and Margaret Mehegan, who came to America in 1842 knowing no one and with only a vague sense of the life this new country might offer. They found themselves at once alone and in good company: theirs was the experience, after all, of thousands of other young women before and after. The journey was physical but also social, an attempt to integrate into a new society and a novel way of life. Respectively the youngest and second youngest of the eight children of Patrick and Johanna Mehegan, they came originally from County Cork. Catherine was born in 1825, Margaret a couple of years before. Patrick Mehegan was a small farmer—a rung or two above the peasant class—who made enough money selling vegetables in Cork to educate his children. The youngest girls supplemented the family income by doing needlework for Cork's moneyed middle class. The Mehegans were conventionally religious; Catherine was the most devout of them. Given to romantic piety and a restlessness for holy adventure, she fretted at the prospect of stitching for ladies for the rest of her life. Thus when Patrick Mehegan died she decided to leave home. His death seemed to sharpen a desire to dedicate herself to some as yet unclear spiritual task: "to go far away from home," she later wrote, "to go far away from home, away from all belonging to me, that I might give myself wholly to God."[52] Perhaps this was more selfish than selfless. It entailed separation from a grieving mother who was not told of the plan. But the impulse to leave was not to be quelled. Catherine left Queenstown (Cobh) for America in early 1842, arriving in New York a couple of months later. Margaret went with her, convinced that she, too, had a religious calling. As it turned out, she had no such vocation. Her chief motive seems to have been a desire to be with her sister on a joint adventure.

After landing in New York, their first instinct was to seek out a Catholic church and a priest. Father William Starrs of old Saint Patrick's in Mott Street quickly realized that, of the two, Catherine's was the more ardent desire for the consecrated life. Margaret went in a different direction, meeting one Thomas Dynan, falling in love with him, and marrying. So much for her dreams of the cloister. Toward the end of her life, Catherine Mehegan recalled this parting of the ways: "I did not oppose her, of course, but when I saw her willing to give up all belonging to her for this stranger whom she had never seen before coming to this country, I resolved that I would work for God alone!"[53] Perhaps a sense of betrayal may be detected here, of shared mission

*Catherine Josephine Mehegan (Mother Mary Xavier) was born in Cork, February 19, 1825. She founded the New Jersey Sisters of Charity.*

suddenly scuppered. Whatever of that, domestic desires prevailed over any need for public or professional acclaim. Margaret and Thomas Dynan remained for a time in America, where they raised their children—their daughters were educated at the Academy of Saint Elizabeth in Madison, New Jersey—but eventually they moved to Australia.

Even as her companion disappeared from the scene, Catherine Mehegan continued to explore the religious life. She became a novice of the Sisters of Charity of Saint Vincent De Paul in New York in February 1847, taking the name Sister Mary Xavier. Assigned at first to a boys' orphanage, then to the newly opened Saint Vincent's Hospital, then to an industrial school for girls in Brooklyn, she spent a total of ten years working as a nun in New York. But New Jersey, not New York, was to be the scene of her life's work. In 1858 Bishop Bayley of Newark, keen to have the services of an order of nuns devoted to the rule of his aunt, Elizabeth Ann Seton, invited five Sisters of Charity from Cincinnati to establish themselves in his diocese. In 1859 Sister Mary Xavier was asked to take charge of the new community. Thus on September 29, 1859, the Sisters of Charity of Saint Elizabeth came into existence, their first motherhouse being the old Colonel Ward mansion on the corner of Washington and Bleeker streets in Newark. The community was entirely Irish: Sisters Mary Xavier Mehegan, Mary Catherine Nevin, Ann Elizabeth Lynagh, Mary Agnes O'Neill, Mary Vincent Daly, Mary Joseph Plunkett, and Mary Cleophas Duffy. Indeed, the novices were also Irish, a welter of Kearneys, Dornins, and Garrigans. Some of the women were daughters of Irish immigrants, but most were Irish born.

The fledgling community rapidly outgrew its Newark home, requiring Mother Mary Xavier to establish another house in Madison in July 1860, which would soon become the motherhouse of the order. Taking over premises occupied by Seton Hall College, which was about to transfer its operations to South Orange, she created the Convent of Saint Elizabeth and with it a select academy for young ladies, the latter to be under the direction of Sister Mary Agnes

*Sister Mary Catherine Nevin, born in Ireland, was cofounder of the Sisters of Charity in New Jersey.*

❧

O'Neill. The school's first enrollment was seven. "Mother Xavier is a plunger," recorded Bayley, knowing she had assumed a debt of twenty-five thousand dollars to buy the property, "but she never gets beyond her depth unless she is sure of a nearby rescuer!"[54] Somehow the money was found. More important than cash, however, were hard work and a sense of shared purpose, the one reinforcing the other. A visitor in 1862 noted her first sight of the convent the groundsman "digging potatoes in the field and the Sisters helping him gather them up and store them in improvised pits."[55] This was not unusual. The women were as tireless as men in performing the physical labor necessary to get a convent, farm, and school up and running.

> When digging was in season . . . the Sisters got together pulling and hauling and pushing the plough [after sundown] until they actually turned up rows of the hard soil for the next day's work. Later they did the same to prepare the ground for the foundation of the girl's building. During [the construction] of this building the Sisters went into the halls and rooms every night before bedtime to clean up the debris, drag out all rubbish and leave the place in readiness for the men to begin work without delay the following morning. . . . The Sisters did all the planting and threshing, and the heavy work of preparing wheat and oats continued up to the year 1882. [Sister Alphonsa] was able to do more than any man on the place and it delighted Bishop [Corrigan] to see her manage the great mass of grain.[56]

*Irish-born Sister Mary Agnes O'Neill was the first director of the Academy of Saint Elizabeth.*

The Catholic Church in America, it is often said, was built by the pennies of the poor. It was also built by the hands of the people, and many of those hands belonged to women.

It was not all work. When time permitted, fun and lightheartedness cheered the day. The same retainer who helped the nuns to gather potatoes in the fall (an Irishman called Mackey) entertained them with sleigh rides in the winter. Generally this was a comic affair. The sleigh, a crudely concocted wooden jalopy drawn by oxen and prone to breakdown, was a familiar sight in the hills around the convent, with ten nuns jammed together in an open cart better suited for five. Once or twice it crashed; occasionally the driver got lost. It was not unusual for the Sisters, excursion aborted, to have to trudge miles through the snow to get home.

Bit by bit and brick by brick, the community founded by Catherine Mehegan began to flourish. The academy succeeded. The convent took in novices and made nuns of them. The mission expanded. From Newark and Madison, Sisters of Charity moved to Paterson, Trenton, Jersey City, South Orange, Hoboken, West Hoboken, Elizabeth, and New Brunswick. Within thirty years of the Madison foundation, nuns from the order were to be found in some eighty towns and cities in New Jersey and beyond. (Before long some ventured as far afield as China.) Working in hospitals, schools, and orphanages, they transformed New Jersey Catholicism, softening its sharper male edges, bringing gentleness and delicacy to thousands of lives. Nor was this their only achievement. Changing the Church, they changed the prospects of many New Jersey women, their own included. The religious life offered a socially sanctioned sphere of female advance; it was a feminism of the cloth that appealed to hundreds of women over the years. Moreover, it was distinctively female, not imitatively male. Half a lifetime after handing over the Seton Hall property in Madison, Bishop Bernard McQuaid of Rochester admitted that "we men could never have done with this place what [the] Sisters have managed to do." This was less commendation than common sense. "It is simply wonderful," he continued, "what these little women can do when they put their heads together."[57] To modern ears the adjective jars, hinting at condescension. Even so, the admiration is not to be doubted. Indeed, Mother Mehegan and her sisterhood had no firmer friend than McQuaid. Addressing the pupils of the Academy of Saint Elizabeth's in 1898, he marveled at a mission that had borne such fruit from such "humble and lowly" beginnings:

> The noblest fruit in this magnificent Church of America, the greatest work that is going on the whole of America over, is the very work in which your teachers, the Sisters, are engaged. Our grand schools, our churches themselves, would be but hollow shams were it not for the soul and the life that we are able, through just such good and noble women, to put into the work.[58]

McQuaid's praise suggested a double journey. Physical distance from Ireland was also social distance from the world of 1842. Toward the turn of the century, for example, women began to chafe at the limited roles they were expected to play; ethnic success had heightened expectations, and entry into the bourgeoisie had

*The Golden Anniversary of Mother Mary Xavier, February 12, 1897,*
*saw a major gathering of Sisters of Charity at Convent Station.*

encouraged the keeping up of appearances, sometimes in rather derivative ways. Think of higher education. Here was the standard goal of second-generation immigrants, functioning both as sign and safeguard of newly acquired social position. But why should it be confined to men? Increasingly, women also wanted to earn degrees, not so much for instrumental purposes, some suspected, as for reasons of fashion. "It is only of late that our Catholic girls are going to College," McQuaid wrote in 1903, noting that the desire had become "a sort of fad."[59] Craze or not, the trend had the important consequence of requiring the Church once again to enter the education market, this time to provide degrees for women of superior intellectual gifts and elevated cultural aspirations. Part of the motivation was to board a train that would have left the station anyway. "Nearly all [the young women go] to non-Catholic colleges," McQuaid worried. "I am setting my face against their attendance at these."[60] It was the characteristic fear: upward mobility could mean dilution of faith and loss of ethnic identity. Though exaggerated, the anxiety was not entirely unreasonable.

The creation of colleges for women was thus the last unfinished task of the nineteenth century and the first substantial achievement of the twentieth. It was also the final gift of Mother Mary Xavier Mehegan to New Jersey. The initial idea was to build on existing efforts, offering advanced courses at Saint Elizabeth's Academy in conjunction with its already well established high school department. Indeed, outside assessors reported in 1895 that the school provided instruction for older girls comparable to anything offered at accredited degree-awarding colleges. Encouraged, the Sisters added other courses and began to recruit young women who specifically wished to earn degrees. A new building was constructed (the impressive Xavier Hall), a curriculum was finalized, and in September 1899 the College of Saint Elizabeth opened for business. The initial enrollment was four, three of them girls of Irish extraction. It was the first degree-awarding Catholic college for women in the United States. The founding president was Sister Mary Pauline Kelligar.

Saint Elizabeth's was not, and was never intended to be, a finishing school. "Music and art are very necessary for a school of young ladies," McQuaid wrote with some asperity to Sister Mary Pauline in 1903, "but these accomplishments do not make a College." The women had brains, he thought, and should be made to use them. "Latin, Greek, Mathematics, and Scientific Studies are the requirement of a college. . . . Severe training, it is true, but [it] will be the making of [the place]." The wider humanities were also important. "You will need professors of French, German, Italian, and Spanish," he told the president. "Even Polish must not be despised." Here was a rigorous program for the women of a new century.[61]

Yet there were limits. Educated women were not expected to enter the world of work. The aim of the exercise, rather, was to return to the traditional domestic role newly aware of its spiritual importance. "Your mission is not to dignify the walks of public life, to dazzle the multitude with . . . eloquence or to pursue the devious paths of politics," Bishop John O'Connor of

*Bernard McQuaid as bishop of Rochester in the 1880s. McQuaid's ministry to Irish Catholics in northern New Jersey was both pastoral and educational in nature. He collaborated closely with Bishop James Roosevelt Bayley of Newark in the founding of Seton Hall College in 1856.*

❧

Newark told the first graduating class of Saint Elizabeth's in 1903. "Yours to fulfill duties more sacred than these—to adorn and ennoble the Christian home." For women to "engage in politics or law or commerce" would be to "nullify" the "very purpose for which civil society is established—the protection of the home."[62] No statement of conventional categories could have been more confident. Yet behind the bishop's words lurked fear. He protested too much, seeming to evoke a world suddenly fading from view. How long would it be, he seemed to wonder, before law and commerce (even politics) would claim these still unravished brides of quietness? It was sooner than he thought. Here was an irony no one anticipated. Catherine Mehegan came to America to advance the Church, and, succeeding, she also advanced the cause of women. But Advanced Women? That was the last thing on her mind.

# CHAPTER 5

# A Trickle Becomes a Flood

## THE IRISH AND THEIR NEIGHBORS

**L**IKE SIGNPOSTS pointing in opposite directions, Catherine Mehegan and James Donnelly seem to epitomize the best and the worst of the Irish in New Jersey, the one a paragon of self-improvement and social betterment, the other a figure from low-life literature or the penny dreadfuls. For a time it seemed as if the latter were more typical. Donnelly's case was a classic of mid-nineteenth-century political theater, performed in a political system finely attuned to fear, bringing out and exaggerating the worst in everything it touched —intolerance in the populace, unfairness in the courts, grievance-stroking in the Irish. Here were the symptoms of a social order in profound transition. As the unfortunate man discovered to his cost, the coming of outsiders changed every equation. Fear of foreigners concentrated the collective mind of white Anglo-Saxon Protestants in Newark and Trenton, Paterson and Point Pleasant. They realized, too late to make much difference, that their state was being taken away from them. Consider the figures. As the population of New Jersey grew, the number of Catholics in the state exploded. Foreign-born residents in New Jersey doubled between 1850 and 1860,

*Bernard Kearney was one of the first parishioners of Saint John's Church in Newark.*

❦

COURTESY: SETON HALL UNIVERSITY
SPECIAL COLLECTIONS CENTER
AND UNIVERSITY ARCHIVES

*Edward Garrigan, trustee of Saint John's Parish, Newark, in 1908.*

❧

from 60,000 (12 percent of the total population) to 123,000 (18 percent of the total). Many of these were Irish. The population of Newark was 48,000 in 1853—three times what it was in 1840. In 1855, there were 40,000 Catholics and 35 priests, 17 of them from Ireland. By 1872 there were 170,000 Catholics, 113 churches, 62 priests, and a seminary, Seton Hall College.[1] This was prodigious growth by any standards. No wonder nativists were fearful.

Ironies abounded in this situation. One was that anti-Catholicism was bigotry masquerading as enlightenment. Critics of the Church standardly condemned its obscurantism and irrationalism, never pausing to wonder if such charges might better be leveled at themselves. Another peculiarity, unrecognized by nativists, was that their criticism of Irish failure to assimilate was precisely the cause of the syndrome they deplored. It was hostility that forced the Irish into ghettos in the first place. In the pestilential rookeries of Jersey City, Hoboken, and Camden, they created a world of their own. Huddled in church or pub—the first place for spiritual solace, the second for liquid—the Irish fashioned a parallel society, comforting, familiar, and safe. Indeed, this network of neighborhood associations suggests a final irony. Ostracized and made to fend for himself, the Irishman could become as American as the next—finding work, knocking on doors, getting by on his wits. Even in the ghetto a kind of assimilation took place. "No Irish need apply" meant that the Irish had to apply themselves. It meant, too, that they had to apply to one another. That more than anything else made them American.

If assimilation was steady, it was also painful. Irish respectability was hard won, not least because one avenue of social advance, the priesthood, tended to confirm the nativist caricature of foreigners in hock to an alien creed. Yet even before second-generation Irish Americans became priests, the first generation had to build the towns where they would minister. They did not have it easy. Every infraction or idiosyncrasy was seized upon to demonstrate fecklessness or eccentricity—the brogue exaggerated to a caricature of comic stupidity, the quirkiness twisted into strangeness, the fondness for drink turned to chronic unreliability. Whenever the Irish offered their enemies ammunition, it was eagerly accepted.

Consider one episode, small in itself but typical of many. In February 1857 Bishop Bayley of Newark recorded in his diary "a terrible riot between the Irish factions engaged in making the [Jersey City] tunnel" in which 1,200 men were said to have participated.[2] To anti-Catholics, this was proof that the reputation of the fighting Irish matched reality. For a time, indeed, Bayley himself seems to have believed it. In fact, the riot was little more than a Saturday night brawl, although, with two hundred participants and forty-seven arrests, an unusually nasty one. More interesting than the fisticuffs was what lay behind it. Nativists liked to speak of the Irish as homogenous—an undifferentiated mass, drunk and dirty—but examined closely the "riot" suggested otherwise. It was territorial and had more to do with property and memory than drink. Gangs from Munster fought gangs from Connacht, apparently because some Corkonians had trespassed on shanties occupied by the men of Connacht. That localism bears examination. When Irish people came to New Jersey they remained among their own kind—and their own kind did not constitute a bloc called "the Irish" but were people from the same county, town, village, or even extended family. This was the more complex social reality missed by nativists. They also missed the paradox behind the particularism: it represented at once a reluctance to assimilate and a means of doing so. Urban life was less oppressive when its burdens were shared with a mate with a Mayo accent, a friend with a familiar set of references. Nativists misunderstood this. For them, boozy belligerence made a better story than social privation or regional memory. Know-Nothings thought they knew everything. They offered a reason—the same reason—for all the social ills of their time. That the Irish were poor, plentiful, and Papist was explanation enough for them. The melee of 1857 was one night of noise whose true significance lay in the echo. The reverberation suggested that almost any story could be told of the Irish and believed.

*Ecclesiastical historian Paul Flynn recorded the Irish contribution to Saint John's, Newark, in 1908. They were clever disputants, he wrote, "able to explain to their Protestant fellow citizens the true Catholic doctrines."*

## PARISH, PUB, AND POLITICS

**C**ARICATURES ONLY work when they contain an element of truth. Despite its crudity, the notion of the Irish as drink-soaked was partially accurate. The lives of the urban poor were sweetened by the saloon but also destroyed by it. The perennial dangers were the pay packet blown on a spree, the job lost because of Saint Monday. This was not a uniquely Irish problem, but a reputation once gained was hard to shake. The Irish did little to dislodge it. As with most working-class groups, for the Irish bars had multiple functions; they were community centers, job providers, employment exchanges, and street theaters, as well as places of escape. Similar functions were performed in other ways by the Church. It, too, provided togetherness, social mobility, a network of charity and self-reliance, and a momentary release from workaday cares. Saturday night and Sunday morning were two sides of the same Irish coin.

Competing for the same audience and offering comparable services, priests and publicans were locked in a complex relationship. The clergy knew how seductive saloons could be and made strenuous efforts to keep parishioners away from them—as much to assert their own authority, perhaps, as to curb an objective social evil. On the other hand, many priests sprang from the same milieu as the clientele of the pubs or the owners of them. They were sons or brothers of publicans, men of an emerging Irish American propertied Catholic middle class who knew that bars were not all bad. To complete the confusion, some priests were themselves known to enjoy an occasional glass. Not every cleric was a killjoy.

This said, throughout the nineteenth century New Jersey's temperance campaigns were led by Irish priests. Patrick Moran in Newark in the 1820s, James McKay in Orange in the 1860s, and Thomas Killeen in Newark in the 1870s were larger-than-life figures in their respective communities. Father Killeen was legendary. On Saturday night, a clerical contemporary wrote, "he was worth a score of policemen" as he single-handedly cleared every bar in his parish before midnight.[3] A cleric of equal dispatch was Father

*Bishop Michael Corrigan of Newark, child of Irish immigrants, strongly supported temperance among his people.*

✥

Patrick Byrne of Trenton, who in February 1872 founded the Catholic Total Abstinence Union of America. Byrne was a native of County Longford, Ireland. Intemperate for temperance, he damaged his cause—even in episcopal eyes—by a zeal that seemed unhinged. "The A.O.H. [Ancient Order of Hibernians] and other societies [are] fast demoralizing the youth of [Trenton]," he wrote to Bishop Michael Corrigan in 1874. "These societies hold annually some nine or ten picnics and many more balls without either pastoral permission or supervision. They are a source of scandal, as was one held last week by the A.O.H. at which there was such fighting and drunkenness, the whole day, as would shame Comanches."[4] Corrigan and Byrne fell out over the Hibernians later that year,[5] prompting Bishop Bernard McQuaid of Rochester to write to Corrigan that Byrne had become "eaten up with pride and self-sufficiency, . . . ruling bishop and people with an iron hand of despotism."[6] He was not the first or last Irish temperance campaigner to lose his sense of perspective in this way.

The fight for Irish sobriety also exercised Corrigan's successor as bishop of Newark, Winand Wigger. In 1884 Wigger ordered that the last rites of the Church

*Bishop Winand Wigger, Corrigan's successor as bishop of Newark, was fiercely hostile to alcohol abuse among the Irish.*

❧

COURTESY: SETON HALL UNIVERSITY
SPECIAL COLLECTIONS CENTER
AND UNIVERSITY ARCHIVES

*Father Thomas Killeen of Bayonne, temperance campaigner extraordinaire.*

❧

COURTESY: SETON HALL UNIVERSITY
SPECIAL COLLECTIONS CENTER
AND UNIVERSITY ARCHIVES

be denied to those who sold drink to minors or drunkards. Wigger was of German extraction, as were most of Newark's brewers. The saloonkeepers were Irish. On this evidence, and because he was a disciplinarian when Irish priests themselves fell from the wagon, Wigger was thought by some to be anti-Irish. The truth was simpler: he knew, as did others, that the Irish in drink were their own worst enemies. (Wigger's hostility to drink, it should be acknowledged, verged on mania. The slightest tipsiness was enough to get a priest sent packing.) To balance the account, Germans themselves were hardly abstainers. Indeed, their Sabbath-day beer drinking was a perennial political issue between 1870 and 1910. On that matter, as we shall see, Irish priests were again in the fore.

The mid-nineteenth-century Irish world was thus dominated by parish and pub. The triangle was completed by politics. All three represented a barrier to integration and a form of it. Self-segregation reinforced separation but also reproduced a community in miniature, allowing hierarchies and structures of power to emerge. Of the three, politics was most contentious because it represented the point at which the separate Irish world came into contact with the host nation. But there was contention *within* the Irish world as well. Priests were also political creatures, unafraid to use pulpit power to curb secular, even radical, tendencies in their flocks. The Church regarded some Irish organizations with suspicion, and others it considered beyond the pale. For a time, the Ancient Order of Hibernians fell into the first category, the Fenian Brotherhood into the second. Irish America may have seemed harmoniously united to outsiders, but behind its own closed doors, and half doors, no such unity existed.

*The board of directors of the Ancient Order of Hibernians in Jersey City adopted a resolution in 1876 condemning the "detestable organization calling themselves Molly Maguires." John Hart, state delegate to the national organization, dutifully wrote to Bishop Corrigan with the good news.*

❦

COURTESY: SETON HALL UNIVERSITY
SPECIAL COLLECTIONS CENTER
AND UNIVERSITY ARCHIVES

# A. O. H.

## OBLIGATION.

I, _____ do declare
and promise, that I will keep inviolable all the secrets of this Society
of Brethren from all but those whom I know to be members in
good standing, except the Roman Catholic clergy.

1st. I also promise, that I will support the Constitution and
By-Laws of the Ancient Order of Hibernians in preference to any
other society.

2d. That I will be true and steadfast to the Brethren of this
Society, dedicated to St. Patrick, the Holy Patron of Ireland, and that
I will duly conform myself to the dictates of my legally elected officers
in all things lawful, *and not otherwise.*

3d. That I will not provoke or fight with any of my Brethren.
If a Brother should be ill spoken of or otherwise treated unjustly, I will
espouse his cause, and give him the earliest information, aiding him with
my sincere friendship when in distress.

4th. I also promise, that I *will not propose or allow to be
admitted* any person of a *bad or suspicious character* into our society;
and that I will endeavor to propagate friendship and brotherly love
among those of my acquaintance whom I may think worthy of such
confidence.

5th. *That I will not attend* any of the meetings of this society
while under the influence of liquor.

6th. That I will at all times be zealous for the interests of this
society, and will not wrong a member to my knowledge.

7th. That I will not join in secret societies with persons of other
denominations, not meaning trades societies, sailors or soldiers.

8th. I, _____ having made
the above promise of my own free will, I hereby acknowledge myself a
member of the Ancient Order of Hibernians. Amen.

*The Ancient Order of Hibernians oath of the 1870s forbade members of the fraternity from joining "secret societies with persons of other denominations" and urged them not to attend "meetings of this society while under the influence of liquor."*

## JERSEY CITY

**J**ERSEY CITY offers clues to this ambiguous pattern of integration. Hudson County was a world where the Irish were expected to fail and yet flourished; where they were forced to play politics and, in so doing, discovered their mastery of it. Straight off the boat, many Irish people found work in Jersey City as laborers and artisans in the middle years of the century. The census of 1860 revealed their strengths and weaknesses. Compared with British and German immigrants they were plentiful—an obvious advantage, but also a weakness, as their numbers prompted a high degree of anti-Irishness. They were poor, unskilled, badly educated (if educated at all), and—worst of all—Catholic. They represented the nativist's nightmare: a *Lumpenproletariat* armed with a brogue and a set of rosary

*The epitome of second-generation respectability. Mary Owens Mulligan, second from left at front, came from Ireland as a girl to serve as housekeeper to her uncle, Father Patrick Leonard of Newark. Having married, she produced a large family of her own, one of whom, Michael Mulligan, became a monsignor.*

❧

COURTESY: SETON HALL UNIVERSITY SPECIAL COLLECTIONS CENTER AND UNIVERSITY ARCHIVES

beads. Over 40 percent of American-born citizens in Jersey City in 1860 worked in nonmanual jobs; less than 7 percent of Irish-born citizens could say the same. Resentment was all but inevitable.

Many in Jersey City wanted to Americanize the Irish by converting them. Popery produced poverty, and Protestantism promised prosperity: this was a well-attested truth on both sides of the Atlantic. Proselytism—that is to say, class warfare by other means—was therefore waged with vigor in Hudson County in the middle years of the century. In 1853 Irish prisoners and inmates in Jersey City almshouses were required to attend Protestant services. In the 1860s members of Protestant organizations used their dominance on school boards to shape an anti-Catholic curriculum. In the 1870s the Monthly Tract Society delivered evangelical literature to every home.

The irony is that these efforts to undermine the faith probably strengthened it. As historians now recognize, Irish Catholicism underwent a sea-change in the decades after the famine—a "devotional revolution" no less—in which every expression of popular piety (mass attendance, reception of the sacraments, the "Forty Hours" adoration) increased. These practices crossed the ocean intact and, transplanted into new soil, flourished. Attempts to eradicate them served only as reminders of historic persecution in Ireland—another reason for holding on to them. Bible Christians who thought that the Irish needed only a scrubbing and a sermon to become good citizens misread their audience. A history lesson might have disabused them.

By the early 1860s the Irish of Jersey City began to recognize the possibilities of politics, especially Democratic politics, as a way to shape a life more to their liking. In 1861 they mobilized to defeat the city recorder, Thomas Tilden, whose record as public prosecutor revealed nativist tendencies. In 1862 they forced the Democrats to nominate an Irishman for police chief, then carried the day for him in the election. These electoral outings were gratifying signs of strength. More surprising, perhaps, was that the Democratic leadership of Jersey City was

*Father Patrick Leonard, born in Ireland, was the founding pastor of Saint Michael's Church, Newark. The parish was created in 1878 to accommodate the overflow from Saint John's Church. Father Leonard died in 1892 and was succeeded by another Irishman, Denis McCartie.*

❧

dominated by former Know-Nothings. Certainly Republicans thought that the Democrats cultivated pliant candidates but took care "to exclude Irishmen of character and intelligence from office."[7] There was a less sinister explanation for the Democrats' success in ethnic politics: they were generous patrons. Irish laborers and policemen depended for their jobs on Democrat control of City Hall and at election time did not forget it. Besides, throughout the 1860s Democrats toned down their nativist rhetoric as it became counterproductive. Increasingly the Irish were a bloc to be courted, not condemned. At the end of the decade, indeed, Jersey City's political sectarianism was turned on its head. The *Evening Journal* reported in November 1868 that the "old Know-Nothing Democrats had once been smart enough to honeyfugle the Irish into doing all the heavy voting and yelling while they took all the fat offices themselves." Now "Pat has worked up to a conscious sense of his power, and demands the offices himself."[8]

This confidence yielded impressive results. In 1870 Jersey City elected nine Irish-born aldermen out of a total of twenty, changing the coloration of local politics. But the victory was short-lived. Unable to resist Irish advances in local government, nativists responded by emasculating local government itself. In 1871 Republicans and some Democrats at state level adopted a new city charter that transferred most local powers to the New Jersey legislature. Deprived of the spoils system, they decided to spoil it for everyone else. It took nearly a generation for the Irish to regain political hegemony in Jersey City. Their enemies, it seemed, still had a few tricks to play.

*Leon Abbett.*

❧

## CIVIL WAR POLITICS:
## THE CASE OF LEON ABBETT

THE LARGER context for this municipal mudslinging was the Civil War. Throughout the state, and especially in larger urban areas, Republicans and Democrats were eager for Irish support but aware that it carried political dangers. Democrats were usually better placed to cater to their client interests. In the presidential election of 1860 Newark, Trenton, Jersey City, and Camden, all with solid Irish populations, supported Douglas; only Paterson supported Lincoln. In 1864 New Jersey was one of only three states to go Democratic, in part because of strong Irish Catholic support for General George McClellan.[9] The Democrat case was unashamedly racial. Why should Irish workers fight to free blacks, they argued, who would then take their jobs? The appeal received a good hearing. In June 1863 draft officers visited Irish sections of Newark only to have local women stone them. New Jersey was spared draft riots—New York was less fortunate—but ethnic tension remained high. One resident of Elizabeth deplored the "fiendish unreasoning cruelty" of the Irish "towards the unoffending blacks."[10] It was a plausible criticism but one that lacked perspective. Irish racism—which is not to be denied—was largely class anxiety expressed in racial terms. (That did not lessen its ugliness.) On the credit side, many Irishmen fought for the Union, some for pecuniary reasons, others for reasons of principle.[11] These extenuations notwithstanding, antagonism between Irish and Negro was a reality, and Democrats knew how to exploit it.

Consider the career of Leon Abbett. A working-class Philadelphian, Abbett moved to Hoboken in 1862 to practice law in lower Manhattan. Possessed of powerful gifts of oratory, personality, and political astuteness, he quickly established himself as a coming man in the Democratic Party. (He later served as governor, becoming the state's "foremost Democrat and . . . undisputed party leader.")[12] Abbett's early years in New Jersey politics established a pattern. In private he cultivated the party machine. In public he supported an array of working-class issues: state's rights, opposition to overreaching federalism, and white participation in elections. It was a winning if at times unattractive combination. Abbett's opponents saw him as demagogue, not Democrat. Perhaps so. Politics was a contact sport, and he certainly played it better than they.

*James Morrissey from County Tipperary was one of thousands of Irishmen who fought in the Civil War. Born in 1831, he left Ireland for New York in 1851, settling there with his family for two years before moving to Paterson, where he found employment in the cotton mills. Immediately upon the outbreak of the war he joined Company G, Seventeenth New York Voluntary Infantry. He was severely wounded in the Battle of Peach Tree Creek in the taking of Richmond. Morrissey remained a military man after the conclusion of the war; he was present at Fort Union when Custer was killed fighting Sitting Bull. His last years were spent in Paterson, where he was heavily involved in Democratic politics.*

Abbett's first run for office came in 1864, when he sought election to the New Jersey State Assembly for the Fourth District of Hudson County, comprising Hoboken and Weehawken. His cause was helped by McClellan's campaign for the presidency, which garnered strong Irish Catholic support. Removed by Lincoln from command of the Union Army, McClellan—a resident of West Orange—called for an end to a war that was going badly for the North. Abbett echoed this. He, too, was impatient with a crusade to abolish slavery that had succeeded only in abolishing the rights of individuals (who were drafted to fight and threatened with jail if they resisted) and of states (whose prerogatives were ignored by the Emancipation Proclamation of 1863). He adopted this position while professing continuing support for the Union, a delicate but necessary balancing act that reflected the ambiguous politics of New Jersey during the Civil War. Abbett was careful to be on the right side of the Irish of Hudson County, who were (as his biographer has it) "intensely anti-black."[13] The first speech of his campaign, delivered in Jersey City, was a racial appeal to the fears of low-income Irish voters.[14] He continued as he began, arguing a states' rights case that everyone understood as code for anti-war, pro-white localism. But he did not campaign with a united Democratic party behind him. In Hoboken there were War as well as Peace Democrats, the former prepared to cross party lines to support Lincoln in the presidential race. In the end these desertions did not deny McClellan the state or Abbett his own smaller victory. He won the seat, albeit with a very slender majority, and thereby laid the foundations of a career that consistently succeeded because of attention to Irish working-class issues.

Abbett had an unusually acute instinct that the appeal most likely to succeed in Hudson County was to ethnic fear. His earliest positions were all negative: opposition to the draft, to the integration of black Americans into the mainstream of political life, to giving Union soldiers

*Father James Sheeran had a notable career not only as a cleric but also as a soldier. Born in County Longford in 1813, he left Ireland for Canada (subsequently ending in New York) at the age of twelve. He was ordained a priest in 1857, served as chaplain to the Third Louisiana Regiment in the Civil War, and was appointed pastor of the Church of the Assumption of the Blessed Virgin in Morristown in 1871. He died in 1880.*

✥

the right to vote in the field, to paying widows of black soldiers the same pensions as white widows, to acknowledging at the end of the war Lincoln's role in preserving the Union. Adopting a tone of lawyerly piety, he maintained that he, not Lincoln, was a better friend to the Union and to slaves: these matters, he argued, should be adjudicated by states, not by a national government in the hands of abolitionist fanatics. It was a relentlessly minatory record, barely enough to secure his reelection in the election of 1865. In the war's immediate aftermath Republicans did well throughout the state, winning the governorship, senate, and assembly. Abbett was nearly swept away, his majority reduced to ninety-five votes and his sense of political security shattered. Whether the margin of victory would have been larger or smaller without an appeal to the social and economic anxieties of the Irish cannot be known.

Abbett's early career as a representative is worth examining because it is itself representative. There were dozens of Leon Abbetts across the state, each carefully calibrating the dangers and opportunities of ethnic politics during and after the war. Republicans played the game, too, always hoping to benefit from anti-Irishness if their opponents should overreach. Consider the Democrats' nomination of an Irishman to be Essex County sheriff in 1862. The Irish were strong in Newark, but most Essex County electors thought this was too obvious an appeal to one ethnic constituency. Republicans exploited the backlash to secure an unexpected victory. In the atmosphere of civil war, their party line—that the goal of politics ought to be assimilation to the mainstream, not division of racial spoils—was powerfully persuasive. To give another example, the state assembly election in 1864 saw the Republican candidate in Gloucester praised by the *Woodbury Constitution* as "not an Irishman: he is a Jerseyman."[15] This was artful: an appeal for ethnic votes (the anti-Irish sort) that deplored ethnicity as a basis for voting. Yet Republicans themselves occasionally looked for Irish votes. One of their themes in the election of 1864—admittedly sounded with no great conviction—was that they were the party of independence for Ireland. This was gesture politics, generally recognized for the sham it was.

The electoral pendulum thus oscillated between tokenism and nativism; Democrats and Republicans each in their different ways were well trained in both. Neither appeal was subtle. Each acknowledged nonetheless that the Irish could not be ignored. They now constituted a voting presence (if not a bloc) of real importance, especially in cities. Democrats had the better of the bargain, as even their opponents conceded. The Republican charge that the Irish marched unthinkingly behind any Democratic banner was one part truth to two parts jealousy. Certainly the party of Abbett and his ilk seemed to command greater loyalty and a formidable ability to get out the vote. (In the election of 1864, for example, Irish voters, Democrats to a man, registered with suspicious speed at the last moment in Newark, Orange, and Jersey City, causing Republicans to cry foul.) Even as they suspected fast work, Republicans may have admired privately the efficiency of the operation. Still, the broader picture suggests that their fears were overdone. Vote-buying notwithstanding, electoral trends were moving in a Republican, not Democratic, direction. New Jersey rejected Lincoln in 1864 but compared to 1860 that election actually marked an underlying shift toward the G.O.P. There was, in other words, a paradox at the heart of Jersey politics. The strength of the Democrats lay in their Irish base; that was also their weakness.[16]

*Jeremiah O'Rourke, architect, was born in Dublin in 1833, immigrating to the United States in 1850. An ardent proponent of the Gothic revival, he designed the chapel of Seton Hall College, the magnificent and extravagant Saint John's Church in Orange, and Sacred Heart Cathedral in Newark.*

## PRIESTS, PARADES, AND POLITICS

THIS STORY of pride and prejudice—of ethnic solidarity provoking nativist response—was commonplace in New Jersey throughout the nineteenth century. As every immigrant came to realize, assimilation to American ways demanded a delicate calculus. On the one hand, ethnicity meant integration—fitting in, going along, toning down, making the system work. On the other hand, it meant differentiation—the assertion of distinctive identity demanding its own electoral and economic reward. Getting the balance right was not easy.

There were other ambiguities. One oddity of assimilation was that it allowed the Irish to see nationality as a mark of honor, not a badge of shame. As they merged into the mainstream it became possible, even necessary, to celebrate identity rather than conceal it. But this was not straightforward. To celebrate identity was to raise a question: which identity? Irish? American? Radical? Conformist? Not every expatriate answered similarly. Think of a thing as apparently simple as Saint Patrick's Day. To commemorate the national apostle was to engage in a political as well as a patriotic and pious act. It was a statement of solidarity, pride, memory, and in-

In July 1886, Joseph Atkinson, president of the Irish National League (Newark branch), thanked Bishop Winand Wigger for his "generous check" and his "hearty words of recommendation." He continued: "They are so many towers of strength to those who are at work in the noble cause of aiding a long-suffering and brave people. And, dear bishop, how superbly the Irish in Ireland are behaving! Now who can doubt their capacity for self-government?" (16 July 1886, Winand Wigger Papers, Record Group 3, 3.36, Clerical and General Correspondence, Box 4, Archdiocese of Newark Archives).

Atkinson's letter came at a crucial moment in Irish political history. In June 1886, British Prime Minister William Gladstone failed in his attempt to pass a bill through the House of Commons that would have provided a degree of Home Rule for Ireland. The proposal split the Liberal party and led to his defeat in the general election of July 1886. Restored to power in 1892, he tried again in 1893 only to see a bill pass through the Commons and be subsequently rejected in the House of Lords.

❧

creasingly confident Catholicism as the Irish began to dominate the streets and wards of New Jersey's cities. Marches had multiple meanings. A parade, properly understood, was a parable. Consider Hudson County. "The Celts of Jersey City are about to pay due honor to the Patron Saint of the Emerald Isle," wrote the organizer of the festivities for 1865, John Pope Hodnett, to the *Daily News*:

> During the day the citizens will be pleased to witness the processions of the various Irish American Associations of our city, the Father Mathew, Hibernians, etc. In the evening, the more youthful and jovial will participate in the grand Irish National Ball . . . given under the auspices of the Fenian Brother-hood. . . . The accomplished Militia Brass Band of Brooklyn, who are specially engaged at very great expense, will pour out sweetest notes of music, and to crown all the Fenian Men have secured the services of Mr. Lawless, the great Irish piper from Cork. His shrill and thrilling notes will convey the exiled Gaels in fancy, back again to the hills and vales of fatherland.[17]

*Bishop Wigger, prepared to support the fund-raising efforts of the Irish National League, was insistent that such events be decorous and sober. "I must not even appear to approve of round dancing," he wrote to Joseph Atkinson, president of the Newark branch of the Irish National League, " or to invite people to attend a place of amusement where it is included."*

✣

Here was the Irish American idyll, an idealized community of the young and the old, the sober and the celebratory, at home in America but still loyal to the land across the sea. Yet all was not jollity. "Let us have a glorious time," Hodnett urged, but let us remember that "the proceeds will go promptly to the succor of the suffering in our own dear Isle. . . . If the sons and daughters of Ireland do not feel for motherland, they cannot expect the children of Italy or France or Germany to feel for her." First fun, then funds. The money was

for the support of the Fenian Brotherhood, a group dedicated to the violent over-
throw of English rule in Ireland. That the Fenians of Jersey City had secured the
services of the well-named Mr. Lawless was appropriate. That was precisely how
their organization was viewed by British authorities in Ireland, to whom Irish
American sentimentalism had a sinister side.

Naturally the Irish saw it differently. The famine generation, torn between relief and regret, gratitude and grief, never shook the sense that America, for all its
opportunities, was a place of exile. They could not forget, and wished to avenge,
the indifference of English administrations to their plight. Fenianism fell on fertile soil in America; more fertile soil, in fact, than in Ireland itself, where for years
after the famine politics had a stunned, somnambulist quality, as of a nation made
dumb by grief. Nor was Fenianism the only expression of Irish American anti-
Britishness. Every organization represented in the Jersey City parade—the Knights
of Saint Patrick, the Friendly Sons of Saint Patrick, the Ancient Order of Hibernians—had an animus against the old enemy. Hodnett's appeal to a certain com-
petitive nationalism was well chosen. It reinforced a message that Irish parades had
a political as well as a processional purpose, and that the politics had to do with Ireland as well as America.

Hodnett overstated his case in one particular. By implying that the community
he described was united and integrated, he glossed over the strong opposition of
some to physical force nationalism as the primary purpose of Irish American politics. The Catholic Church viewed with distaste the politicization of Irish nationalism; many bishops saw the Fenians and the Ancient Order of Hibernians as
dangerously radical, threats to religion as well as to the state. Bishop Bayley, an avid
newspaper reader, kept a clipping of Hodnett's announcement and annotated it
thus: "Father Darnen who believes Fenianism the Devil's special work, got all his
hearers one night at Saint Mary's to promise they would not go to this Ball."[18] Nor
was he alone in thinking that the quasi-revolutionary character of some Irish organizations put them beyond the pale. His successor as bishop, Michael Corrigan,
had similar qualms. In the case of the Fenians, his anxiety had justification; with the
Ancient Order of Hibernians it was excessive. But both Bayley and Corrigan recognized the indignation that animated Irish radicalism and sought to channel it pos-
itively. Above all they hoped to retain a semblance of clerical authority over groups
of self-willed laymen.

This was a difficult balance to achieve. During his years as bishop, Bayley was
much occupied by Irish affairs. In 1863 he ordered a collection to be taken
throughout the diocese for the poor in Ireland. Over $8,500 was collected. He en-
couraged Irish organizations, expressing pleasure at their devout Catholicism
and—undercutting the point a little—surprise at their sobriety on festive occa-

sions. But he drew the line at Fenians. "Lectured at Orange on Saint Patrick and the mission of the Irish people," he wrote in his diary in June 1866. "Good audience—gave a good strong rap at Fenianism."[19] This was a constant theme with him. In fairness, Orange was a special case. Its pastor, a young Dubliner called James McKay, had fallen foul of the bishop, and this may have sharpened the latter's impatience with Irish politics. McKay opposed the drafting of Irish immigrants into the Union Army in the Civil War, a stance in Bayley's eyes more political than pastoral. Worse followed. During a visit to Ireland in 1865 McKay wrote pseudonymously a series of articles extremely critical of the United States government. Incensed, Bayley removed him from his post, and as a result he never returned to the United States. (He ended his ministry in the Diocese of Derry.) McKay's mistake was less his association with Irish causes than his too obvious relish for the political arena. Bayley preferred his priests in the pulpit, not in the public prints. The "good strong rap at Fenianism" was as much a warning against clerical involvement in politics as against Irish radicalism in particular. If the thought occurred to him that his own opposition to Fenianism was itself a form of involvement in politics, he kept it to himself.

Bishop Michael Corrigan faced similar challenges. As we have seen, at the beginning of his episcopacy the Diocese of Newark was home to 170,000 Catholics—more than enough for ethnic tension and administrative anxiety.[20] The Irish dominated, with Germans and Italians also strong. Corrigan himself, the child of Irish immigrants, was something of a boy wonder: Doctor of divinity at twenty-five, president of Seton Hall College at twenty-nine, bishop of Newark at thirty-four, archbishop of New York at forty-one. "Dr. Corrigan has learning enough for five bishops," Bishop Bayley wrote, "and sanctity enough for ten."[21] His career reflected the gifts of a superb academician and administrator. (It also captured another truth of the Irish immigrant experience. America was a channel of social mobility, but so, too, was the Church. Corrigan would have succeeded almost anywhere as an ecclesiastic. Rome, not New York, was the making of him. Catholicism may have kept some immigrants back—hostility remained strong for decades—but it pushed others forward.)

The obverse side of abundant talent was prickliness. Corrigan was impatient with those less able than himself and had a martinet's consciousness of episcopal rights. Both sides of his ecclesiastical personality—the pastoral and the peremptory—were obvious in his dealings with the Irish. Like Bayley, he was distressed by the unending suffering of Ireland. Crop failure, poor weather, and eviction brought famine to the country in the late 1870s and early 1880s. Moved by this, he organized a collection throughout the diocese and recorded its success with characteristic precision:

June 1880. The collection for Ireland during these past months of terrible distress for that afflicted country amounted in this diocese to over $20,000. The amount reported in the *Freeman's Journal* . . . is $19,365.50 but this account is incomplete for the reason that some Rectors failed to report their offerings to the Chancellor.[22]

This was impressive by any standards, a tribute to Irish American compassion and to the formidable organization of the Diocese of Newark. But purposes other than charity were served by such efforts. They reinforced solidarity between priests and people, binding shepherd and flock in common purpose. American Catholics

*An extraordinary figure in Paterson Catholicism, William McNulty was born near Ballyshannon, Ireland, in 1829. Immigrating to America in 1850 to pursue a religious vocation, he studied at Fordham and Emmitsburg before being ordained priest by Bishop J. R. Bayley in Newark in 1857. McNulty's first appointment was as dean of discipline and vice president of the recently established Seton Hall College at Madison. When the college moved to South Orange in 1860, he remained at Madison as chaplain to the Sisters of Charity. This ministry was also brief. In October 1863 Bayley appointed McNulty pastor of Saint John's in Paterson, a post he held until his death in 1922. Two three-year appointments were thus followed by one of fifty-nine years, the latter a record in the state's Catholic annals.*

*McNulty, indefatigable promoter of Catholic interests in a rapidly growing city, was named dean of Bergen and Passaic counties in 1886. Presiding over his own parish, he also assisted in the formation of "daughter" and "second-generation" ethnic parishes in Paterson. Many schools, hospitals, and charitable institutions also owe their existence to him. He rebuilt his own parish church on a scale sufficiently grand that it became the cathedral church of the Diocese of Paterson when the latter was formed in 1937. By then McNulty was fifteen years dead: "the last of the pioneer priests," as local newspapers aptly dubbed him.*

❦

helped Ireland survive. Irish Catholics returned the favor by giving the American Church an opportunity to grow.

Corrigan's concern with Irish matters was confined to alms and admonitions. Like Bayley, he thought his duty was to lead his flock in prayer, not politics, and so Irish groups that ventured beyond the spiritual or charitable were suspect to him. Part of the problem was that some Irish Catholics seemed more interested in Irishness than in Catholicism. An encounter in 1877 captured this concern:

> In the afternoon [he recorded in his journal for October 17] we visited Colt's Neck, six miles from Freehold, and addressed the people in Mrs. Maguire's house, and afterwards Big Woods. The people were earnestly urged to build a small church, which they promised to do, and a subscription list was opened on the spot. . . . That night a committee came to see me about getting an Irish priest, if possible. They were composed of drinking men and careless Catholics, members of the A.O.H.[23]

For Corrigan, careless Catholicism and membership in the A.O.H. were almost synonymous. From the beginning of his episcopacy he regarded the organization as a boozy brotherhood and a potential challenge to his own authority.[24] This assessment lacked charity, as perhaps he later came to realize. Yet the Colt's Neck meeting, a minor matter, stood for a larger whole. Clerical leadership of an ethnically diverse laity required tact and delicacy. Bishops, happy to urge the building of a church, were not so happy to be urged themselves to provide a pastor of a particular nationality. Corrigan momentarily forgot that without the priest whom the laity itself had requested the practice of the faith could only be casual. Of course, Irish priests usually ministered to Irish flocks, but that decision belonged to the bishop alone.

Corrigan also objected to the Hibernians because of their secrecy. As a private, oath-swearing organization, they seemed like a Celtic version of the Freemasons or, worse, one of those revolutionary groups in Europe explicitly condemned by the Church for their anti-Christian activities. Some bishops allowed Catholics to join; others did not.[25] Corrigan's first instinct was prohibition. "As to the Ancient Order of Hibernians," he wrote privately to Father Patrick Byrne of Trenton in 1874, "I have felt compelled to abstain from all ecclesiastical sanction or recognition of them. . . . They bind themselves in advance to obey superior orders, [and the] Head Officers are to be the judges of the lawfulness of the orders given. . . . A Catholic cannot in conscience bind himself by any such obligation." This was not, however, his settled judgment. As we have seen, Father Byrne was no friend of the Hibernians, and he used Corrigan's letter to deny them participation in his parish's Saint Patrick's Day parade. This deepened the bishop's embarrassment. A further letter followed. Condemning the increasing secularism of Saint Patrick's Day, Corrigan nonetheless modified his position:

> For motives of prudence [I hoped] that the question of the Ancient Order would be settled before the next recurrence of the anniversary. In this I am disappointed; and I am much embarrassed between the fear of encouraging the A.O.H. by a spirit of opposition on the one hand, and the fear of alienating from the Church on the other those who clearly do not come under the ban of the Church.

This anguish was reflected in a compromise. In July 1874 the clergy of the Diocese of Newark were instructed "not to recognize the A.O.H. in Catholic procession or to admit them to the Church as a society with regalia and banners." (No sooner was the instruction issued than it was ignored. Two months later one thousand Hibernians attended the laying of the cornerstone of Saint Mary's Academy in Newark.) Further embarrassed, Corrigan issued a final instruction. Members of the order, he said, "must not be debarred from the Sacraments (in this Diocese) for the mere fact of their belonging to that Society."[26] This lawyerly solution, saving face as well as souls, satisfied the delicate sensibilities of both parties.

Oath-taking and drinking were not the only problems. Rightly or wrongly, the Hibernians were associated with radical labor movements, especially the Molly Maguires. The A.O.H. cannot be blamed for its wayward brethren, but there was certainly overlapping membership in the two organizations. Corrigan fretted about this connection. It undermined the Catholicity of his people, implicating them in criminality and impeding their integration into the larger American community. In the western part of the state—the area on the Delaware River around Phillipsburg and Easton, Pennsylvania—the Mollies and the Hibernians were strong. The result was tension in January 1876 when a member of the A.O.H. called Michael Doyle was put on trial in Mauch Chunk, Pennsylvania, for the murder of one John Jones, a foreman for the Wilkes-Barre Coal Company.

It was widely believed that the A.O.H. had connived in the crime. Whatever of that, the accusation inaugurated a protracted period of bitterness between the Irish community and the local church and between Hibernians in New Jersey and Pennsylvania. Seeking to ease anxiety, the "heads of several Irish societies" (the *Easton Sentinel* reported in January 1876) canceled Saint Patrick's Day parades in Pennsylvania. This, they argued, would show respect for the national centennial. Hibernians in Warren County, New Jersey, and in neighboring Pennsylvania decided to parade anyway. They planned a march in Phillipsburg, the first in the town's history, and one in Easton, so that "everybody may have a chance to see the Order and the character of the men who compose it."[27] The local pastor, Father Cornelius Reilly, knew already the character of the A.O.H. and had no time for it. Indeed, his relations with Hibernians collapsed as a result of their accumulated impertinences—the labor radicalism, the parading without permission, the seeming indifference to clerical direction. Corrigan was forced to visit the parish to bring both sides together. "The parties seemed well-disposed at the time," he wrote in his journal in February 1876, "but the next Sunday things were worse than ever; so that a riot in the church was imminent."[28] In fact, no such riot occurred. The tenor of Corrigan's mediation is unknown, but if he hoped that Hibernians would cancel their march he was disappointed. The parade went ahead, "a very imposing affair," the *Easton Daily Express* reported, with five hundred marchers and four bands, all looking and behaving well. Unmollified, Father O'Reilly the following month denounced the Ancient Order of Hibernians from the altar, only to have one of their number answer the charge from the congregation. By then, however, the row had petered out, the success of the parade having cooled tempers. Corrigan revisited Phillipsburg in June and found the atmosphere more agreeable. "The excitement caused by the A.O.H. in this Parish has subsided," he recorded in his journal.[29] There the matter rested. The dispute had as much to do with personality as politics. O'Reilly was not the first or last priest to get on the wrong side of his flock. Moreover, although his quarrel was with Hibernianism it might have been with almost anything. Still, the episode was a reminder that when some Irish Americans were invited to show loyalty to the Church Militant they preferred a militancy of their own making.

## IRISH PRIDE, IRISH PREJUDICE

THE FENIAN Brotherhood was politically radical, socially advanced, and marginally Catholic, if Catholic at all. The Ancient Order of Hibernians was different. Within a few years, episcopal suspicion of the Hibernians disappeared. At the Annual Meeting of the Archbishops of the United States in 1904, for example, the archbishop of Saint Louis presented a petition from the A.O.H. urging the study of Irish history in parochial schools. It was received by the archbishops "most favorably."[30] Although distinct in character, the two organizations had a similar effect. Each provided practical and political support for the Irish in Ireland while also allowing communal solidarity to flourish among the Irish in America. These aims did not always sit easily with each other. At least at the beginning, Fenianism expressed a nationalism of exile and of revenge. Sullen and embittered, some Irish continued to fight in America the war against England they had lost at home. This hindered their full integration into the American way of life. For many, Ireland became a romantic idyll, sepia colored in memory, a land of lost content. (For others, of course, it was a place they were only too happy to leave.) This long-distance longing could be benign or malign. The Irish of New Jersey gave money for famine relief and Fenianism, not always distinguishing between the two. As for communal solidarity, that, too, was problematic. Associations and confraternities softened the life of the ghetto, but they could also make it permanent. When an ethnic redoubt became comfortable there was no reason to leave it. Nor was this the only paradox. Americans, as Alexis de Tocqueville famously noticed in 1831, were great joiners. They loved their parishes, their clubs, their local organizations. The moment Irish people arrived in the New World, they discovered in themselves precisely the same enthusiasm. They were never more American than when they banded together to proclaim their Irishness.

These tensions reflected the complexity of the world Irish Americans created for themselves. Of the various curiosities of their in-between state, most striking was that religious identity was compounded of equal parts pride and prejudice. This was true of most immigrant groups throughout the United States. Consider how Catholicism became a national church: by the efforts of different nationalities preserving an old faith in a new country. Nativists never understood the significance or irony of this: that far from proving the disloyalty of Catholics it proved the opposite. The Church was the means by which immigrants could demonstrate commitment and new belonging, attachment to their adoptive land. Indeed, the Church was an institutional mirror of America itself, embracing ethnicities and recognizing distinctiveness while also requiring conformity to certain general norms. Religion acted as a double bridge—between the Old World and the New, and between this world and the next. It fashioned people worthy of two cities, of God and of man. Catholics of all nationalities were rightly proud of their achievements in nineteenth-century America.

This, then, was pride. What of prejudice? That came in the form already noticed: distaste for foreigners and a foreign creed, indignation at their ambiguous loyalty (Rome first, then America), and hostility to those who

*Englewood Irishmen—the Blackbirds Minstrel Troupe—in 1899.*

❧

COURTESY: SETON HALL UNIVERSITY
SPECIAL COLLECTIONS CENTER AND UNIVERSITY ARCHIVES

A TRICKLE BECOMES A FLOOD    **119**

would steal American jobs or do no work at all. These resentments helped build the American Church, reinforcing identity, requiring self-reliance. Catholics became American precisely because many doubted their Americanness. But another prejudice, less frequently noticed, should also be mentioned: the hostility of Catholics to each other. A Church that balanced ethnicity and universality sometimes found equilibrium elusive. In New Jersey, racial problems were often intramural. True, they were rarely dangerous—family squabbles, not civil wars—but all the same, they showed the potency of ethnic tension inside as well as outside the Catholic community.

A little episode in Bordentown in 1856 makes the point. Three years into his episcopate Bishop Bayley received a complaint from "the Catholics of Bordentown," or at least twenty-one of them, all with Irish names. With the careful script of the recently literate, they described their plight:

> We believe we are mortally aggrieved by the fact of Father Biggio now introducing a female teacher into our school. After supporting a male teacher for the last four years the majority of the parents of the children here are entirely opposed to this measure and will be obliged thereby to send their children to an infidel school. . . . We are willing to support a good school. But Father Biggio is trying to bully us out of it by treats [*sic*] and tells us to send our children to the Devil . . . and all this on Sunday in the hearing of Protestants. . . . Now in conclusion we humbly request your Lordship to removed Father Biggio and send us an Irish priest whom we will understand. . . . Father Biggio has publically [*sic*] insulted the founders of Catholicity here. . . . [He] calls us ignorant but he wants to make our children ignorant. If we are ignorant we are generous.[31]

*Irish-owned businesses began to flourish in the late nineteenth century.*

❧

There was nothing unusual about the complaint—bishops received letters like this all the time—but precisely for that reason it commands attention. It was, in fact, a classic of the form, with much of the Irish experience in America—their encounters with bishops, priests, education, and class—captured in its few sentences. Here was a laity undecided between assertion and acquiescence: witness the mock solemnity ("mortally aggrieved"), the patriarchalism (elsewhere in the letter they noted that "some of the children . . . are now far advanced in Philosophy, Mathematics etc. and a female will not be qualified to instruct [them]"), the self-righteous claim of scandal ("in the hearing of Protestants") the injured honor ("the founders of Catholicity here"), and the final hint of threat ("If we are ignorant we are generous"). The complaint was real but articulated in ways that revealed more than the complainants intended. The Irish of Bordentown in 1856 inhabited a nether region between respectability and rejection: a minority in a Protestant world and objects of suspicion to their neighbors, but also anxious for recognition of some prerogatives within their own Church. Paradoxically, to complain about a priest was not a sign of anticlericalism but its opposite. So close was their identification with the peasant priesthood in Ireland that any other kind of priest in America was unlikely to satisfy. As a matter of practical common sense, most bishops recognized the value of Irish priests for Irish parishes. They drew the line at making it mandatory, certainly at making it a matter decided by parishioners themselves. As for the Bordentown petition, Bayley took note of it but declined to act.

If the Irish were touchy it was because they sensed a degree of clerical condescension and a hint that their generosity was sometimes taken for granted. In 1865 the parishioners of Saint Patrick's in Elizabethport complained of their pastor on both those grounds. Rising to the full height of their indignation and hardly pausing to draw breath, they addressed the bishop:

Annex is a statement of the grievances of the Parish and of the Rev. Father Werzfeld['s] neglect of duty since the early

*Saint James's Parish in Woodbridge was largely Irish. In 1895 such was their attachment to the old wooden church that they had it placed on a scaffold and physically removed to its new location in the parish.*

☘

stages of the parish until the present day. First that of not being able to give a True account or at least of refusing to do so of moneys collected in the parish by districts when committees were appointed for that purpose and of not making a true report of moneys collected at Fairs and Pic-Nics and not putting the same to good use by Paying off the debt of the Church in place of loaning out to his own countrymen the moneys thus received and reduce the debt and interest on the church and they the very men who would fain pay a dollar for any such purpose but would laugh at what they call folly for Irishmen to be such fools. Next the squandering of the moneys thus raised from the Poor Liberal Irish by Father Werzfeld calling around him the Dutchmen and drinking wine and lager beer to a shameful extent, and never having the least respect for a poor Irishman contributing to the same but treat him in such a manner as to say to him Poor Irishman if he wanted any business with him while in the act of enjoying himself with his own class such as Dutch Protestans [*sic*] and cold Dutch Catholicks that he the Poor Irishman should wait until he got ready no matter on what Emergency.[32]

Page upon page it proceeded, the pent-up anger of a long failed marriage.

The cleric in question had complaints of his own. Werzfeld assured Bayley that his critics were "so-called Catholics," unrepresentative of the parish as a whole. Worse, they were tainted with infidelity and radicalism:

> None but a Finian [*sic*] is connected with the matter. The Finians of this place spoyled [*sic*] our Pic-Nic for the school by arranging one for themselves, and ours would have been a Complete failure had it not been for some of my in-fluential *Protestant* friends. . . .
>
> They have raised such a talk and have invented such stories about me that even Protestants are scandalized at them, and all for no other reason than be-cause I am not in favor of Finiainism. Deeply as I felt their ingratitude I for-give them.[33]

This was astute. The easiest way to win Bayley's endorsement was to suggest that one's opponents were motivated by Fenianism. (The embrace of martyrdom was also a nice touch.) In the scheme of things the dispute was trivial—parochial in every sense of the word. In its own time and place, however, this *was* the scheme of things. The little world of the parish mirrored the wider world of American Catholicism as a whole, in which lay ethnicity and clericalism sometimes chimed, sometimes clashed. The picnic was picayune, but the forces it called forth were not. They were, in fact, the two strongest impulses of an immigrant church on its way to becoming a national institution.

The passage of time did not eradicate Irish irritability. Any priest who offended them was likely to know their collective wrath. In 1888 the pastor of Elizabeth wrote to the third bishop of Newark, Winand Wigger:

> I have never been liked by the Irish part of the Congregation, who even invented a nickname for myself and my family. An affair between the Sisters and a person who had taken up her residence in the convent was made the ground of direct hostility towards me, although . . . I had nothing to do with the matter and always entertained the warmest feelings towards that community.[34]

Two years before, Monsignor Robert Seton of Saint Joseph's in Jersey City had a different grievance. Seton, distinguished scholar and martinet, never mastered the ethnic touch. "You know what the Irish are," he wrote to Wigger, "how they will always want fun and excitement and will spend their money when any priest calls for it."[35] If this seems strange—a clergyman deploring generosity—it was also understandable: the people in question were not his own parishioners and were raising money for another priest. Seton was certainly right about canon law, but in his fussiness we glimpse a wider point. The Irish were good to their friends, he realized, and dangerous to their enemies. As for their taste for fun and excitement, virtually every priest in the diocese could testify to it. In September 1889 Father John Sheppard of Passaic warned Wigger of a convention of the Ancient Order of Hibernians about to be held in his parish. "I have not the slightest doubt that if [a letter from you] reaches them a resolution will be passed doing away with all night picnics."[36] Wigger was the last person to need prompting in this regard.

*Faces in the crowd: baseball fans from Saint James's, Newark, 1912.*

❧

COURTESY: SETON HALL UNIVERSITY
SPECIAL COLLECTIONS CENTER
AND UNIVERSITY ARCHIVES

## TOWARD THE END AND THE BEGINNING OF A CENTURY:
## A CHURCH IN MONTCLAIR

**S**ETON AND Sheppard were not unfair. They viewed the Irish through a set of commonplace expectations that were often crude but occasionally compelling. In a state whose ethnic mix grew more intricate by the year, racial caricatures were the beginning—and sometimes the end—of wisdom. Stereotypes were never subtle, but in a complex world they provided a kind of clarity: the Irish as convivial or morose, Germans as punctilious, Italians as extravagantly emotional. As working approximations of a more varied social truth, they sufficed. Their power derived less from rough-and-ready accuracy than from the fact that the groups themselves tended to believe them. The caricatures created the very reality they claimed to describe. People behaved in particular ways because they embraced, wittingly or unwittingly, the social roles already established for them.

Class was another element in these behavioral expectations. By the end of the century the Irish had lost their hungry look. The children of the famine had begun to make their way, inching toward respectability. They were white and could speak English—no small advantages in the 1890s and early 1900s. As Italians, Hungarians, Austrians, and Poles flooded into New Jersey, and as blacks moved from south to north, the Irish seemed less alien than before.[37] Slowly, one set of caricatures had to be replaced with another. In the middle of the century there had been poverty; now it was beginning to be concealed by a lace curtain.

A vignette from Montclair in northern New Jersey reveals these *fin-de-siècle* trends. It has to do with the building of a new Catholic church in the town in the early 1890s, a decision in which considerations of race and class blended so perfectly that we see not only a house of worship but a glimpse of New Jersey's past and its future. Settled in the late seventeenth century by the English and the Dutch—the former in an area called Cranetown, the latter in Speerstown—Montclair was part of Newark until 1806, then a section of Bloomfield until 1868, when it became an incor-

*Father Joseph Mendl of Montclair.*

❧

porated town in its own right. Proximity to the Morris Canal and to New York aided its development. Employment in the middle of the century was provided by small mills and light manufacturing. By the end of the century Montclair was a suburb where wealthy New Yorkers spent the summer, where an underclass attended to their domestic needs, and where a black community (many of them those same domestic servants) had recently established itself.

The siting of a church ought not to have been controversial. Father Joseph Mendl, Austrian-born pastor of the parish, had labored for twelve years in a church at Washington Street, which was now too small for a Catholic population of approximately fifteen hundred. Besides, the social profile of the parish had moved up a notch or two, with the result that the existing location seemed to be *infra dignitatem*. Common sense suggested that the church should move uptown, closer to the center of things. Considerations of convenience, however, were secondary to those of class. Father Mendl explained the situation to Bishop Wigger. The problem with one proposed location, he noted, was that there were "only a few Catholic servants" living there:

> Would it not be more sensible to have the new church near the centre of the town [he wrote] so as to make it almost equal distance to all parishioners? Besides the Catholics in the upper part of the town have given most of the money for the new church. From the very first time I began to collect for the Building Fund I insisted that every person should write his name on the envelope for the *very reason that* in the case of any dispute about the location of the new church the reasonable wishes of those who contributed most might be weighed in the balance of justice. . . . Does not justice *demand* that the people *who have given most of the money* collected should have *the church at least as near to them* as those who contributed but a small fraction?

And there was another argument. What of those Catholics of neighboring Bloomfield who attended mass in the existing Montclair church despite the fact that a new parish had been formed for them fourteen years before? This was not a problem, Mendl assured Wigger. The numbers involved were minor: "only two Catholic families and they are Italian."

Mendl had yet to explain the most significant objection to the suggested site of the church. To build close to the existing location would be folly, he argued. Consider how the neighborhood had changed:

> The street below the church is now swarming with colored people; a Mrs. McGarry owns three double houses, all of them occupied by black people, be-

cause the catholic people are moving to the upper part of town. The colored church is just opposite ours, and the shouts and yells from there are heard plainly in our church, particularly at the morning service. I presume that it requires no argument to prove that the Irish people who live around the church are *not anxious to have a church alongside the colored persuasion.*

The Catholic societies were offered time and again the use of the basement of the church gratis for their meetings; but they rather pay rent uptown because it is nearer for most of the members, and besides they do not want to meet in that part of town which is nicknamed "Harper's Ferry."

He ended with a flourish:

There is only one way of keeping the parish together and avoiding endless trouble and that is by building the church in the centre of the town. . . . The people will be enthusiastic as soon as they find out that a site has been secured for the new church in the heart of the town and in the midst of the parish, instead of in the outskirts . . . where the "niggers" are.[38]

Carl Hinrichsen, historian of the diocese of Newark, has remarked that at the end of the nineteenth century "some Irish pastors made the Italians very unwelcome and had little good to say about them."[39] That is true. He might also have remarked that some Austrian pastors had very little good to say about anyone.

Mendl's remarks demand context. A generous reading is that they represent an account of social prejudice, not approval of it. That seems implausible. Mendl shared the views he reported and did little to lead his flock to a different gospel.[40] A more realistic assessment is that, in reporting and to some degree representing end-of-century Montclair, Mendl described the social arrangements of a world in flux. A new dispensation was beginning to take shape. At the top stood a professional and mercantile elite, philanthropic but remote in its private realm; then came the Irish; then the Italians; finally the blacks. Each except the last had the pleasure of looking down on the rest. Each except the first had the ambition to supplant the set above.

Something bigger than the building of a church was at work here. Pride and prejudice came in many forms, race and class being two of them. But when did one form end and the other begin? Father Mendl, Montclair's social geneticist, saw how the two could breed and blend. The desire of ethnic groups, he seemed to intuit, was to be thought of not in ethnic but in class terms. Social arrival meant the shedding, or shading, of immigrant skin. By that standard, at the end of the century in some parts of New Jersey the Irish almost passed for white.

# CHAPTER 6

# The Twentieth Century: From History to Heritage

## HISTORY, HERITAGE, AND THE IRISH AMERICAN MEMORY

Eᴛʜɴɪᴄ ᴍᴇᴍᴏʀʏ may be long or short depending on its object. With Irish people it is thought to be elephantine. Only in Ireland could it be joked that the old eventually forget everything—except the grudges. The past weighs so heavily in politics, religion, and social relations that the present seems squeezed out, haunted by ghosts that refuse to depart. History, James Joyce's Stephen Dedalus once suggested, is the nightmare from which the Irish are trying to awake. The difference between Ireland and other countries, it has often been noticed, is that everywhere else the past is over; in Ireland it is still going on—an exaggeration, but the idea is not completely foolish.

As with the Irish in Ireland, so also with the Irish in America. At the beginning of the twentieth century they straddled a line between gratitude for a new life and resentment of a life slow to fulfill its promise. For a generation or two after the famine their experience was of doors closed, work withheld, and religion reviled. Other immigrants were treated similarly,

*Thomas Fitzgerald, journalist, was born in Tullamore, County Offaly, and came to New Jersey as a young man.*

❧

COURTESY: SETON HALL UNIVERSITY
SPECIAL COLLECTIONS CENTER
AND UNIVERSITY ARCHIVES

*Commodore Martin Attic Adams was a Jersey City poet, philosopher, and eccentric. Born in Kilkenny in 1847, he immigrated to America in 1868.*

❧

COURTESY: SETON HALL UNIVERSITY
SPECIAL COLLECTIONS CENTER
AND UNIVERSITY ARCHIVES

*The parents of Princeton lawyer Michael Dunn were emigrants from County Cavan, a county of small farms in the Irish midlands.*

❧

COURTESY: SETON HALL UNIVERSITY
SPECIAL COLLECTIONS CENTER
AND UNIVERSITY ARCHIVES

but that was little comfort. A temptation to bitterness was not always resisted. Witness the political martyrdom of James Donnelly. The significance of the episode rests less with the crime and punishment—though the story is a study in anti-Irishness—than in its endurance in local memory and the protracted rancor it provoked. Donnelly, never allowed to rest in peace, was trundled out year after year, a grievance as familiar and comfortable as an old pair of slippers. For the promoters of his posthumous cause, calculation lay behind the complaint. Victimhood paid dividends in the politics of sulk. Of course, nursing anger to keep it warm ran the risk that resentment might itself be resented. Thus the dilemma of ethnic politics: the Irish complained about anti-Irishness, and their complaints merely encouraged it. It was a price worth paying. Ward politicians mustered reliable votes with a reminder that the party—invariably the Democratic party—could protect the faithful in a hostile world. Yet permanent self-pity was also a form of infantilism.

Ethnic grievance may have been a political bonanza for bosses, but it was a social cul-de-sac for their tribe.

Still, grudge-bearing does not tell the whole story. In obvious ways ethnic memory in America was shorter than in Ireland. The New World *was* a new beginning, another chance. A grievance could be maintained for only so long. (Try a thought experiment. In 1900 two northern New Jerseyans, Laurence Fell, former mayor of Orange, and Judge Daniel A. Dugan formed the Friendly Sons of Saint Patrick of the Oranges. How would they have fared had they decided to form the Unfriendly Sons of Saint Patrick?) As the urban experience gave way to suburbanism, and as the class structure became less of an obstacle and more of an opportunity, the collective memory changed. History—raw and elemental, an unfinished nightmare—gave way to comfortable, unthreatening Heritage. History was for those who crossed the sea, who lived in tenements, who faced refusals. Heritage was for those who heard their story; it was immigration for those who never endured it, secondhand parables for second-generation patriots. Think of Irish parades in America, which gradually came to represent the changing community they celebrated. For newcomers, fresh off the boat, they kept together a frightened, threatened people. For their children and grandchildren—less threatened, more confident, a people who had experienced the promise and fulfillment of America—they were festivals of a new culture, not funerals for the culture left behind. Immigrants commemorated a past recently (and rightly) abandoned; their children celebrated the same past at an ocean's and generation's distance from it.

One reason for celebrating the past was relief that it was over. Who would want to repeat Ireland's miseries? For every homesick Irishman there were hundreds happy to have escaped. (Much of the homesickness, paradoxically, was experienced by those who stayed at

*Irish Americans did more than sentimentalize Ireland. They also sought to promote its well-being. In 1903 the Celtic Club of Newark tried to raise funds for the improvement of Irish agriculture.*

❧

COURTESY: SETON HALL UNIVERSITY
SPECIAL COLLECTIONS CENTER
AND UNIVERSITY ARCHIVES

home. The ballads of longing and separation were mostly sung in Ireland, where the sadness of the "American wake" was not only for the leaving of a loved one but also for the loss that departure represented for the town or village.) When American-born children of immigrants explored their Irishness, they discovered a heritage that could be enjoyed and sentimentalized. Nor was this fraudulent. It was simply how one generation came to understand the forces that shaped its predecessor. The need to make sense of the past was also a need to put it in its place; to get the measure of the parental or grandparental experience and make it into myth.

Bayonne at the turn of the century, for instance, was a working-class town a short ferry ride from New York, strongly Irish, Catholic, and, in the best way,

*The stories of individual families are at once unique in themselves and typical of the experiences of many. Consider Thomas Earls. Born in Limerick in 1870, he came to Hoboken as a young man and worked in a furniture factory there for much of his life. Diagnosed with a serious illness, he gave up work and was cared for by his wife who opened a small confectionery store to provide for the family. The first photograph (top left) shows Earls as a child, the second (top middle) as a youth, the third (top right) as an adult, the fourth (right) depicts his widow in her retirement in Rockaway.*

☘

COURTESY: REVEREND THOMAS PENDRICK

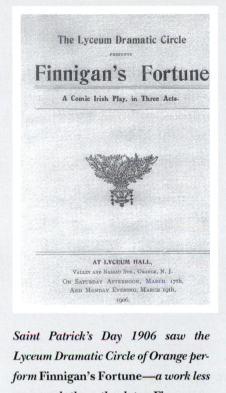

**The Lyceum Dramatic Circle**

PRESENTS

# Finnigan's Fortune

A Comic Irish Play, in Three Acts.

AT LYCEUM HALL,
VALLEY AND NASSAU STS., ORANGE, N. J.
ON SATURDAY AFTERNOON, MARCH 17th,
AND MONDAY EVENING, MARCH 19th,
1906.

*Saint Patrick's Day 1906 saw the Lyceum Dramatic Circle of Orange perform* **Finnigan's Fortune**—*a work less renowned than the later* **Finnegans Wake** *but more entertaining.*

❖

*Once in America, some Irish emigrants were never heard from again. In April 1929 John Condon of Mitchelstown, County Cork, sought the help of Bishop Thomas Walsh of Newark in tracing his lost New Jersey relatives.*

❖

parochial. At the end of the nineteenth century Bayonne's social life consisted of parades, fairs, and amateur theatricals. Thus in 1886 the Young Men's Catholic Lyceum of Saint Mary's Church performed *The Irish Lion* and *The Irish Patriot*; two years later they staged *Robert Emmett*.[1] Such community theater perfectly expressed the aspirations to respectability of the skilled working class and the petit bourgeoisie just above them—clerks, office managers, schoolteachers, and the like. Here was the Church once again as a means of integration, not an obstacle to it; a channel of upward mobility for those who had passed through the first stages of social admission. The plays themselves, forgotten and forgettable, were standard crowd-pleasers of the day, satisfying Irish Americans inclined to find fault with all things English as well as the rest of the audience, the majority most likely simply wanting an evening's entertainment. In this way the Young Men's Catholic Lyceum

*Henry Quinn of Dromore and Bayonne beginning to make his way in American business. He was sufficiently successful to be able to afford a second home in Katonah, New York, probably to be closer to the Fargo family, who had been his chief sponsors and patrons in America.*

❧

COURTESY: WILLIAM QUINN

provided Saint Mary's parishioners with a stage for nationalism and for stage-nationalism: history and heritage for the price of a ticket.

In the rest of New Jersey, too, the road from rejection to respect passed through strange territory. Even as they came to be accepted, the Irish remained colorful, eccentric, and larger than life. Strangeness still attached itself to them. In 1918 one William Lehman of Somerset County, a private in the Seventy-eighth ("Lightning") Division, wrote to his sweetheart from Camp Dix, where he was undergoing training before joining the American Expeditionary Forces in France. Describing his fellow recruits, he spoke of a certain Callory, who was Irish. "He has the real Irish accent on his speech and it sounds awful funny to hear him speak."[2] Brogues never failed to raise a laugh. Even Woodrow Wilson engaged audiences with Irish caricatures. During his 1910 gubernatorial campaign he joked of "the Irishman who [when] digging a hole through a cellar wall [was] asked, "Pat . . . are you . . . letting the light into the cellar?" [and] replied, "No, I'm letting the darkness out."[3] This was fairly harmless, offensive only to those quick to take offense, but it presumed a notion of the Irish as entertaining oddities, inhabitants of their own idiosyncratic universe.

The Irish went along with this and even at times reveled in it. Wilson's joshing worked because it contained an element of truth. Irish anecdotes seemed always to reduce to stories of amiable whimsicality. "I know an Irishman who came into the saloon to telephone," recalled a resident of Newark's Twelfth Ward in 1939:

> It was the first time he used a phone. He wanted Bill Brennan. Another Irishman in the saloon told him just to ask for Bill Brennan. The Irishman called up Brennan. The operator asked for the number. "Number be damned," he said. "I want to talk to me delegate Bill Brennan. He lives at 240 Springfield Avenue. Ye ought to know him."
>
> The same man came to vote. The challenger challenged his vote. He said

Henry and Minnie Quinn of Bayonne honeymooning at Niagara Falls in 1898. Born in Dromore, County Sligo, to small farmers, Henry Quinn left Ireland in 1888 at the age of sixteen, finding work in New York before settling in New Jersey. He managed property for the Fargo family of New York, including the real estate that later grew into the American Express Company. (Minnie Quinn later headed American Express's fraud investigation department; she was the first woman employed by the firm in more than a menial capacity.) The Quinns prospered; Henry became a substantial property owner in Bayonne before his death at the early age of forty-two.

❧

*Bayonne in 1929: confidently Irish and Catholic.*

❧

*Music played an important role in the social life of Irish Americans. The band of Saint James's Church, Newark, was one of the best in the city.*

❧

*The conferral of the pallium on Archbishop Thomas Walsh of Newark, April 27, 1937, was another occasion of growing Irish American pride. The procession of papal knights included former governor Al Smith of New York, second from the rear.*

❧

he wasn't a citizen. He brought the door of his closet with the citizen papers pasted on it. He couldn't take off the papers.[4]

Such quirkiness formed the basis of many a taproom legend over the years. And why not? The Irish knew their reputation and played up to it. The quick-witted turned themselves into endearing oddballs or lovable misfits. That was the easiest way to win a friend, cadge a drink, or escape a scrape—necessities which might have been avoided, of course, if the behavior had been less bizarre in the first place.

Yet the story reveals more than the teller intended. The narrator was himself the child of Irish parents, although with a shaky grasp of their history: "I can't tell you when they came over here. . . . As a matter of fact, Mother and Father didn't know their own ages." He possessed the kind of immigrant memory that was able to embrace ethnicity without endorsing its more eccentric manifestations. The Irishman with his papers posted to a door was not the same Irishman who could tell the story with a cheerful, affectionate condescension. America had socialized the latter. He had moved beyond the naiveté of his parents' youth. If Saint Patrick's Day saw him Irish again, for the rest of the year he was as American as the next.

This distance between immigrant generations—the parents uncouth, the children urbane—occasionally manifested itself not in affection but embarrassment, even contempt. Often it appeared as historical amnesia, a dulled sense of one's own origins. With little prompting Irish Americans could boast of their roots and social arrival while forgetting that others sought the same acculturation. Consider the recollections of another Newarker at the beginning of the Second World War:

> My grandfather was born in Cork. My grandmother was born in Kilkenny. On my father's side it was McCarthy, and on my mother's side it was Fitzpatrick. My father was born in Newark and my mother was born in New York. In those times they came over in sailboats; there was no steam. There isn't much that I know about them. They came over here to get anything they could, like we do now. My grandfather had a hide and fat business. The fat house was on the corner of Norfolk Street and Thirteenth Avenue. He was there for years. That's the Fitzpatrick I'm talking about now.

So far, so familiar: here was the immigrant story in miniature. But that was not the end of it. The next question—did you have a happy childhood?—produced an unexpected answer:

> Oh, sure, that's the trouble. I had it too easy. If I had had to work a little harder, maybe I would have got somewhere. Look at how these foreigners come over and make good.[5]

*William Hughes, born in Ireland in 1872, came to Paterson in 1872 with his father, a foundryman. Variously a mill worker, court reporter, soldier in the Spanish American War, labor organizer, and lawyer, Hughes, a Democrat, served in the U.S. House of Representatives (1903–1905, 1907–1912) and the U.S. Senate (1913–1918). His funeral in 1918 was one of the largest in Paterson's history.*

COURTESY: SETON HALL UNIVERSITY
SPECIAL COLLECTIONS CENTER
AND UNIVERSITY ARCHIVES

Missing the irony, the respondent sounded a note of what might be called second- or third-generation nativism. He revealed, too, another aspect of acculturation. With erasure of ethnic identity could also come loss of social status. Grandfather Fitzpatrick was "worth over one hundred thousand dollars" when he died; the grandson, disinclined to educate himself, became a carpenter. America's appeal

WILLIAM B. GOURLEY.
COUNSELLOR AT LAW,
CORNER MAIN & WARD STREETS.

PATERSON, N.J. June 18th, 1898.

Right Rev. M. W. Wigger,

My Dear Bishop:-

I have a cousin in
Ireland who is very anxious to come to America to complete his
studies for the purpose of being ordained. He is twenty-three
years of age and was matriculated at the Royal University of
Ireland, some years ago. He is at present attending the Marist
College at Dundalk and has finished his second year in philosophy. He would prefer to come to America if it can be arranged. His
eldest brother has been ordained some years and is at present
attending to his duties at Drogheda. He has two younger brothers
preparing for the church, but who will remain in Ireland. All his
sisters--three in number-- are in religious orders. The consequence of this is that his father feels himself unable to pay
anything here for his tuition. I write to ask whether it would
be likely under these circumstances that he could attain his object here. I know little about such matters at Seton Hall at the
present time. I have not consulted any of my clerical friends
here, but have preferred to write directly to you. Will you kindly
let me know whether you can aid him in his laudable effort

Very Respectfully

William B Gourley

*Bishop Winand Wigger of Newark was occasionally—and unfairly—thought to be hostile to the Irish members of his flock. For all that, his patronage remained important for those who sought to place their Irish cousins in America.*

✤

*The owners and employees of the McGann Company (Transfer Agents) of Newark in 1917.
As the Irish moved into business, their social arrival was marked by (among other things)
the ability to employ those of a less regarded class. Notice, for instance, the solitary black face.*

❧

for immigrants lay in its social mobility, but mobility, as some discovered, was a stairway going down as well as up. The real irony was role reversal: the parents were urbane, the children uncouth. If roots were celebrated as a way of acknowledging successful distance from them, failure brought resentment that others, "these foreigners," had done better.

When did immigrants begin to see others, not themselves, as outsiders? It varied from case to case, class to class. Much depended on other ethnic groups: the more exotic, the less alien seemed one's own by comparison. Witness a first-generation Irishman interviewed in Newark in 1939. Recalling a childhood spent in that city's Ironbound district, he noticed the importance of ethnicity as a measure of social distance:

> Irish and German. I remember when there wasn't an Italian in it, this side of the railroad. There was only four families of Jews. . . . Those were the good old days. We didn't realize it. Lots of times we'd be diving from lumber piles at Clark's lumberhouse, when a policeman would come along. We'd swim across the Passaic and sit on the other side until he went away. The old Down Neck, when the Irish and Germans were here, was the best place in New Jersey—no, I mean in the world.

TOP LEFT: *Saint Catherine's Church in Spring Lake was a notable early twentieth-century monument to Irish piety and prosperity. Funded by the fabulously wealthy Martin Maloney of Philadelphia to memorialize his daughter Catharine, who died returning from a trip abroad to restore her health, its artwork consisted of depictions of ancient, medieval, and modern Ireland. The cornerstone was laid March 17, 1901, by Bishop James McFaul of Trenton; the artwork took another twenty-five years to complete.* TOP RIGHT: *Martin Maloney and Bishop Thomas Walsh at Spring Lake.* ABOVE: *Ballingarry, Martin Maloney's residence, was one of the great houses of the eastern seaboard: a fitting home for one whose wealth was estimated at three hundred million dollars.*

Why the change?

> Since Father came here we have every nationality on the face of the earth—
> everyone. . . . The Slovaks, the Poles, and the Lithuanians—yes, all except the
> Spaniards and the Portuguese are all right. When the Spaniards and the Por-
> tuguese moved into the neighborhood, the kids would rush home with their
> lanterns, and when they got to the door, they wouldn't stop ringing until
> someone came to the door. They sure used to be scared.[6]

The significance lies less in the nostalgia (no novelty in recollections of childhood) than in the fact that the nostalgia was ethnicized. In a world swamped by
Spaniards and Portuguese, the Irish were no longer foreign. They had paid their
dues and could speak English. "The neighborhood was mostly German and Irish
in those days," a third Down Neck Irishman recalled. "People did not bellyache the
way they do today."[7] Here was another missed irony: the remark seemed much like
a bellyache itself.

## IRISH AND GERMANS IN EARLY TWENTIETH-CENTURY NEWARK: SUNDAY OBSERVANCE AND "CAHENSLYISM"

LONG OR short, ethnic memory could play tricks. Seen from late middle age,
turn-of-the-century Newark was an Irish and German idyll, a city confident in
its national cultures because both had learned to share a common space. It did not
seem that way at the time. In the late nineteenth century and the early twentieth,
the Germans and Irish were quarrelsome neighbors who clashed sharply before finally making their peace. Two matters exercised them: Sabbath-day observance
and ways of worship within the Catholic Church. Yet for all their fierceness, the arguments were signs of ethnic success. German and Irish immigrants had been on
the margins of Newark life in the early nineteenth century, but they found themselves at its center at century's end. They jostled for power in municipal and ecclesiastical politics no longer as the unwashed but as would-be members of the
establishment. If they were spoiling for a fight, at least they were now fighting for
spoils.

Notice, however, a distinction. Germans were first to achieve political dominance in Newark, a position subsequently challenged by the Irish. The Irish were
first to achieve ecclesiastical dominance, and this in turn was resented by Germans.
Why the difference? The two phenomena were connected. In local politics, the
Irish tended to be Democrats, the Germans Republican, and this linked the latter

*William Tierney was president of the Holy Name Society in Englewood in the early 1900s.*

❧

to the economically influential sections of the community. Germans were also mostly Protestant, another advantage when it came to assimilation. Lastly, Germans came to wealth faster than the Irish. For these reasons, City Hall was a more welcoming place for them well into the second half of the nineteenth century. Even so, mass migration in the middle of the century meant that the numbers increasingly favored the Irish. By 1870 they "had become sufficiently strong to force native politicians to grant them better treatment in matters of municipal patronage."[8] In Church politics it was the other way around, with Germans attempting to supplant an early-achieved Irish hegemony. The Irish disadvantage in Newark's social arrangements—that they were Catholic—was a boon in the narrower world of ecclesiastical affairs. Newark Catholicism was largely Irish until the last three decades of the nineteenth century. There were German parishes, of course—three in the whole of New Jersey in 1853—but "Germanness" in the Church did not become apparent (and contentious) until the 1890s. Snubbed at City Hall, the Irish held tightly to the keys of the sacristy. When Irish and Germans clashed in municipal politics, the dispute was between denominations; when they fell out in ecclesiastical politics, the dispute, obviously, was within one. In both cases, however, the tension was real.

Weekend drinking sparked the trouble. For Germans, Sunday was the best day of the week. Work completed, they abandoned themselves to the postponed pleasures of sport, dancing, singing, and beer. Unfortunately this offended long-established Newark residents who regarded such entertainments as blasphemies requiring extirpation or, at least, strict control. Throughout the 1870s nothing generated more heat than efforts of German Americans, now electorally consequential, to relax Newark's Sunday observance laws. Indeed the subject rumbled on well into the following decades.[9] This offered the Irish an opportunity to score an ethnic point. The leadership of Newark's temperance movement was dominated by priests from Ireland, or of Irish parentage, who found themselves improbably allied with native puritans of traditional stripe. *Fin-de-siècle* anti-drink

*Father R. A. Mahony and the children of Saint Patrick's Parish, Chatham, 1922.*

campaigns now appear comically extravagant in their rhetoric, Victorian morality teetering toward self-parody. This was one such case. "Newark," thundered the Reverend James Brady in 1891, following a German song festival, "supplied herself abundantly with her most odoriferous and gummy fluid; tricked in her most variegated finery, and flouting in her red, white, and blue bunting presented herself to dance obedience to the Sabbath-befouling sackbuts of the Sabbath-defiling Teuton."[10] Beer was wasted on Brady: words alone could intoxicate him. Perhaps the language, for all its moral certainty, contained a hint of desperation, an intuition of ultimate defeat. Temperance won a victory in 1906 when the New Jersey legislature passed the "Bishop's Law" raising the fee on liquor licenses. But that was its last hurrah, at least until Prohibition. Public reaction to the law was hostile. The 1908 election saw those associated with it—Republicans mostly—receive a drubbing. This may not have been unwelcome to some Irishmen, not averse to entertainments of their own.

Temperance offered one proof of respectability, leadership in the Church another. With Irish American bishops constituting the bulk of the ecclesiastical establishment, newer immigrants often felt outsiders in their own church. Most resentful were Germans. Driven from their homeland by the threat of conscrip-

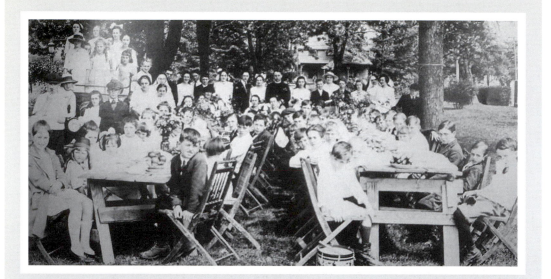

*Saint Virgil's Parish in Morris Plains, named for an Irish saint (Fergal or, in Latin, Virgilius), served the needs of many Irish families. Its pastor in 1919 was Father John Culliney, pictured at the rear of the graduation party for the parish elementary school.*

❧

*An Irish outing in Morris Plains, 1917: Danny Myers, Blondy Coffey, and John Byrnes with Margaret Devine, Ethel Kapinos, Alice Doody, Helen McErlane, and Mary Myers.*

❧

tion, by economic need, and by the *Kulturkampf*—Bismarck's assault on the Church's autonomy in the years after 1871—German Catholics came to America, and New Jersey, in large numbers in the last two decades of the nineteenth century. Nationally, a million and a half arrived in the 1880s and another half million in the decade that followed. This pattern held regionally. In the portion of northern New Jersey covered by the Diocese of Newark there was an increase of some 12,233 foreign-born Germans in the 1890s, most gravitating toward places with already established communities—Newark, Paterson, Jersey City, Union

*Father J. C. McCormick, Sister Clara Teresa Valentine, and the children of Saint Patrick's, Chatham, in the early 1900s.*

Hill, and Elizabeth.[11] The size of the influx brought difficulties. The newcomers mostly took their faith seriously: it could hardly have been otherwise if the *Kulturkampf* had been one reason for emigration. Some, however, were poorly instructed. Father Nicholas Hens of Paterson complained in 1884 that those of his flock who had come from German manufacturing cities were "corrupted and without religion": fathers kept sons from mass and never dreamed of crossing the church threshold themselves. The idea that urban, industrial America weakened a uniformly strong immigrant faith should be rejected. In some cases the faith was gone already.[12]

From an Irish clerical point of view, Germans were either too Catholic or not Catholic enough; they were too attached, that is to say, to distinctly German forms of religious practice or too detached from them. This posed a dilemma. The sharpest religious controversy of the 1890s was "Cahenslyism," a movement that promoted German-speaking parishes, German-speaking schools, German devotional forms, and German bishops within the American Catholic Church. The idea originated from Peter Paul Cahensly from the Rhine province of Nassau. Cahenslyism, at least in its moderate form, made a certain amount of sense, but some saw it as a mockery of the Church's claims to universalism. New Jersey's Irish priests fell into the latter camp. Father Patrick Corrigan of Hoboken condemned it as a conspiracy to "Germanize the country by means of the Church."[13] Father Thomas Killeen of Bayonne denied that Germans had "a right to a church of their nationality any more than have the Irish or any other race."[14] Corrigan even argued that Germans, escaping one religious persecution, might create another:

> The newly arrived German priest [tramps] from house to house . . . vilifying the parish church as "Irish" and hostile to Germans.
>
> This policy of antagonism does its deadly work on the German-American youth, who becomes disgusted with this phase of religion and seldom go [*sic*] to Mass at all; and it creates a spirit of insubordination that almost paralyzes the authority of the pastor of the English-speaking church. This strikes at the very root of the Church. . . . These men must understand that we have no Kulturkamp [*sic*] here, and that the American Church does not authorize them to instigate one.[15]

This was not the most extravagant claim. Cahenslyism was "more dangerous to this country," proposed Corrigan, "than the introduction of the leprous Chinese."[16] Such rhetoric weakened a case never strong in the first place.

*Father William Tighe and the altar boys of Saint Agnes's Parish, Atlantic Highlands, in the early 1900s.*

❧

Hyperbole aside, Corrigan hinted at a crucial question. Was the purpose of the Church to Catholicize Germans or to Americanize them? In obvious ways its first duty was religious. Yet wider acculturation was also important. "We are all Americans," urged Father Killeen of Bayonne, a remark partly directed at his own bishop, the supposedly German-favoring Winand Wigger. (Wigger's pro-German, anti-Irish bias was a myth. His sternest critic, Father Hugh Murphy, accused him of being "opposed to Irish priests" and of giving Germans all the plum appointments. In fact, Wigger was opposed chiefly to Murphy himself whose major failing was a weakness for the bottle.) Killeen's remark captured the true and paradoxical significance of the movement. Nativists had long complained that Catholicism was un-American. Killeen and others were able to use Cahenslyism to assert that Catholics in general, and the Irish in particular, were as American as the next. "Cahenslyism is dead in America forever," he wrote after a German-Irish dispute in his Bayonne parish in 1892, "and every American will rejoice with me that it is." His comrade-in-arms Father Corrigan was also confident: "It is astonishing how selfish and clannish these men are, and how hard it is to Americanize them. They actually entertain the absurd notion of Germanizing the country and the Church."[17] Equally astonishing was the lapse of memory. Not so long before, similar things had been said of Corrigan's crowd.

*The Duff family of New Jersey pictured in 1914. Standing far right is John Bernard Duff (1900–1968), whose children went on to achieve distinction in the world of scholarship. Peter and Tom Duff taught at Seton Hall University, and John Duff served as provost of Seton Hall before becoming chancellor of higher education for the state of Massachusetts.*

Cahenslyism was short-lived, but its implications were of longer duration. Whatever threat it posed, the "Germanizing" of the Church was only an exaggerated form of a truth no one disputed: parishes were almost always defined along national lines. The genius of New Jersey Catholicism was its capacity to retain this strong ethnic element while avoiding the ghettoism that went along with it. Historically the Church was the most impressive of the various engines of Americanization. Thus the extravagance of Corrigan's language: he was alarmed that anyone should question so obvious a fact. To that extent, the failure of Cahenslyism anticipated a double phenomenon of the twentieth century: the capacity of Catholicism to assimilate itself to the practices of multiple ethnicities and the related ability of the Church to assimilate those ethnicities to a wider American community. Killeen was right. Irish Catholics *were* all Americans; indeed, in their confident patriotism, they were all-American. For that they had Germans, Poles, Italians, and Hungarians to thank.

## TOWARD AN EVER GREATER UNION—THROUGH UNIONISM

**A**s the Church asserted its institutional distinctiveness, then, it also represented a means of acculturation. Catholics were separate but not singular. They had their own schools, parishes, newspapers, and social activities, but these posed a threat to no one. On the contrary, they were precisely the ways by which aliens became Americans. As the historian of the Irish in Camden County has written, clergymen "served the familiar Irish role as middlemen between the new immigrants and Anglo-Saxon culture," inculcating civic as well as Christian virtues.[18] If this meant that Irish Americans became "less and less Irish and more and more Catholic," state and nation could hardly complain.[19] True, anti-Catholicism remained an occasional ugliness in New Jersey life, a reminder that not everyone accepted the polite restraints of pluralism. Crosses were burned in Camden and Gloucester in the 1920s. There was a Ku Klux Klan riot in Perth Amboy in 1923 to cleanse the town of the "pollution" of Romanism.[20] Al Smith's presidential bid in 1928 evinced strong opposition. A market always existed, sometimes bearish, sometimes bullish, for old-fashioned bigotry. Witness the letters that appeared in nearly every clerical mailbox:

*Bishop John O'Connor of Newark.*

❧

COURTESY: SETON HALL UNIVERSITY
SPECIAL COLLECTIONS CENTER
AND UNIVERSITY ARCHIVES

> For years [wrote a correspondent to Bishop John O'Connor of Newark in 1903] the public schools were good enough for the Paddys and Germans. . . . I remember how 'umble some 30 years ago an Irish Catholic priest was—Uriah Heep wasn't in it. Today he swells like a toad with rum and conceit and power—but can't handle our public school money. . . .
>
> A priest is of all things selfish and the principal thing the Catholic Church wants is the money to feed and support a lot of non-productive hypocrites. . . . [Look at] old Skull and Crossbone yclept Pope Leo XIII making Cardinals. Paper says no Americans named. God forbid—paper means Irish. If the old Nibs named some-*one* in this country he would have to kiss the Pope's Arse.[21]

Rabelaisian anti-Catholicism of this kind never died: it simply became less acceptable in civilized company. By the middle of the twentieth century, overt sectarianism began to fade, not least because Irish Americans, far from being alien, were highly patriotic. They fought in the First World War, making common cause even with the British as proof of loyalty to America. After the Second World War their Catholic anti-communism matched the mood of the day. They may have been intemperate in some enthusiasms, but their Americanism was never in doubt.

The Church was not the only avenue of integration and mobility. Politics and trades unionism also offered ways for the Irish to become American. Ecclesiastical leaders sometimes worried about this, especially the appeal of trades unionism. If unionism meant socialism, they wanted nothing to do with it. "Crude socialism has bankrupted itself," suggested Bishop O'Connor toward the end of his episcopate. "Human nature conquered it." O'Connor (himself the child of Irish parents) was bishop of Newark from 1901 to 1927—the era when socialism emerged from the seminar to become a world-transforming movement. In matters of social reform he naturally preferred Church-sponsored organizations such as the National Catholic Welfare Council, which combined "the best economic thought with the principles of revealed religion [to] raise human life to new standards of decency and comfort."[22] This was unexceptionable, but given a choice between the social gospel and the gospel of socialism, some Irish workers chose the latter. Perhaps we should not register surprise. Even in Ireland the same tension was apparent. The Easter Rebellion of 1916, for example, was born of mixed parentage—the romantic nationalism of Padraic Pearse, with its lurid imagery of a people crucified and born again in blood, coupled with the theoretically sophisticated (if inappropriate) Marxism of James Connolly, who embraced the Gaelic Revival of the late nineteenth century for reasons of class rather than culture. Irish Americans were never so conflicted—Marxism had no appeal for them—but comparable fault lines could be seen just below the surface.

*Irish dominance of the hierarchy: In June 1942 at Seton Hall College Archbishop Thomas Walsh (seated) was photographed with the four men he had consecrated as bishops. From left to right: Thomas Boland, Frank Monaghan, John Duffy, Thomas McLaughlin.*

❧

*Children of Our Lady of Mount Carmel Parish, Ridgewood, in the 1920s.*
*Most of the parishioners were Irish.*

☘

Trades unionism was an economic necessity and a social religion. (The latter was one reason for clerical concern.) Membership in a union was the only way for many to protect legitimate economic interests, as the Church was first to acknowledge. "I was born of Irish parents who had come from England," recalled one Newarker in 1939:

I got married in 1931. I settled down and took up organization as a life work. I was just a bartender when I started. I found that a union is the only way a man can get decent wages. With an organization behind him, a man has a backing. It is not a question of pressing an employer with a whole lot of grievances. We settle grievances by arbitration and by co-operation between employee and employer. First, it is our duty to keep our men employed—to see to it they get proper remuneration. We never force a man to join our union. We sit down with a man and explain to him how a union benefits him. If he doesn't understand, we don't want [him].[23]

This kind of unionism benefited employer as well as employee. "A union bartender always knows his business and . . . knows that he has to be honest to keep his job."[24] It even recognized the limits of unionization. "We advocate a union in every bar [but] we never ask a family who operates their own tavern or saloon." Some of those families joined the union nevertheless.[25]

Labor organizations varied from trade to trade and employer to employer, and in some industries—textiles, for example—there was a greater history of militancy and bitterness. Irish workers who took part in the Paterson silk strike of 1913 were following a precedent set by their forebears in the same town in 1835. Irish workers were also involved in the Gloucester City trolley strike of 1919 and the Camden shipyard strike of 1934. In one respect, of course, a union's strength was revealed not in its capacity to strike but in its choice not to do so. A stoppage was a sign of failure, not success; a last, not a first, resort. The true measure of achievement lay in making strikes unnecessary. In that sense, the textile industry had shown improvement over the years:

THE PARISH REVIEW
(Issued Monthly)
*Official Organ of*
ST. JAMES' CHURCH
Newark, N. J.
Rev. JOHN J. MURPHY, Rector
1st Asst., Rev. John J. Gormley     2d Asst., Rev. Matthew J. Toohey
VOL. XIV.          FEBRUARY, 1922          . No. 7

ST. JAMES' PARISH NOTES.

*Saint James's Church in Newark in 1922: a sacrament mill run by three Irish priests.*

COURTESY: SETON HALL UNIVERSITY
SPECIAL COLLECTIONS CENTER AND UNIVERSITY ARCHIVES

> I was born in the old country [a Newark woman remembered in 1939]. I was almost thirteen years old when I came here. . . . In those days children went to work young. Today they can't go to work until they are eighteen. In Amsterdam, New York, fifty years ago, I recall a young Irishwoman of nine years of age working in the Sanford mills from six in the morning to six at night. . . . Women built up that mill.[26]

This was powerful testimony. It was through their power to ameliorate such con-

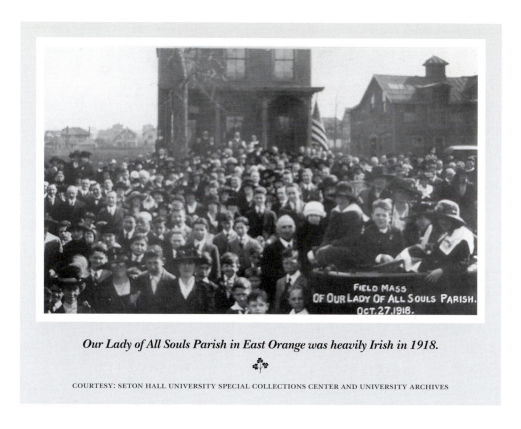

***Our Lady of All Souls Parish in East Orange was heavily Irish in 1918.***

ditions that unions made claims on the emotions as well as the intellect. Rightly or wrongly, they demanded and received the loyalty owed to any tribe or religion:

> My father was Irish, my mother was Irish, and so I am Irish. I am a union man and proud of it. I was in the Building Trades Council. I was in a union ten years before I came to this country and twelve years in this country. I worked as a laborer when I was first here. I belonged to a laborers' union. I was in a bartenders' local in Dublin—the best there was. I never scabbed in my life. I was a bartender at Number One, Mill Street, Dublin. I'd rather go on relief instead of taking low wages. I'd always stick by the union and the Irish.[27]

Sticking by the union and the Irish was the secular faith of thousands. In the early years of the century, immigrants or their children made steady progress up the ranks of union leadership: Arthur Quinn of Perth Amboy as president of the Brotherhood of Carpenters;[28] Joseph McComb and John Farrell of Camden as vice presidents of the local AFL and CIO.[29] The list could be extended. As a minor curiosity, it meant that the Irish had to learn a new political vocabulary. In

Ireland, Catholics were republicans and nationalists; in America, they were Democrats and unionists. The two countries, yet again, were separated by a common language.

## THE POLITICS OF THE MACHINE:
## FRANK HAGUE AND JERSEY CITY

STRUGGLING AGAINST bosses was all very well, but Irish people also wished, in a political sense, to be bosses themselves. Some succeeded. In the early and middle years of the twentieth century the Irish American genius for ward organization became apparent in men such as "Little Bob" Davis of Jersey City, "Big Jim" Smith of Newark, Thomas McCran of Paterson, and—*capo di tutti capi*—Frank Hague of Jersey City. The machines they controlled dominated urban New Jersey politics for decades.

"Bossism" has had a bad press. The squeamishness of a later age finds its coercive methods hard to stomach. Many contemporaries were also repelled by it. The journalist Dayton David McKean complained in 1940 that the Hague organization "alone among American city machines . . . systematically utilized terrorism, infiltration of groups, suppression of criticism, and the hierarchical principle of leadership [characteristic of] fascist regimes in Europe." This seems overheated: Hague was no Hitler. Still, as McKean's reaction suggests, the organization evoked strong affection—and disaffection—among those who came in contact with it. Representing power in its rawest form, the machine could make or break lives. It often did. Yet distaste is only part of the story. Political machines should be understood for what they were: channels of welfare and group protection, even (when occasion demanded) progressive instruments of urban reform. Moreover, the Irish dominated them for perfectly honorable reasons. Unlike more recent immigrants, they spoke English; they had had political experience in Ireland; they had been in New Jersey for a

*In the early years of the twentieth century the Jersey Shore gained a new clientele: second- or third-generation Irish immigrants who had attained a more elevated social status than their parents or grandparents.*

☘

COURTESY: PROFESSOR THOMAS HUGHES,
KALAMAZOO VALLEY COMMUNITY COLLEGE

*Ushers for the first mass at the new Church of Our Lady of Victories, Jersey City, in April 1917.*

❧

couple of generations; they had stayed longer in the wage-earning class. The notion of machines as menacing, which contains an element of truth, needs to be set beside their sometimes enlightened politics. In the Progressive era "a considerable number of machine politicians in the New Jersey General Assembly lent their names to a surprising array of political reforms," often fracturing the unity of the machine in the process. Bossism was not all good; it was not all bad either.[30]

Nowhere was this more evident than in Jersey City. In the 1860s the Irish struggled against the established order; two generations later they constituted it. This change of fortune mirrored a social transformation. Between 1880 and 1910 Jersey City's population grew by over 120 percent, most of the rise coming from immigrants from southern and eastern Europe. In an urban working-class mix that increasingly comprised Russians, Italians, and Poles, the Irish had the marginal advantage of having been on the block for a while. It was not a major boon, but it was sufficient to give them a head start in urban politics. Jersey City's Irish mainly lived in the downtown First Ward, a polyglot slum where poverty recognized few ethnic distinctions. The social and economic needs of these immigrants were met largely by the Catholic Church, which found itself almost overwhelmed. In 1905 the Catholic Children's Aid Society (established in 1903) dealt with cases involving 700 families with 2,300 children under the age of fifteen, most involving parental

*The annual communion breakfast of the Holy Name Society of Saint Aedan's, Jersey City, May 1937.*

☘

neglect or cruelty.[31] With so many parishioners "destitute, illiterate, and largely un-skilled," priests and nuns struggled urgently against problems that threatened to swamp them.[32]

Political amelioration was also a possibility. The symbol of Jersey City's altered politics was Mayor Frank Hague. From 1917 to 1947 he turned Hudson County into a personal fiefdom, dispensing favors and delivering votes with the confidence of a boss courted by presidents and parish priests alike. Born in 1876 in the "Horseshoe," a gerrymandered downtown district into which Republicans squeezed as many Democrats as possible to keep other areas clear of them, Hague inched his way through saloon politics to a job in City Hall in 1908 and eventually the mayoralty in 1917. Hague's Irishness was never in doubt—he played up his lowly birth and flawed grammar when necessary—but he was never a gladhander in the mold of, say, James Michael Curley of Boston. In looks and manner he was more patrician puritan than Paddy. Nonsmoking, nondrinking, personally devout, he resembled the Boston Brahmins whom Curley despised. There was severity in his politics, too. "I know the people want a clean city and I give it to them. I do not allow nightclubs or dance halls where liquor is served. That recommends me to every respectable home in the city."[33] Hague and the Irish were well matched: he gave them respectability because he wanted it himself. He was also

*Monsignor McGinley, first pastor of Saint Aedan's, Jersey City, with the graduating class of 1935.*

❦

good for City Hall: efficiency, not charm, was the key to his municipal success. A master at cajoling money from Trenton or Washington, then supplying votes to the benefactor in return, Hague presided over a system that worked to general satisfaction until after the Second World War. If corrupt, at least the arrangements were honestly—that is to say openly—corrupt. Besides, most residents of Jersey City were prepared to accept some sharp practice if in return they were guaranteed a well-lit street, a safe neighborhood, and trash collection every week. There have been worse Faustian bargains. "You'll notice I'm still here," Hague remarked in an interview in 1936. "And why? Organization and good government. I've played square with the organization and the customers. That's why."[34]

Playing square with the organization and the customers: here was electoral honesty, Jersey City style. Hague understood politics as commercial transaction, the voters so many clients eager to buy and be bought. This was hardly unusual, in Jersey City or anywhere else. The mayor was simply better at it than most. For the transaction to be possible a machine was needed, and Hague's was Irish to the core. His slate for the quadrennially elected city commission never varied: four Catholics, one Protestant, all Irish. The solitary Protestant constituted, it may be supposed, a kind of diversity. Other ethnic groups quietly, then not so quietly, seethed. Hague was indifferent. He recognized the first principle of electoral politics: the need to protect the base. Sweets for the opposition could come later, if at all.

Some of this was gesture politics. Hague forced the Board of Education to remove "pro-British" textbooks from city schools, a simple but effective acknowledgment of the nationalist sentiments of his constituents. (This was not difficult.

Few would have disagreed with the bishop of Newark that "there is not a single argument in justification of England's course in Ireland. . . . The conflict seems to be one nation's legitimate aspirations combating [another's] groundless fears.")[35] Hague also played on prejudice. In his lexicon Republicans were always "black Protestant Republicans," supporters of a party hostile to strangers and minorities. But these gestures only worked because they were not empty. Hague put his money—or City Hall's money—where his mouth was. Indeed, he proved himself a new kind of patron, his client base reflecting changed social circumstances. "He paid particular attention to the Irish lawyers," suggests his biographer, and in so doing perfected what might be termed second-generation jobbery. "The old immigrant patronage posts (policemen, firemen, and sanitation workers) were of little value [to the creation of a machine] so the Boss turned to 'bourgeoisie' patronage"—judgeships, receiverships, and the like. "Patronage provided the political glue to hold them in the organization . . . even after they moved . . . out of their downtown flats onto the heights."[36]

This is not to say that Hague forgot his roots. The gritty, colorful Horseshoe of his youth remained the linchpin of the machine. Year in and out the Irish did their duty by him, voting early and often, fulfilling an obligation as natural and unchanging as eating fish on Friday. They did not warm to him—he was too severe for that—but they recognized and respected power when they saw it. As one historian of Hague's mayoralty has noticed, the machine did more than generate votes. It defined an entire way of life:

> The Democratic organization, as perfected by Hague, was the sponge which absorbed this teeming society. Its ward clubs, the saloons, provided the main outlet for social intercourse. It found or made jobs; it taught citizenship requirements; it treated the sick; mourned the dead; it whitewashed crime short of rape or murder; it aided and was aided by the clergy; it performed a myriad of other favors ranging from finding housing for families to finding families willing to house gambling on a per diem basis.
>
> The opposite side of the coin was party loyalty. There were other requirements to be sure, such as turning out for public demonstrations, helping to get out the vote on election days, and not quibbling on "Rice Pudding" day [when] 3% or higher of one's publicly earned salary was kicked back to the organization. These were not entirely unpleasant experiences, however. In the former case, the worker . . . was often rewarded with free food and drink, and in the latter case the kickback was rarely protested [but] was regarded as a political fact of life, a cementing of tenure. [To refuse was] simply an oblique way of submitting one's resignation.[37]

Attention to detail was the key. Hague's watchful personality superbly qualified him for the small chores of bossism. A call from Trenton in the morning, a wake or ward meeting in the evening: these were the day-to-day details of his life. Opponents chafed at massive power acquired in minor ways but could do little about it. In the 1920s the machine could turn out twenty thousand votes in Jersey City alone. In the 1930s the number was more like thirty thousand. In addition there were some four thousand to six thousand votes gained by fraud or voter suppression. Except in presidential election years, Republicans virtually conceded Hudson County "before they printed a pamphlet."[38] Even in presidential years their hopes were never high.

A machine so formidable was unlikely to be sentimental. Irishness did not guarantee immunity from the wrath of Hague: loyalty and obedience meant more to him than ethnicity. Those of his own race who opposed him did so at their peril. Consider a letter written by a small businessman in Jersey City in 1930 to Bishop Thomas J. Walsh of Newark. Poignant and pugnacious, it conveys the force and insidiousness of the Hague operation. The writer began with his bona fides:

*Senatorial candidates in the Democratic primary of 1958 made their respective pitches in characteristic fashion. Mayor John Grogan of Hoboken expected to win the Irish vote in Hudson County.*

☘

> I have always taken an active part in the welfare of our Church, having been President of [a division of] the Ancient Order of Hibernians, . . . an organizer of the Knights of Columbus Building and Loan Association [and of] the A.O.H. Building and Loan Society. [My children] are in Catholic schools and colleges.

Credentials established, he described his recent history:

> I have committed one unpardonable sin, politically speaking, that of seeking public office as a Commissioner of Jersey City. . . . When I held public office in the Board of Freeholders,

my Catholic colleagues, now identified with the Hague regime, felt that I worked too hard for the interests of the inmates of the Hudson County Hospital for the Insane, 90% Catholic, instead of for their benefit; consequently every one of them hold high positions in the Hague Cabinet today.

The result of this *lèse majesté?*

Since I have been a candidate against Mr. Hague and his colleagues, I have been punished very hard by them in my business, for they have gone to my customers and demanded that their work be taken from me, and then substitute in my place Protestant members of the Hague order. . . . I often wonder how the good priests of the State of New Jersey feel when they think that the son of the leader of the Democratic party is a student at Princeton University. . . . Thank God my children are in the care . . . of the Church.[39]

The communication put Walsh in a difficult position. Although it had the ring of truth he could not take sides in a private political dispute. Nor would he wish to denounce Hague's apparatus. However crude, its methods were effective, in Church as well as city matters. (The mayor's piety was public as well as private: he identified closely with the ecclesiastical establishment.) Walsh wrote an anodyne response, regretting "the alleged treatment" and suggesting that the local pastor might be in a better position to help. The complainant could not have expected more. Fair or not, the grievance illustrated the nature of Hague's sovereignty. He ruled by a hundred little fears, and even bishops were loath to take him on.

Given this strength, the real struggle for power in Jersey City was within the Democratic party, not between Democrats and Republicans. Hague did not go unchallenged—the election of 1929 was especially sharp—but for thirty years he prevailed. Yet nothing lasts forever. Hague's power declined in the 1940s when the "great Trenton job drought" (as the *Newark Sunday Call*

*Monsignor Daniel Brady, pastor of All Saints in Jersey City and member of the Seton Hall class of 1891, was born in Gowna, County Cavan, in 1868. He served, among other places, in Paterson, Newark, and Bayonne before his appointment to Jersey City in 1937. He died in May 1956.*

❧

*The children of Saint Michael's, Jersey City, in 1916.*

❧

termed it in 1946) began to take its toll. "Six years without . . . the thousands of little [state] jobs which keep a political machine functioning," wrote the paper's political reporter, "have hurt Hague deeply."[40] He might have survived had he broadened his electoral base. He resigned the mayoralty in 1947 but handed power to his nephew Frank Hague Eggers, thinking to retain power through family connection. This offended Jersey City's Italians, Poles, and Slavs, who thought (and who was to blame them?) that the Irish had ruled long enough. In 1949 the anti-Hague freedom ticket of John Kenny defeated Eggers. "Here Lies the Remains of the Hague Machine," read one sign on election night. "36 Years of Age."

Hague's mistake was not so much to outstay his welcome as to misunderstand its nature. Irishness alone was a shaky platform on which to build political appeal. The weakness of the platform was twofold. It excluded all groups except the Irish. It also assumed that ethnicity was indeed the key to political identity. The latter belief was becoming anachronistic in the late 1940s and 1950s when class and status—the chief components of party loyalty—were defined in ways that had little to do with the immigrant history of parents or grandparents. (It should be acknowledged, though,

*The model family: Irish, American, Catholic, middle class: Mayor Thomas Whelan of Jersey City with his wife and children in 1967.*

❧

*The new establishment: Monsignor Leo Martin, Father John J. Nolan, Father James B. Sullivan. Monsignor Martin (1900–1965), a Bayonne native who ministered mainly in Jersey City, was famed for his wit, his booming voice, and his apparently insatiable thirst for tea.*

❧

that Irish bossism did not end with Hague: John Kenny's machine ruled the city until Kenny himself was jailed for income tax evasion in 1972.) Hague's fall thus had wider significance. To the irony of a potentate without potency may be added another oddity. It was an exodus of WASPs that allowed the Irish to dominate urban politics in the years before the Second World War: in effect, the first flight to suburbia left the cities in Irish hands. After the war, the second flight to suburbia was of the Irish themselves. Hague disappeared, in other words, because his world disappeared. That was the paradoxical price of long-hoped-for *embourgeoisement*. The cities were left to others, and the cycle of assilimation began anew.

## AN IRISH PARISH IN JERSEY CITY

H AGUE'S DOMINANCE of Jersey City was such that children joked about it in the streets. To generations of youngsters he was a local god, the object of playground catechism:

Teacher: Who made the Jersey City Fire Department?
Pupil: Mayor Hague.
Teacher: Who made the Jersey City Police Department?
Pupil: Mayor Hague.
Teacher: Who made the world?
Pupil: God made the world.
Chorus of Pupils: You dirty Republican!

The mayor, as one who knew him remembered, was "a bigger phenomenon of his times than Boss Crump of Memphis or Boss Pendergast of Missouri," a man who lost only those fights "he secretly chose to lose."[41] It would be wrong to imagine, however, that he constituted the entirety of existence in Jersey City. Other realities shaped daily life—the parish, the priest, the school, the shop—and touched people in ways that were more profound than the doings of City Hall. Hague was a distant figure. Most citizens preferred the world of family and friendship, knowing that a life wholly patterned by politics is hardly a life at all.

*Father LeRoy McWilliams of Saint Michael's, Jersey City, ministered to an Irish parish in its heyday and stayed long enough to see the beginnings of its decline.*

❧

Think of the role of the parish in Jersey City life. Here was an association more immediate and intense than any provided by politics. The perennial things—birth, schooling, marriage, and death—were parochial. Indeed, for many people all those rites of passage took place within the same parish, mobility being the dream of a later generation who preferred lawns and yards to blocks and corner stores. Local loyalty was intense. Social identification, less a matter of street or ward than of school and church, was unashamedly religious. To come from Saint Bridget's or Saint Michael's or Saint Aedan's was to say all that needed to be said. Parochial affiliation was a matter of pride, or occasionally of shame as social ambition outgrew social circumstances. (Even clergy sometimes felt the pull of a better class of congregant.) An integrated world, a miniature universe, was contained within earshot of the Angelus bell.

Saint Michael's Parish, where Hague was born and bred, is a case in point. From its beginning in the 1870s as an immigrant hub, a downtown streetscape of tenements and taverns, it was Irish to the core. When Archbishop Bayley—formerly of Newark, latterly of Baltimore—laid the foundation stone of the church on 29 September 1872, the Jersey City *Evening Journal* captured the ethnic quality of the day:

> In the line of march were 6,000 members of the Ancient Order of Hibernians, also about 6,000 members of the St. Patrick's Mutual Alliance Benevolent Association, besides . . . St. Bridget's Shamrock Working Men's and numerous other temperance and benevolent organizations. . . . The ancient Gallow Glasses attracted much attention in their peculiar uniforms, long beards, helmets, broad axes. Frank McDonald . . . as Grand Marshall . . . was the admiration of all the good-looking Irish girls along the route.[42]

As it began, so it continued. At the turn of the century, and well into it, the area of the parish known as Cork Row teemed with newly arrived or recently settled immigrants from Ireland. "These Irish were not rich, lace-curtain Irish," recalled the priest who knew them best. "They were big men with rich brogues who had hands like hams and who worked in the sugar refinery, or down at the docks, or in an oil refinery in Greenville. They worked hard and they drank hard, and they all married angels who had the tolerance and the temperament to keep them on God's holy path."[43] Here were Hague's battalions, the army trained to do his will.

*The effortless Irish dominance of Church and state: Archbishop Thomas Boland and Mayor Leo Carlin of Newark in the 1950s.*

❧

By the time they outgrew each other the conjoined worlds of Church and City Hall had all but come apart. Eventually Hague came to feel more comfortable in Florida than among the flock who supported him; for their part, the Irish came to realize, with the force of sudden revelation, that the master might be opposed with impunity. The divorce was more dramatic for its unexpectedness. Equally unforeseen was that the Irish themselves, even in this moment of self-assertion, were no longer the force they once had been. Hagueism was toppled, but the Horseshoe was also in mortal danger. Its immigrant close-knittedness began to recede as recession and relocation took their toll, as streets were leveled to make way for highways, and as the old died unreplaced by children, who now lived uptown or out west. Slowly but perceptibly it became a neighborhood without neighbors, a community without a common bond.

A fine account of this lost Irish world was published in 1953 as the fingers of mortality were already upon it. Father LeRoy McWilliams ministered in Saint Michael's Parish for over thirty years, arriving as a newly ordained priest in 1918 and becoming rector in 1938. His memoir *Parish Priest* resembles the people he served—sentimental and affectionate, aware of human frailty as well as human strength, eager to charm, and occasionally mawkish. He described a more genial Jersey City than that of Hague's fearful reign: a place where families, against the odds, stayed together; where schools, with modest resources, produced girls of "poise and grace and wisdom" and "big strong fellows unafraid of life"; where charity, among and toward the poorest, was second to none. Saint Michael's was no downtown Eden: drink destroyed lives; murder and suicide happened from time to time; the usual human sorrows obtained. But knowing the "coarse violence [and] . . . ungodliness" of the modern city, the parish survived them nonetheless.[44]

McWilliams, born in Paterson in 1894, was a product of the world he described. His father was an Irish Catholic, his mother an English Episcopalian who became Catholic on the eve of her son's ordination. His childhood was dominated by stories of Wexford, Cork, Tipperary, and Galway. Discerning a vocation to the priesthood, he entered Seton Hall College in 1911 and the Immaculate Conception Seminary four years later. Most of his teachers bore Irish names: Father Clarence McClary, the college vice president, famously tight with money; Father Thomas McLaughlin, later bishop of Paterson, so severe a grammarian that even the prose of Cardinal Newman, surreptitiously incorporated into exercises, came back marked and corrected; Father Frank McCue, nicknamed "Baldy" because of his wig. His classmates and juniors were of the same

*Annual parish events such as the Holy Name Society parade were occasions of pride and formality. Pictured here are Roger Brennan, Thomas Cumiskey, and Joseph Brennan from Saint James's Church, Newark, in 1935.*

❦

*The Church defined a multigenerational world complete unto itself. This is Saint Henry's, Bayonne, in the 1930s.*

stock—an array of Bolands, McNultys, Flanagans, and Barretts. Seton Hall, he conceded, was a priest factory but for all its austerity a remarkably successful one.[45]

Newly emerged from the seminary, McWilliams was appointed to Saint Michael's. He discovered in his first rector, Monsignor John Sheppard, a legendary figure among priests of the Newark diocese. In the manner of a school prefect he demanded to know his priests' whereabouts at all times, constructing a notice board in the rectory to allow them to convey the information. (It had four options: IN-OUT-CHURCH-SCHOOL.) Fellow curates likened the household to a police station; McWilliams thought it resembled a boardinghouse with good food—in that respect an improvement over Seton Hall—but with very few privileges. As vicar-general of the diocese the rector bore the letters *V.G.* after his name: some thought they stood for vinegar and gall. McWilliams knew differently. Beneath the formidable exterior he was kindly and paternal—a *sagart aroon*, as the Irish say, a priest of the people. He was also cunning. Sheppard used his connection with Hague—

*Return to ethnic roots: John McNulty, future priest and president of Seton Hall University, behind a horse-drawn plow in the 1930s.*

☘

*Seton Hall College.*

☘

whose career he helped launch with some words of praise in the parish newsletter—to secure top jobs for parishioners and land for a new school, all the while insisting on the dignity and impartiality of his priesthood. Asked to adjudicate the political shrewdness of the two, McWilliams gave the palm to the rector.[46]

If life inside the rectory seemed a continuation of the seminary, life outside could not have been more different. Alive with noise and color, the Horseshoe of the 1920s and 1930s was a place where several Irish worlds met and mingled: the church, the pub, the police station, the firehouse. For a young cleric making his way, the boundaries were not always easy to discern. Should a priest be seen in a tavern, for instance? Certainly not, if the purpose was to drink; perhaps, if the purpose was to stop others from drinking; certainly, if pastoral necessity demanded it. One of McWilliams's sharpest memories was of a night he was summoned to Sweeney's Bar to give communion and the last rites to a man who had collapsed:

> The moment I entered I began to wonder whether I was right or wrong. The place smelled of stale beer and whiskey. But on the bar, directly over the victim, were the crucifix and two lighted candles. Every drunk in the place had moved away from the bar, and, the moment I entered, all hats were removed, and every man dropped to his knees. . . . Those men . . . felt that I carried God on my person, and they knew instinctively what to do in His presence.

Such was an Irish parish: a place where sin and sanctity mingled, where "true love and fear of God are not always found in church."[47] The striking juxtaposition of the sacred and the profane confirmed the naturalness of religion in the lives of the people.

McWilliams came to delight in this easy religiosity. For him there was not oddity in the uniformed department of the Hudson County police force receiving communion en masse, each coming to the altar with "loaded guns swinging from the hips." Mary Bradley would "swing her old shillelagh" to demolish anyone who spoke ill of the cloth; Gene Sullivan, owner of Sullivan's Saloon, bequeathed a handsome sum to Saint Michael's—only for it to be discovered that he had gambled it away before he died.[48] At times the balance of perfection and imperfection seemed to favor the latter. Late one evening Pat Kane and two bodyguards arrived at the rectory.

*An Essex County outing for Newark priests: a pastoral interlude in an increasingly urban life. Bishop John O'Connor (bishop of Newark, 1901–1927) is standing, far right.*

☘

> "Father," he said in a whisper . . . "I clean forgot that this is St. Blase Day, and
> I wanted to know if you'd bless me t'roat."

The priest complied, making Kane a happy man:

> "Father," he said seriously, "any time you want anything done, just let me
> know. If you want someone bumped get in touch with me and I'll take care of
> it."[49]

In addition to the usual array of characters contained in any parish were those who crossed the line into invincible eccentricity. Priests as well as parishioners fell into this latter category. A surprisingly high number of McWilliams's colleagues were practical jokers: monsignors who liked to offer guests exploding cigars or collapsing chairs, curates looking to do the same. Father Edward "Bullets" McGuirk caused uproar at one clerical dinner when he replaced the contents of his pastor's

*The funeral of Bishop John O'Connor of Newark, 23 May 1927, was the largest Irish American gathering of the year.*

❧

whiskey bottle with insecticide.[50] McWilliams himself on one occasion convinced his fellow curate John Ratigan he was about to be visited by the Imperial Wizard of the Ku Klux Klan.[51] Real eccentricity, however, was usually confined to the flock: the Irishman who carried a door on his back, claiming it was knocked from its hinges by an overeager census-taker; the heavy-drinking McInerney, whose nose was said to resemble a gas meter, registering more than it consumed; the irrepressible Tom Boyle, crony of John Kenny and member of the Hudson County Board of Freeholders, who had a miraculous way with forged baptismal certificates to be used to get jobs for people.[52] These were the types who delighted the rest of the parish.

For all its charm, a note of melancholy pervades the book. McWilliams chronicled a world he knew to be passing away. Threatened by secularism and suburbanism, forces it scarcely understood, the old Horseshoe began to disappear during his lifetime. He was fortunate, he said, to have entered the ministry "at a time when the Irish priest was still the administrator of his flock's daily well-being, in addition to their spiritual health."[53] That function was becoming a thing of the past. Nothing escaped his notice in the early days: settling disputes, contriving jobs out of thin air, haggling with Hague, acting as a go-between for those in trouble with the law. He was a politician as much as a pastor, his power unchallenged within an eight-block domain.

Eventually, however, some problems resisted even clerical intervention. The Wall Street crash and subsequent Depression destroyed whole families. Overnight "the rich became poor and the poor became destitute," and charity seemed unable to cope.[54] The parish was never the same again. Property owners, unable to pay taxes, forfeited their homes to the city. The new occupiers cared little for them, the city even less. Equally devastating was the opening of the Holland Tunnel and its feeder ramps. At a stroke Twelfth Street was destroyed, hundreds of families, "the very heart of the parish," having to move elsewhere.[55] (The irony of the tunnel was that it both required and permitted them to do so.) When the recession ended, a permanently scarred cityscape remained—no competition for the classier uptown sections or leafier towns to the west. McWilliams, writing in 1953, predicted a protracted death scene of "another twenty or thirty years" for the neighborhood where he cut his clerical teeth. Even that may have been optimistic. Other forces, unforeseeable in 1953, would also transform church and neighborhood in the generation to come. *Parish Priest* is more than one man's memoir. It is also an elegy for a vanished era and an indefatigable people: "The grandeur is gone, and . . . as it dies a bit of me dies with it, because this was an old-fashioned Irish section about which one could write books and movies. Anything that could possibly happen— and some things which couldn't—have taken place in the Horseshoe."[56] The farewell seems fitting, even comforting. After all, if a requiem is to be sung, it is well that a priest should sing it.

## FROM CITY TO SUBURB: A FAMILY STORY

THE STORY of the Horseshoe was not singular. It happened throughout New Jersey—indeed, throughout the country—in the middle years of the twentieth century. Nor was it wholly unexpected. On the contrary, the road from city to suburb, from one class to another, represented that transformation of fortune of which every immigrant dreamed. It was a complex process, a blend of political and economic forces as multifarious as America itself. Yet if the social transfiguration reflected factors larger than the people themselves, it was also, first and last, a series of personal stories. Social history is family history writ large. There are faces behind

*Essex County Court Judge Daniel A. Dugan with his wife Anna Davis Dugan and their children at Coney Island in the early twentieth century. From left are son Paul (rear admiral in World War II), son Augustus (lieutenant general in World War II), Judge Dugan, daughter Anna, son Frank, daughter Dorothy (later Mrs. Bernard Degnan), Anna Davis Dugan, daughters Madeleine and Clarissa.*

❧

*Mayor Ben Degnan of West Orange and his wife, Dorothy Dugan Degnan, in the early 1940s.*

❧

the forces. Consider, as only one example, the Irish American odyssey of Peter Duignan and his descendants. Duignan was a nineteenth-century immigrant. His twentieth-century children and grandchildren seem to personify the promise of the New World. Without much stretching, the history of this one family may be made representative of many.[57]

Little is known of Peter Duignan except that he was born in Ireland, came to New Jersey as a young man, and Americanized his name to Degnan. This gesture of assimilation marked him as eager for success. He married Elena Boylan, whose family were small but successful farmers from County Cavan. (The farm had been continuously worked since 1715 and is still in family hands.) They had six children: Mae, John, Frank, Bernard, Jerome, and James. Each of those children seems to represent an aspect of Irish American advance—marrying well, making careers, burnishing the family name. Consider Bernard, third son of the Degnan-Boylan union, universally known as Ben. A volunteer for the Marine Corps in the First World War, he was so slight that only a diet of bananas brought him up to the required weight. Once enlisted, he fought with the Second (Indianhead) Division in France and was twice wounded, the second time severely. As the child of immigrants fighting alongside the British in France he typified, even as a young man, the unforced patriotism that made the Irish into Americans. Returning home at the end of the war, he went to work for the Standard Oil Company of New Jersey and became chief clerk in the Perth Amboy office.

Ben Degnan's ambitions were not satisfied by a chief clerkship. Preferring self-employment to a salary, he ventured into real estate and in 1923 established Bernard M. Degnan, Inc., a firm that eventually expanded to cover the entire state. To succeed in real estate required a good brain, shrewdness, a degree of luck, and social skill. Degnan was endowed with all of them. These were also talents that might also launch a political career. A Democrat, Degnan resigned in 1934 as Newark manager of the Home Owners Loan Corporation to run for West Orange town commissioner. He won overwhelmingly and was reelected, equally handsomely, four years later.

After this second election Degnan was chosen by his fellow commissioners to serve as mayor of West Orange, a post he held for fourteen years along with the locally significant position of administrator of the Department of Parks and Public Property. He could have served longer as mayor but resigned to take the prestigious appointment of postmaster of Orange and West Orange. His final public position was as clerk of the Essex County jury commissioners. For a generation, Ben Degnan's combination of personal skill and political connection made him West Orange's leading citizen. An Irishman and a Democrat (the terms were almost synonymous), he mastered a relatively small world and made it his own.

Other children of Peter Degnan also achieved distinction. Ben's younger brother James became a real estate lawyer and a judge, serving as West Orange police recorder for thirty-three years; his sentencing, according to family tradition, tended to be gentle. As with many children of immigrants he never felt a need to move from his hometown. Social mobility, he reckoned, was more impressive when older neighbors could remember family origins. James Degnan was Man of the Year of the Irish-American Society of the Oranges in 1960.

Two final Degnans demand mention, the sons respectively of James and Ben and therefore first cousins of one another. Jim Degnan's third son, John, became attorney general of New Jersey. A distinguished academic career was capped by a degree from Harvard Law School in 1969 and a clerkship with New Jersey Supreme Court Justice John Francis. John Degnan, a Democrat in the family tradition, was appointed chief counsel to Governor Brendan Byrne in 1976 and attorney general in 1978. He was thirty-three years old, the youngest person to hold the office. (That Byrne was also an Irishman from West Orange did his cause no harm.) His tenure was marked by the opening of the New Jersey State Police to women (controversial then, commonplace now) and by the deregulation of the liquor industry.

John Degnan was loyal to Byrne when other Democrats had their doubts.

Unpopular because of the imposition of a state income tax, Byrne nevertheless won reelection in 1977, confounding critics who dubbed him "One-Term Byrne." (Byrne's wit was a political asset. Asked on leaving the governor's office how life had changed, he remarked that in parades people now waved at him with all five fingers.) Having paid party dues, John Degnan began to formulate his own gubernatorial ambitions. He resigned as attorney general in March 1981 to fight the June primary. He was endorsed by the *New York Times* but not by the electorate. (James Florio won the primary, Tom Kean the subsequent general election.) Yet Degnan's post-electoral career showed the distinction of his early promise. He returned to private practice, then joined the insurance company Chubb & Son in 1990 as senior vice president and general counsel; he became its president in 1998 and vice chairman of the Chubb Corporation in 2002. This success, striking in itself, contains a symbolic footnote. The founder of the company, years before John Degnan's birth, was Hendon Chubb, who resided in Llewellyn Park, West Orange. Among his domestic staff was a part-time gardener who lived locally—an immigrant Irishman called Peter Degnan.

The last grandchild of Peter Degnan to warrant attention is Daniel, third child and first son of Mayor Ben Degnan of West Orange. As with many of the extended family, law played an important part in his life. So also did the Church. Unusually gifted as an academician, Dan Degnan did undergraduate work at Georgetown and took a law degree from Seton Hall. He then served as a naval quartermaster from 1944 to 1946. Returning to civilian life after the war he entered general legal practice, eventually becoming an associate of the Newark law firm of Gilhooly, Yauch, and Fagan. His life then took a different turn. In the late 1950s he heard a calling to the religious life and entered the Jesuit order. Dan Degnan was ordained priest in 1966.

Father Degnan achieved high distinction as a member of the Society of Jesus, combining his legal, academic, and spiritual training in a career of unusual breadth and depth. Within two years of ordination he accepted a teaching appointment at the Harvard Law School (where one student was his cousin John). Thereafter he taught law at Syracuse and Georgetown universi-

*West Orange Municipal Court Judge James Degnan was surrounded by his family when he took the oath of office. Left to right: wife Anne Gould Degnan, father Peter Degnan, James Degnan, mother Elena Boylan Degnan.*

COURTESY: JOE RUSH

ties and served as academic vice president of Loyola College of Maryland before becoming dean of Seton Hall Law School in 1978. Other positions followed before he became president of Saint Peter's College in Jersey City in 1990. His five years as president of Saint Peter's saw substantial increases in the college's recruitment, graduate programs, and fund-raising.

There are dangers in making family history, especially the history of a successful family, stand synecdochally for wider social trends. The sample skews the results. Achievement tends to be remembered, failure forgotten. Those who record dynastic deeds believe those deeds to be worthy of record. We ignore—because we are ignorant of—those who came from humble beginnings and, after a couple of generations, remained humble. Yet even granting these qualifications, the Degnan story provides testimony of remarkable mobility, indicating the opportunities available not only to a family but to an entire social category. To be sure, it is foolish to speculate on what might have been had Peter Duignan remained in Ireland. (Some of the family *did* stay in Ireland, and their lives are not to be discounted or diminished.) But within two generations two movements occurred that are hard to imagine in County Cavan. Degnans shifted from country to town (indeed, from one country to another) and from town to suburb. Luck and talent made it possible for the son of an immigrant to become a mayor, his grandsons to become an attorney general or college president. But luck only occurs in context. Three social realities of the mid-nineteenth century—law, politics, and religion—were once obstacles to the Irish. Now they were opportunities. Clan Degnan may be said to personify that change.

*Mary Degnan Flynn, the Reverend Daniel Degnan, S.J., and Pattie Degnan Flynn visit the early Boylan homestead in Kilmaleck, County Cavan, Ireland. The building is now used as a storage shed. Elena Boylan married Peter Degnan.*

COURTESY: JOE RUSH

CHAPTER **7**

# The End of the Journey

## THE IRISH IN SUBURBIA

**T**HE DECADE and a half that followed the end of the Second World War was an American golden age. The generation that led the world's fight against tyranny returned home to claim its crown and make the world anew. The economy, sluggish throughout the thirties but transformed by the war, provided ample work for those who wanted it. Husbands and wives began long-delayed families. New schools opened to cope with the boom of babies; new and old colleges expanded enormously to welcome a victorious army of GIs. The farms that hemmed America's cities were gobbled up by a vast, unstoppable march: fields turned into suburbs, meadows laid low to become golf courses. The only cloud—in the shape of a mushroom—was the Cold War. Yet even this was turned to advantage. Communism reinforced a sense of American exceptionalism. The world created by the "greatest generation" provoked envy and demanded protection. Moscow and Peking made Peoria worth protecting. And so, under the leadership of Harry Truman and Dwight Eisenhower, America prospered. A nation at peace had turned its swords not into plowshares but into 5-irons.

With suburbs stretching to every horizon, Irish Americans surveyed a landscape radically different from that of their parents and grandparents. Tenements gave way to picket fences; backyards became homegrown Edens. A family such as the Degnans could prosper to such a degree that within two generations of Peter Duignan's coming to America his descendants moved in an entirely different world. Tellingly, some of that prosperity was based on real estate. Suburbia—the "crabgrass frontier"—was settled by children of immigrants: it was also bought and sold by them. Not everyone grew rich, of course, but many did. The promise of New Jersey was a cookout in the summer and a Christmas trip to Radio City.

From city to suburb represented more than a physical journey. Ethnicity itself was transformed. As the Irish became bourgeois, their Irishness changed. The pig in the parlor was now porcelain; the curtains were now made of lace. If they had yet to reach the ranks of the truly genteel, fewer now had dirt under their fingernails. For most, this social ascension was welcome, it being, after all, the very point of their parents' coming to America. Others were not so sure. Perhaps something beautiful had been lost with arrival into the middle class, some authentic ethnicity, some essential national characteristic. When America got its hands on a culture, purists argued, it cheapened it, cheered it up, or made it into a commodity. There was an element of truth to this. Every March an efflorescence of green proclaimed a community sufficiently self-confident to parody itself, as if, by some strange mid-Atlantic alchemy, the Irish had become what they had never been in Ireland: optimists. Replete with corned beef and cabbage, they contemplated a vision of Ireland more agreeable than the Ireland their forebears had left behind.

*Irish heritage represented a rich commercial opportunity for the American greeting card industry. This Saint Patrick's Day postcard dates from 1908 and was designed by M. W. Taggart of New York. Providing words and music of "The Harp That Once thro' Tara's Halls," it was at once more useful and tasteful than later leprechaunish offerings.*

The purists missed the point. Here was not inauthentic Irishness so much as authentic Irish Americanness. Irishness had to do with history; Irish Americanness had to do with heritage. Between them was all the difference in the world. Eoin MagUidir, associate editor of the monthly review *The Monitor*, complained to Bishop Thomas Walsh of Newark in 1931 that Irishness in America had become trivial and debased:

> Doubtless you are not aware of the fact that some of the largest as well as some of the smallest stores in Newark and in other cities throughout the country make yearly displays of insulting mockery against both the Irish race and the Catholic Church, around each succeeding St. Patrick's Day. Just picture the "honor" that is offered the Apostle, Patrick, and the Faith which he preached, in exhibitions of pigs painted green; in figures of both men and women, bedecked in green colors but with faces like gorillas' and clay pipes in their mouths; figures of cats with green hats on their heads and clay pipes in their jaws etc., etc.!!!

MagUidir sniffed a larger cultural assault:

> If such green monstrosities were only placed before the statue of St. Patrick in one of our city churches, just how would you feel about it, or how could any Catholic in America feel about it? But the displays are publicly shown in "honor" of the Irish, in "honor" of St. Patrick and in "honor" of the Faith which Patrick brought to the Irish, and everyone seems far too timid to protest against the wanton insult and ridicule. If a pig were decorated with the Jewish flag and exhibited in "honor" of Moses and Abraham, there is not a Rabbi in America who would not speak out for the whole world to hear him.

*Eugene Kinkead was born in Buttevant, County Cork, in 1876 and came to the United States in 1880. He graduated from Seton Hall College in 1897, the year he became a U.S. citizen. Kinkead had a varied career as financier, soldier, and politician. As sheriff of Hudson County, he helped to persuade Woodrow Wilson to run for the governorship of New Jersey in 1910. He also fought in the First World War, ending his military service as a major.*

☘

If the pig were shown carrying the Italian flag, in "honor" of St. Anthony, the outrage against Catholicity would soon be condemned and abolished.[1]

This was the cry of a crank, the moral indignation of one for whom the highest form of heroism was a letter to the editor. Walsh chose not to take the hint. The communication received a perfunctory response, and the outrage remained uncondemned.

MacUidir's indignation was overdone, but he was right to recognize that Irishness had been turned to a valuable commercial purpose. His mistake lay in assuming that the Irish themselves greatly cared. As chief buyers and sellers of vulgar cheerfulness, it was they who had commoditized Irishness the moment they landed in America. That was the only possession some of them had. They played

*More than respectable: Monsignor Michael Mulligan of Bayonne considers portraits in oil of his parents, Michael and Mary. Mary Mulligan (née Owens) came from Ireland to serve as housekeeper to her uncle, Father Patrick Leonard (see page 104). The family's money came from quarrying in Clinton.*

❧

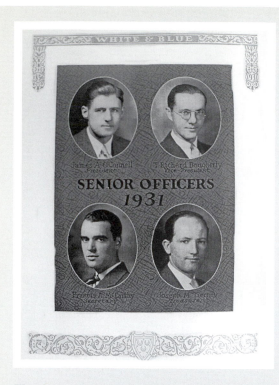

*The Irish of Paterson in the 1930s: Mary Clune Loughrey and three children on East Eighteenth Street.*

❧

*The names of the senior officers of Seton Hall College's class of 1931 (O'Connell, Dougherty, McCarthy, and Tierney) and of 1933 (Fleming, Fitzsimmons, Finn, and Connors) captured the heavy Irish presence in that institution.*

❧

their allotted parts in America's ethnic play—as amiable rogues, lovers of freedom, ward politicians, or priests—with a panache that deserved and expected reward. Stage Irishness was not, as MacUidir thought, a form of cultural self-hatred. It was clever calculation. Besides, America was a big enough theater to accommodate even the likes of MacUidir—a Gaelic-speaking puritan, Malvolio with an Aran sweater. He, too, had a part to play.

The value of Irishness, MacUidir failed to realize, lay in its versatility. It was a protean identity. As immigrants discovered, America offered new ways of being Irish as part of being American. In the Cold War, the fight against communism offered Irish Americans an opportunity to demonstrate their distinctive immigrant patriotism. In 1947 the organizer of the Saint Patrick's Day Parade in Newark wrote to the vicar-general of the archdiocese: "As you probably know, the parade this year will be a marching protest of the Irish of this Archdiocese against the spread of Communism, and undoubtedly the co-operation of the Archbishop will be most helpful in the success which it is hoped we will attain."[2] The merit of green, in other words, was that it was not red. Certainly the archbishop of Newark needed no prompting in the matter. The Church took the lead in anti-communist crusades, and the Irish were more than eager to follow.

## THE ANCIENT ORDER OF HIBERNIANS

NOTHING CAPTURES so clearly this movement—from ghetto to suburb to establishment—as the Ancient Order of Hibernians. In the 1870s Bishop Michael Corrigan of Newark wondered if a Catholic could join such an organization. In 1898 Irish-born Bishop James McFaul of Trenton welcomed the national convention of the order to his diocese, grateful that it would meet "on soil rendered sacred, in revolutionary days, by the blood of our fathers."[3] In the 1960s Archbishop Thomas A. Boland of Newark served as its national chaplain. Once on the margins, the Hibernians were now at the center of Irish American life—well-connected, socially conservative, fiercely patriotic, and conspicuously Catholic. The coldest of cold warriors, they represented a political disposition so close to the American mainstream as to be indistinguishable from it. Viewed from one angle, Hibernianism was hardly political at all. Members of the order got on with the business of being American— running companies, tending patients, teaching classes, opening stores, and going to offices. To read their newsletters—*The National Hibernian Digest, The New Jersey Hibernian, The Hudson County Hibernian*—is to enter the lost world of midcentury middle America, an era of solid certainties between the two McCarthys, Joe and Gene. Accounts of their modest doings—a dance in Bayonne in 1958 enlivened by "the delightful footwork of the Peggy Smith Steppers [and] little Miss Sheila Ferry, a communion breakfast in Elizabeth sponsored by the Daniel O'Connell division, a talk organized by the Ray-

*The Ancient Order of Hibernians remained unwaveringly Catholic and anti-communist throughout the 1960s.*

❦

TOP RIGHT: *John F. Connolly (back left) at his grand-daughter's graduation from Middlebury College, Vermont, 1948.*

ABOVE: *John F. Connolly with his daughter, niece, and grandchildren at a dinner party in North Arlington, New Jersey, in the early 1950s.*

☘

COURTESY: JOHN J. CONNOLLY

Family history tells of Irish entry into the middle classes. John F. Connolly (1870–1956) came from Moyduff, County Monaghan. A carpenter by trade, he came with his entire family to New Jersey while still a young man. Married and widowed twice, he was left to raise four children while at the same time developing his own business. Two of those children predeceased him. His grandson, John J. Connolly, remembers him thus: "He was a devout Catholic and his faith never wavered. He loved nature which seemed strange to me as a kid, as I had no understanding of the Irish rural tradition. He played both the fiddle and the tin whistle, and made me listen to his tunes more often than I would have liked. Although he grew up in Ulster and had no knowledge of the Irish language, he had a number of Protestant friends. While not bigoted in any way, I often wondered if he really believed Protestants could be saved. I lived with him and his unmarried daughter, Mary, after my father died. They saw to my education and arranged for me to attend Notre Dame, which they believed was the best Catholic college in America. My aunt Mary loved Notre Dame. When visiting me there, she appeared to be experiencing the Beatific Vision" (letter to the author, 17 October 2002).

*Paying court to the Irish: the Friendly Sons of Saint Patrick, Mayfair Farms, West Orange, 17 March 1953, with Archbishop Thomas Boland, U.S. Chief Justice Arthur Vanderbilt, and Associate Justice William Brennan.*

❧

*Dr. Joseph Mahoney, director of the New Jersey Catholic Historical Records Commission, and Bishop John J. Dougherty, auxiliary bishop of Newark, were deeply proud of their Irish Catholic heritage. In September 1976 the New Jersey Catholic Historical Records Commission met for the first time.*

❧

mond Ryan division in Newark on "the Israel-Arab situation and the Marxist rule under which half of the world's population now exist—carried the confident knowledge that wholesome values would last forever."[4] Soon that confidence was shaken, but for a time it was serene.

Lectures, entertainments, charity, and religious devotion were at the heart of Hibernianism in New Jersey as elsewhere. But to prescind from politics was to embrace irrelevance. Father John Lawlor, chaplain of the New Jersey Hibernians in the 1960s, warned that the organization should not become "just an Irish social club [promoting] dances, card parties, parades [and] dinners." Matters of greater importance demanded attention. Father Lawlor wanted Hibernians to display greater spiritual seriousness —more "pilgrimages, retreats, Corporate Com-

*The newsletter of the Chaplain's Institute of the Ancient Order of Hibernians was called* An t-Sogart *(The Priest), an indication that the promotion of the Gaelic language was more than a token commitment on the part of some Hibernians.*

❧

*The Peggy Smith School of Irish Dancing was one of the best in the state.*

☘

COURTESY: SETON HALL UNIVERSITY SPECIAL COLLECTIONS CENTER AND UNIVERSITY ARCHIVES

munions, Days of Recollection, Vesper Services." Others understood the call to mean public advocacy of particular causes. As the 1960s unfolded, the general relaxation of popular morals exercised Hibernians in New Jersey and beyond. "Manufacturers of obscene and indecent literature are peddling their filth in greater quantities than ever before," complained Jeremiah J. O'Callaghan, a Corkman who graduated from the John Marshall Law School in Jersey City and became national president of the A.O.H. in 1958. "This material is being circulated with the deliberate intention of so weakening the moral fiber of all Americans that devotion to and even belief in Almighty God will be destroyed."[5]

Constitutions thus compromised could offer little resistance to the next assault: Communism itself. Shelved beside the *Little Red Book* was *Lady Chatterley's Lover.* As a sign of its commitment to traditional values, Irish America was unstinting in championship of the Vietnam War. "We of the Ancient Order of Hibernians are proud to pledge our support to our President Lyndon B. Johnson for his

United Irish Societies of New Jersey
QUEEN OF ANGELS CIVIC HALL
230 ACADEMY STREET :: :: NEWARK, NEW JERSEY

FEIS - TAILTEANN

Great Irish Cultural and Athletic Contests
TO BE HELD AT

NEWARK SCHOOLS STADIUM
ROSEVILLE & BLOOMFIELD AVENUES, NEWARK, NEW JERSEY

Sunday, Oct. 17, 1948
Over 80 Events
FEATURING CONTESTS IN
Irish Step and Figure Dancing,
Singing Gaelic and English,

Music, War Pipe Bands, Brass and Reed Bands,
Fife and Drum Bands, Uileann Pipe, Piano,
Harp and Violin Solos.

Gaelic Language, Art and Essay Contests.

Field Events, Gaelic Football, Hurling, Running,
Jumping, Tug of War, Weight Throwing, etc.
FEATURING OLYMPIC CHAMPIONS

**LEFT:** *The United Irish Societies of New Jersey were interested especially in the promotion of "great Irish cultural and athletic contests" in 1948.*

**BELOW:** *The iconography of the Newark Saint Patrick's Day parade of 1967 was a perfect marriage of American, Irish, Celtic, and Christian symbols.*

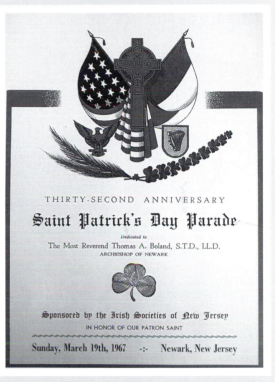

THIRTY-SECOND ANNIVERSARY
Saint Patrick's Day Parade
Dedicated to
The Most Reverend Thomas A. Boland, S.T.D., LL.D.
ARCHBISHOP OF NEWARK

Sponsored by the Irish Societies of New Jersey
IN HONOR OF OUR PATRON SAINT

Sunday, March 19th, 1967 -:- Newark, New Jersey

**ABOVE:** *Saint Patrick's Day in Newark, 1965.*

**ABOVE:** *By the 1960s "Irishness" appealed beyond racial lines. An African American girl was a member of Peggy Smith's School of Irish Dancing.*

JAMES W. KELLY, JR.
PRESIDENT

GEORGE L. RIPLEY, JR.
TREASURER

# St. Patrick's Guard of Honor of New Jersey

536 BROAD STREET
NEWARK, N. J.

December 3, 1968

**RECIPIENTS OF HONORS**

1940 - JOHN W. McGEEHAN, JR.
1941 - JUDGE JOSEPH E. CONLON
1942 - BERNARD M. DEGNAN
1945 - HUGH J. DEVORE
1946 - RT. REV. MSGR. JAMES F. KELLEY
1947 - JOHN J. CONNOLLY, M.D.
1948 - THOMAS F. FITZPATRICK
1949 - CHRISTOPHER J. DEVINE, SR.
1950 - BERNARD M. SHANLEY
1951 - JOHN R. COONEY
1952 - JUSTICE WM. J. BRENNAN, JR.
1953 - DAVID J. CONNOLLY
1954 - JOHN J. CLANCY

**RECIPIENTS OF HONORS**

1955 - JUDGE GERALD T. FOLEY
1956 - JOHN E. FARRELL
1957 - JOHN J. FLANAGAN, M.D.
1958 - MAYOR JAMES W. KELLY, JR.
1959 - RT. REV. MSGR. THOMAS J. CONROY
1960 - JOHN E. JOYCE
1961 - JOHN C. HENDERSON
1962 - JOHN A. COUCH, JR.
1963 - PRESIDENT JOHN F. KENNEDY
1964 - RUSSELL M. WILLIAMS
1965 - DENNIS F. CAREY
1966 - JUDGE JAMES T. OWENS
1967 - JUDGE LAWRENCE A. WHIPPLE

Fellow Member of the Guard of Honor:

The 1968 Annual Christmas Award Luncheon Party of the Guard of Honor will be held on Saturday, December 14th, 1968, at Mayfair Farms, West Orange. Cocktails will be served from twelve noon until one thirty p.m. Luncheon will follow immediately.

Your selection committee has designated Honorable Brendan T. Byrne as the "Outstanding Irishman of 1968." Brendan is a lifelong resident of West Orange and is the son of Essex County Tax Commissioner Francis A. Byrne and Genevieve Brennan Byrne, both born in Orange. His grandparents were born in Ireland. He is married to the former Jean Featherly. The couple has six children.

Our recipient is a graduate of West Orange High School, Seton Hall University, Princeton University and Harvard Law School. He is an Air-Force Combat veteran of World War II. He was admitted to the Bar in 1951.

In the short space of seventeen years as a lawyer, Brendan has had a phenomenal career in public life. In 1955, Governor Robert B. Meyner appointed him Deputy Attorney General. Later that same year he resigned to join the personal staff of Governor Meyner from which he resigned to accept the appointment in 1959 as Essex County Prosecutor. In January, 1968, he resigned upon his appointment by Governor Richard J. Hughes to be President of the Public Utility Commission of the State of New Jersey which position he is now holding.

Meantime, he has found time to practice law as a member of the firm of Teltser, Byrne and Greenberg in East Orange. He is also Chairman of the Board of Directors of Inter-Continental Life Insurance Company of Newark.

*Brendan T. Byrne was "Outstanding Irishman of 1968."*

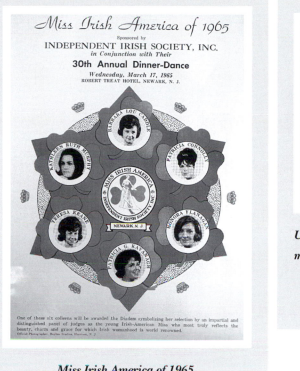

*Miss Irish America of 1965.*

♣

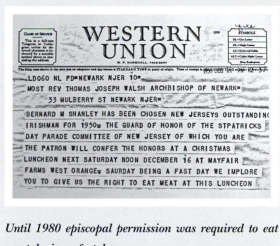

*Until 1980 episcopal permission was required to eat meat during a fast day.*

♣

actions in Viet Nam and elsewhere against the evils of Communism," wrote Michael Delahunty, state president of the New Jersey Hibernians in 1965. "We salute our fellow Americans who are making the supreme sacrifice to preserve the freedom which we so proudly cherish."[6] Even as disenchantment with the war set in, Hibernians remained firmer than most in their support of it.

## IRISH NEW JERSEY AND THE NORTHERN IRELAND PROBLEM

**A**NTI-COMMUNISM WAS as natural to Irish Americans as the air they breathed, but it was not a specifically Irish crusade. A narrower stage for political involvement was Ireland itself. In the late 1960s the familiar certainties of the Irish American world began to crumble. The election of President John F. Kennedy marked a pinnacle: his assassination, and that of his brother, shattered the idyll. Vietnam caused a national soul-searching that puzzled, even appalled, traditional patriots. The Second Vatican Council transformed the practice of Catholicism, bewildering congregations. The civil rights movement demanded for black America what was taken for granted by white, portending an unsettling activism

*Irish America comes of age: President John F. Kennedy speaking on behalf of Richard Hughes in 1961.*

❧

in cultural and identity politics. This was a new world, and some Irish Americans, to their discomfort, represented the old establishment against which it was pitting itself.

If civil rights were contentious at home, they were admirable abroad. When Northern Ireland"s Catholic population demanded its own version of civil rights in 1968—equality in the electoral system, better housing, and an end to discrimination in employment—Irish Americans had a cause they could embrace. Many Irish people remained second-class citizens in their own country, seeming proof of the nationalist agrument that British presence in one corner of Ireland lead to oppression. In 1958, a decade before Ulster's dam burst, Hibernians in New Jersey had four goals: to increase their membership, deepen their Catholicism, buy Irish goods, and by "daily prayer . . . abolish the unnatural border in Ireland [held in place] by the whims of an alien occupaton force."[7] This simple faith did not survive the ferocity of Irish politics ten years later. Prayer had to be supplemented by alms and, from time to time, by arms. And if good intentions were insufficient, so too was the analysis behind them. It was too easy to blame the border for all of Ireland's problems, and absurd to imagine its continued existence to be the result of imperialist caprice. For a time, however, that shibboleth stayed standing.

What precisely was this Ulster problem? In its twentieth-century form it dated from the Easter Rising of 1916 when Ireland (still within the United Kingdom) was proclaimed a republic by a motley group of poets, professors, Gaelic revivalists, and Marxists under the command of Padraic Pearse (schoolmaster and barrister) and James Connolly (trades unionist and socialist intellectual). A military fiasco—it lasted a week, after which its leaders were executed—the rebellion was a political triumph. It galvanized anti-British sentiment throughout the country and produced a new generation of martyrs on whose memory Irish nationalism could sustain itself for years to come. Irish Americans supported the rising and in its aftermath

**TWO OF MANY**

LEFT: *Luke Farrell patrolling the streets of South Orange in the early 1940s. Born in Ballymahon, County Longford, in 1889, he came to the United States as a young man, joining the South Orange Police Department in 1923. Farrell became a local legend, handing out some twenty thousand tickets in twenty-five years of traffic duty.*
RIGHT: *Mike Meehan patrols Ferry Street in Newark, October 1978.*

(LEFT) COURTESY: JOE GARAFOLA  (RIGHT) COURTESY: JAMES LOWNEY

*Atlantic City hosted the Ancient Order of Hibernians and Ladies Auxiliary National Convention in 1937.*

❧

endorsed Eamon De Valera as leader of the Irish provisional government in 1919. This set a pattern. At every turn the leadership of the Irish revolution could rely on Irish American support. Indeed, many Irish Americans favored it against their own government, being enraged, for example, by Woodrow Wilson's failure to press for Irish self-determination at Versailles. Afterward they raised over $5.5 million for the War of Independence (1919–1921) by purchasing Irish Bond Certificates. The American Committee for the Relief of Ireland raised another $5 million for victims of the war. The Irish diaspora was thus involved politically and financially in the affairs of the homeland for the first twenty years of the twentieth century.

In 1921, however, all urgancy ceased. The Anglo-Irish treaty brought the War of Independence to an end and inaugurated, as its Irish signatories feared, a civil war. Under the terms of the treaty Ireland was partitioned; twenty-six counties became the Irish Free State, and six counties remained under British control as Northern Ireland. No nationalist supported partition—independence for the entire island was the very definition of nationalism—but some accepted it as a temporary expedient. The civil war (1921–1923) was therefore fought between those who thought that Britain should be made to yield Northern Ireland immediately and those who expected to see it surrendered at an unspecified later date. The anti-treaty forces were led by De Valera, the pro-treaty forces by Michael Collins, his former comrade-in-arms. The Protestant population of the North, defiantly unionist, was not consulted by the warring factions. As early as 1914 partition had been suggested as a way of protecting their self-perceived Britishness. Now, somehow or other, they were expected to live happily in an all-Ireland republic, which hitherto they had resisted to the point of arms.

The War of Independence excited Irish Americans, but the civil war left them unmoved. Partition offended them, but they were prepared to live with it. This matched the mood in Ireland itself, where little appetite existed even among nationalists to force Ulster Protestants into a polity for which they had shown only hostility. The war's viciousness embittered Irish politics for years to come and, across the ocean, caused most Irish Americans to disengage entirely from nationalist activities.[8] At its conclusion, when De Valera's defeated forces accepted the reality (if not legitimacy) of partition, a kind of normality settled over politics. The institutions of the Free State took root. De Valera broke with the Irish Republican Army, established the Fianna Fail party, led it into Parliament in 1927, and formed a government in 1932. Meanwhile, the institutions of Northern Ireland—a judiciary, police force, House

## Irish Bond Holders Will be Repaid

CATHOLIC UNION AND TIMES, THURSDAY, JULY 11, 1929

Dublin, July 10.—Payment in full will be made by the Irish Free State to the American holders of Irish Republican bonds issued in the United States before the Anglo-Irish treaty of 1922, Ernest Blythe, Minister of Finance, has declared.

Informed that many persons were holding the bond merely as souvenirs, under the impression that they cannot be converted into cash, Mr. Blythe said they were mistaken.

"It is the settled policy of the Free State Government that the American subscribers to the Dail Eireann shall be paid, not merely 60 cents on the dollar but to the full extent of the dollar," Blythe said.

"The Free State Government is now awaiting the completion of the receiver's task in the American courts. When the American courts certify that all the funds held by the court have been refunded, on whatever percentage basis may be arrived at, the Free State Ministry of Finance proposes to establish machinery in New York to make good to all subscribers the balance of the sums subscribed."

Irish-Americans to the number of 175,000 will benefit by the new action of the Free State Government. They are part of the subscribers—the total number 303,000 —who had enabled the Irish Government to float a loan of $5,800,-

*Some 175,000 Irish Americans bought Irish Republic bonds during Ireland's War of Independence, 1919–1921. The government of the Irish Free State later announced that the bonds would be honored in full. From* **The Catholic Union and Times,** *11 July 1929.*

❧

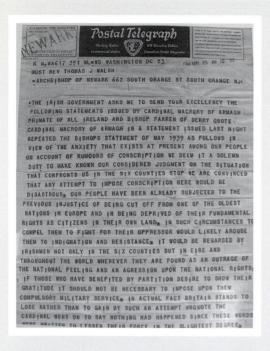

*Richard Hughes and Richard Cushing, one a governor, the other a cardinal. Irish America benefited from the leadership of such men—quick-witted, charismatic, and, above all, close to the instincts of their own people.*

❧

*Irish bishops were keen to enlist their American counterparts in support of the Catholic population of Northern Ireland. In 1939 Archbishop Macgrory of Armagh and Bishop Farren of Derry told Newark's Archbishop Walsh that members of their flock faced the possibility of conscription.*

❧

of Commons and Senate, prime minister, and cabinet—began to function. However, Roman Catholics, 40 percent of the population, showed extreme reluctance to accept the legitimacy of the arrangements. Northern Ireland, in the words of one prime minister, Lord Craigavon, possessed "a Protestant parliament for a Protestant people." For fifty years it remained that way.

As they had at the outbreak of the civil war, after its conclusion most Irish Americans considered partition a sentimental grievance: offensive, certainly, but not a cause of lost sleep. With roots in the Free State, many considered Irish independence more or less to have been won. Northern Ireland hardly entered their minds. Occasionally Ireland intruded into American politics but in ways that disinclined them to take it seriously. Thus the policy of Irish neutrality in the Second World War bewildered them. An independent Ireland would be a "strong ally of the United States," Irish America had once thought: clearly not.[9] Worse, when De

Valera as Ireland's prime minister in 1945 sent the German government a telegram of condolence on the death of Adolf Hitler, most Americans thought he had taken leave of his senses. Under such leadership the nationalist cause, once so compelling, seemed narrow, provincial, and bizarre.

## THE "TROUBLES" BEGIN

AMERICAN NEGLECT of Irish politics ended in the late 1960s. For years the Catholic minority in Northern Ireland suffered discrimination in employment, at the workplace, in access to affordable public housing, and in the electoral system itself.[10] Resentment boiled over in October 1968 when baton-wielding policemen broke up a civil rights march in Derry, Northern Ireland's second-largest city. The march had wide support—Catholic doctors, lawyers, teachers, and businessmen walked alongside factory workers, students, and unemployed—so it could not be called a revolt of the underclass. On the contrary, it revealed a political system dangerously stagnant and unrepresentative.

The crisis worsened in 1969: troops arrived in the streets of Belfast and Derry, and the IRA resumed a campaign to force Britain to withdraw from the last part of Ireland still under its control. The latter was a crucial development. The civil rights

*To the extent that New Jersey's Irish societies had a political agenda it was nationalist: to bring about the reunification of a country divided since the partition of 1921. Some groups, such as the United Irish Society, took this aim more seriously than others. The Independent Irish Society, for example, was mainly a social club.*

❖

movement began as a demand for political equality. Now it was caught up in the older question of national self-determination. The border, a divisive but dormant issue throughout most of the history of Northern Ireland, returned to scupper the chances of real social democracy. Catholics came to believe that if the two halves of Ireland were reunited their second-class citizenship would disappear. Protestants, all the while denying that Catholics *were* second-class citizens, insisted that the Union was the best guarantee of their own political rights. Both analyses were flawed. Even if immediate reunification had been an option, it was unlikely to have been the boon that Catholics thought it would be. As for the assertion that both communities enjoyed equal rights, the facts simply did not sustain it.

Where did this leave Irish Americans? The resurgence of the "troubles" allowed many of them to rediscover a political radicalism that had been dulled by the exodus to suburbia. Some were made uneasy by repeated assertions that the Ulster Catholic experience was analogous to that of American blacks. Others may have felt that support for civil rights in Ireland excused lack of support for them in America. These qualifications apart, the Catholic cause in Northern Ireland was one they could wholeheartedly support. With the immediacy of television, the Bogside and the Falls Road entered their living rooms; equally immediately, those places could be transformed with a signature on a check.

Yet a problem remained. Defined as a struggle for basic human decencies, civil rights won easy Irish American support. Defined as a demand for fundamental social transformation, it was controversial, as can be seen in the reaction of Irish America to Bernadette Devlin, the best-known civil rights figure in the early days of the "troubles." Devlin was a celebrity on both sides of the Atlantic: student radical, leader of the left-wing People's Democracy, member of Parliament at age twenty-two, firebrand orator. To the Washington correspondent of the *Irish Times* she was "the best envoy Ireland ever sent to America . . . the brightest, the freshest, and of course the prettiest Irish politician to come to these parts in living memory." But the acclaim was troublesome. Devlin was a revolutionary, her ideological fervor masked by pert affability and a certain colleen charm. She recognized the irony of the situation: "In America the word socialist is a smear you apply to other people. You never get up and say you are a socialist yourself. All the men in the big green suits cheered and roared when I mentioned James Connolly, until I started quoting what he actually said."[11] This contempt for the men in green suits was shortsighted. Consorting with the class enemy in order to pick its pocket, she was herself an ambiguous figure. The sentimental patriots of suburbia may have seemed absurd but so, too, in her own way, was the Marxist-Leninist as corporate fund-raiser.

Devlin represented a moment of truth for Irish Americans, and some recog-

*Bernard Shanley, distinguished New Jersey Irishman and special assistant to President Eisenhower, welcomed the lord mayor of Dublin, Robert Briscoe, to the White House in March 1957.*

❧

COURTESY: SETON HALL UNIVERSITY
SPECIAL COLLECTIONS CENTER AND UNIVERSITY ARCHIVES

*Raising funds and consciousness, moderate Catholic politician John Hume addressed a friendly crowd in McGovern's Bar, Newark, at the beginning of the Northern Ireland "troubles." To the left is Michael Delahunty.*

❧

COURTESY: JAMES LOWNEY

nized it. In troubling ways she revealed the inadequacy of a naive nationalist interpretation of Irish history, even if, in its place, she proposed a naive socialist one. Prompted by her visit, the Ancient Order of Hibernians in New Jersey conducted a debate about how best to support civil rights in Northern Ireland. Prominent in the discussion was Eugene Byrne, state president of the organization, who concluded that Devlin was a dangerous figure. Writing in the *New Jersey Hibernian*, he outlined her offenses: she was an advocate of international proletarian revolution; she repudiated the leadership of moderate Catholics such as John Hume; she regarded the reunification of Ireland as a means toward the greater end of a socialist republic; she consorted with the worst elements in the American politics—Eldridge Cleaver of the Black Panthers, Jessica Mitford and her husband Robert Treuhaft (the latter "repeatedly identified as a member of the Communist Party"), and so on. Byrne's approach smacked of the blunderbuss—among Mitford's delinquencies was authorship of a book sympathetic to Dr. Benjamin Spock—but he scored some hits. "In all likelihood," he concluded, "I will be characterized as

*Worthy of a book in itself, McGovern's Bar in Newark was a popular watering hole for many of New Jersey's Irish community, serving as a place of entertainment, political headquarters, fund-raising operation, and venue for occasional mayhem.*

having . . . harmed the cause and served the aims of British imperialism."[12] That risk he was prepared to run.

Byrne's excoriations provoked the reaction he anticipated. Some continued to to be bedazzled by Devlin; others began to discover her true purposes. Still it remained the case, as even Byrne recognized, that "real and substantial grievances" existed in Northern Ireland that demanded amelioration. If miniskirted Marxism would not work, what would? The answer was fund-raising on behalf of working-class Catholic communities. The same issue of the *New Jersey Hibernian* that condemned Devlin also announced a national campaign, sanctioned by the Catholic hierarchy, "to raise one million dollars for the relief of victims of recent rioting in Northern Ireland." The money was to be delivered to the archbishop of Armagh, Cardinal Conway, who would decide on its disbursement. Although the drive was national, it was essentially a New Jersey operation. The honorary chairman was Archbishop Boland of Newark (national chaplain of the A.O.H.; his people were small farmers from Mayo), and fundraiser-in-chief was Michael Delahunty (national president), who lived in Montclair. In effect, the campaign was a Church collection in five dioceses and archdiocese in the United States—Newark, New York, Trenton, Providence, and Chicago.

Fund-raising has value beyond the raising of funds. It also raises consciousness. Moribund chapters may be brought to life; hibernating Hibernianism may be prodded from sleep. That was the hope. The reality was different. Although professional fundraisers were consulted, most of the work devolved to Delahunty. This should have been a boon, he being an indefatigable promoter of all things Irish, but even his energy was unequal to the task. Large sums were raised—a check for $100,000 was handed to John Hume on 4 July 1970—but there was never a chance that a million dollars would accrue. Peter Busatti, consultant to the operation, wrote to Archbishop Boland in September 1970 that "the recently concluded A.O.H. campaign was certainly an unhappy event for Your Excellency and also ourselves."[13]

Wh y the disappointment? One reason may have been disillusion with Devlin. Another may have been confusion as to the destination of the money. Yet given the reslpectability of a campaign endorsed by three cardinals, this does not suffice as explanation. The deeper truth is that the drive failed in its primary purpose of raising one million dollars because the time for its secondary purpose—to reanimate local organizations—was long past. Irish America was not a standing army ready for action; it was a few sergeants trying to drill a platoon of sleepy volunteers. At the campaign's halfway point, Cardinal Conway wrote to Archbishop Boland on 5 March 1970 to express delight that "upwards of a million dollars had be collected by the A.O.H. for relief in distress in Northern Ireland." The following day Boland received a more accurate account of progress. The campaign, Busatti

*Mike Delahunty of Montclair was a formidably energetic Hibernian.*

❧

COURTESY: JAMES LOWNEY

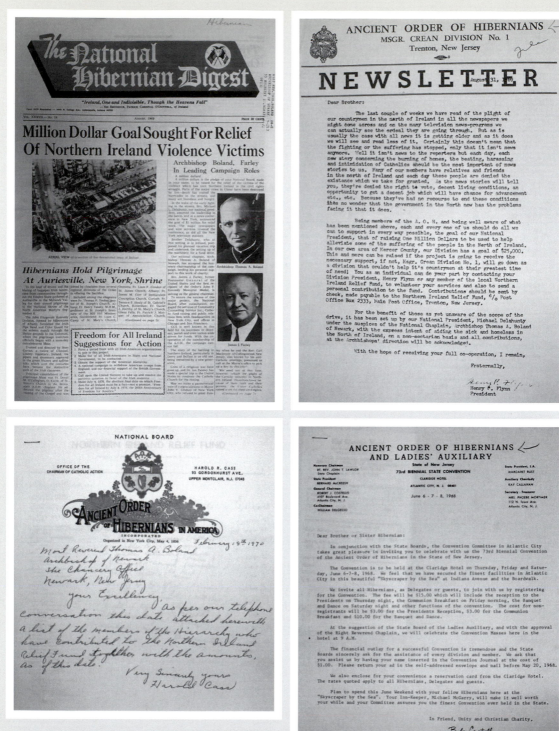

*A flurry of Hibernian newspapers, circulars, and letters announced the ambitious goal of raising a million dollars for suffering Northern Irish Catholics in 1970.*

assured, remained ambitions: "324,000 contribution envelopes and flyers have been distributed throughout the nation with no Division or area receiving an excess. In most cases this distribution was personally made by Mr. Delahunty and ourselves." But troops on the ground were lacking:

> Memorandums . . . requesting reports of progress and information has [*sic*] met with a response of only 11% of the A.O.H. Divisions.
>
> Of the 249 Divisions represented in the United States only 20% have reported any funds. Constant requests . . . brings [*sic*] no response. . . . Why the 80% refuses to co-operate continues to be a mystery.

The poor return could not be attributed to Delahunty, who worked "most diligently on the campaign and [left] no stone unturned." Nor was wider organization lacking: the A.O.H. had a national structure, as had the Church. But these arrangements counted for little:

> *Trenton Diocese:*
> To our knowledge, only those parishes in the Trenton city area are being visited.
>
> *Archdiocese of New York:*
> Assignments were made for parish visitations in all counties in which the A.O.H. is represented.
>
> *Diocese of Providence, Rhode Island:*
> To our knowledge no visits to pastors have been made.
>
> *Archdiocese of Chicago:*
> To our knowledge no visits to pastors have been made.
>
> *Archdiocese of Newark:*
> The Elizabeth Hibernians have worked most diligently under the leadership of Mr. Frank O'Hara.
>
> The Kearny area under the leadership of Mr. Thomas L. Duffy likewise has accomplished similar results.[14]

And that was that. Busatti reported that UNICO, an Italian American organization, also "indicated . . . interest" in the campaign, but if Irish associations were indifferent to Ireland, Italians were unlikely to come to the rescue.

Unremarked in these explanations was the central difficulty. The Ancient

*Saint Patrick's Day, Newark, 1969.*

❧❧

Order of Hibernians was not the only group looking for money, nor the most vigorous. To some Irish Americans, especially younger, unskilled immigrants, they were terminally respectable, churchy, and sentimental: more ancient than Hibernian, the kind of outfit one's father joined. This clash was generational but also ideological. The Hibernian philosophy of devotion, charity, and nonviolence disappointed those who believed that Ireland's most pressing need was guns. Other groups competing for funds were sharper-edged: the National Association for Irish Justice had links to the Black Panthers; the Irish Northern Aid Committee (Noraid) sponsored an American tour by IRA veterans Sean Keenan and Joe Cahill. The money raised went toward the purchase of weaponry. "We deliver the money in Ireland," remarked Michael Flannery of Noraid. "We don't earmark it for anything."[15] This was disingenuous. Members of the IRA who toured America had a training manual for prising cash from their Hibernian hosts:

> It was in the United States that our main funding efforts were conducted [recalled Maria McGuire, who eventually defected from the Provisional IRA] and visiting speakers were carefully briefed on how the audiences should be played. There should be copious reference to the martyrs of 1916 and 1919–21—the period in which most of the audience would be living. Anti-British sentiment, recalling Cromwell, the Famine and the Black and Tans, could be profitably exploited. By no means could anything be said against the Catholic Church and all references to socialism should be avoided.[16]

Money from the 1969–70 Hibernian campaign went to families in need. Other cash found its way, after circuitous meanderings in bank accounts in Antwerp and Trieste, to dealers and shippers of arms.[17]

To disparage the Hibernian accomplishment is to forget that over $100,000 was raised through the efforts of a handful of volunteer activists and that groups such as Noraid were hardly more impressive in their achievements. Unlike the A.O.H., for whom fund-raising was a secondary activity, Noraid's *raison d'être* was to

Archbishop Boland Personal

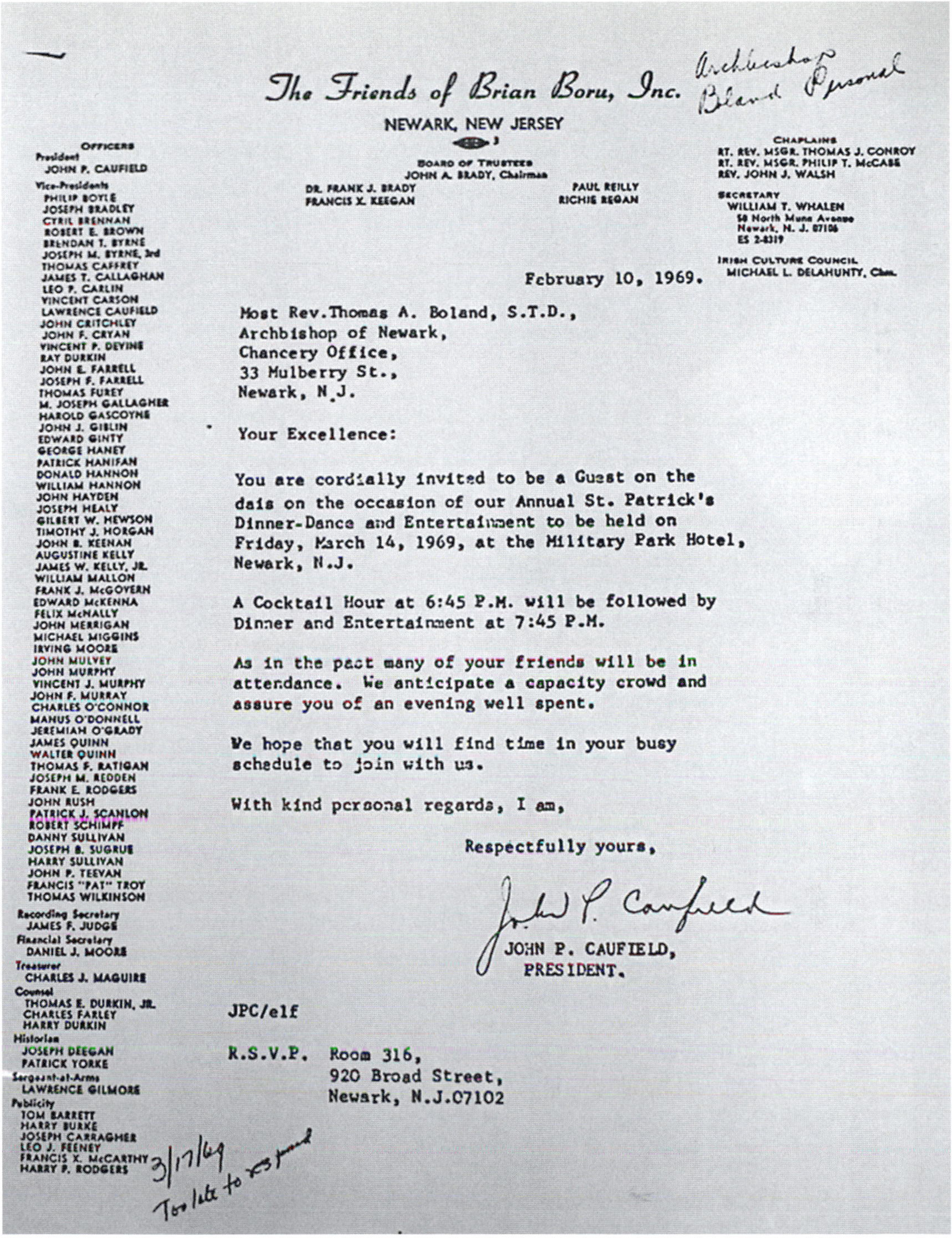

# The Friends of Brian Boru, Inc.

NEWARK, NEW JERSEY

BOARD OF TRUSTEES
JOHN A. BRADY, Chairman
DR. FRANK J. BRADY
FRANCIS X. KEEGAN
PAUL REILLY
RICHIE REGAN

CHAPLAINS
RT. REV. MSGR. THOMAS J. CONROY
RT. REV. MSGR. PHILIP T. McCABE
REV. JOHN J. WALSH

SECRETARY
WILLIAM T. WHALEN
58 North Munn Avenue
Newark, N. J. 07106
ES 2-8319

IRISH CULTURE COUNCIL
MICHAEL L. DELAHUNTY, Chm.

OFFICERS
President
JOHN P. CAUFIELD
Vice-Presidents
PHILIP BOYLE
JOSEPH BRADLEY
CYRIL BRENNAN
ROBERT E. BROWN
BRENDAN T. BYRNE
JOSEPH M. BYRNE, 3rd
THOMAS CAFFREY
JAMES T. CALLAGHAN
LEO P. CARLIN
VINCENT CARSON
LAWRENCE CAUFIELD
JOHN CRITCHLEY
JOHN F. CRYAN
VINCENT P. DEVINE
RAY DURKIN
JOHN E. FARRELL
JOSEPH F. FARRELL
THOMAS FUREY
M. JOSEPH GALLAGHER
HAROLD GASCOYNE
JOHN J. GIBLIN
EDWARD GINTY
GEORGE HANEY
PATRICK HANIFAN
DONALD HANNON
WILLIAM HANNON
JOHN HAYDEN
JOSEPH HEALY
GILBERT W. HEWSON
TIMOTHY J. HORGAN
JOHN B. KEENAN
AUGUSTINE KELLY
JAMES W. KELLY, JR.
WILLIAM MALLON
FRANK J. McGOVERN
EDWARD McKENNA
FELIX McNALLY
JOHN MERRIGAN
MICHAEL MIGGINS
IRVING MOORE
JOHN MULVEY
JOHN MURPHY
VINCENT J. MURPHY
JOHN F. MURRAY
CHARLES O'CONNOR
MANUS O'DONNELL
JEREMIAH O'GRADY
JAMES QUINN
WALTER QUINN
THOMAS F. RATIGAN
JOSEPH M. REDDEN
FRANK E. RODGERS
JOHN RUSH
PATRICK J. SCANLON
ROBERT SCHIMPF
DANNY SULLIVAN
JOSEPH B. SUGRUE
HARRY SULLIVAN
JOHN P. TEEVAN
FRANCIS "PAT" TROY
THOMAS WILKINSON
Recording Secretary
JAMES F. JUDGE
Financial Secretary
DANIEL J. MOORE
Treasurer
CHARLES J. MAGUIRE
Counsel
THOMAS E. DURKIN, JR.
CHARLES FARLEY
HARRY DURKIN
Historian
JOSEPH DEEGAN
PATRICK YORKE
Sergeant-at-Arms
LAWRENCE GILMORE
Publicity
TOM BARRETT
HARRY BURKE
JOSEPH CARRAGHER
LEO J. FEENEY
FRANCIS X. McCARTHY
HARRY P. RODGERS

February 10, 1969.

Most Rev. Thomas A. Boland, S.T.D.,
Archbishop of Newark,
Chancery Office,
33 Mulberry St.,
Newark, N.J.

Your Excellence:

You are cordially invited to be a Guest on the dais on the occasion of our Annual St. Patrick's Dinner-Dance and Entertainment to be held on Friday, March 14, 1969, at the Military Park Hotel, Newark, N.J.

A Cocktail Hour at 6:45 P.M. will be followed by Dinner and Entertainment at 7:45 P.M.

As in the past many of your friends will be in attendance. We anticipate a capacity crowd and assure you of an evening well spent.

We hope that you will find time in your busy schedule to join with us.

With kind personal regards, I am,

Respectfully yours,

John P. Caufield
JOHN P. CAUFIELD,
PRESIDENT.

JPC/elf

R.S.V.P. Room 316,
920 Broad Street,
Newark, N.J.07102

3/17/69
Too late to respond

*Yet another Irish fraternity: Newark's Friends of Brian Boru, 1969. Its letterhead carries the names of many of the leading Irish Americans of the state.*

COURTESY: SETON HALL UNIVERSITY SPECIAL COLLECTIONS CENTER AND UNIVERSITY ARCHIVES

*In December 1970 Governor Richard Hughes was guest of honor at the Saint Patrick's Guard of Honor lunch in Mayfair Farms, West Orange. A veteran Hibernian, Victor Kilkenny, presented him with a commemorative gift. Other guests are pictured below.*

funnel cash to radical republicans. In the first half of 1971, Noraid raised about $16,000; between August 1971 and January 1972, $128,000 was delivered to the IRA; in the first seven months of 1972, $312,700 made its way to Ireland.[18] Through a network of working-class Irish bars, especially in New York, Noraid appealed to a more militant clientele. For all that, it was not vastly more successful than the ad hoc and middle-class Hibernians.

Conclusions are in order. The outbreak of violence in Northern Ireland caught Irish America unprepared, revealing that community's new complexity. A canyon of difference separated Noraid and the Ancient Order of Hibernians. The former was attractive to the "New Irish": second- and third-generation immigrants who preferred political engagement to bourgeois assimilation and who saw Ireland as an outlet for social activism, not social activities. The latter attracted the "Old Irish": integrated, socially consequential, conservative Catholics. They took to the streets once a year to the sound of bagpipes. Noraid supporters were the types to take their Irish holidays in the Bogside or the Falls Road: explorers of the ghetto, collectors of the rubber bullet. Hibernians preferred Connemara or the Ring of Kerry. Neither group understood or cared for the other. Inclined to sentimentalize Ireland, the Hibernians put the sham into shamrock; inclined to brutalize it, Noraid put the rock.

Yet both groups had one thing in common. Their work was done by a tiny number of activists. In 1980 nearly 41 million Americans claimed to be of Irish descent. (A majority of them were Protestants of Scots-Irish lineage.) In no sense did they constitute a political, social, cultural, or religious bloc. There was no Irish vote, only lots of Irish voters. So large and heterogeneous a collection cast its ballots and gave its charity on grounds that had nothing to do with ethnicity. To be Irish was to be so American as not to be Irish at all.

## A CULTURAL HOMECOMING

I T IS BEYOND the scope of this volume to trace Irish American involvement in Northern Ireland in the last three decades.[19] The experience of Delahunty in the early 1970s indicates well enough the limitations of enthusiasm, goodwill, and political innocence. The energy of activists could not conquer general lethargy. Nor could anyone have known that the conflict would prove so intractable. Its seeming endlessness has encouraged most Americans to leave well alone. They have not lacked generosity over the years. Indeed, the depth of their pockets has been extraordinary. But they have come to realize, as have most people, that a solution must be home-grown if it is likely to work. When asked, they remain nationalist in their reading of Irish history, but, like nationalists in Ireland, they do not expect reunification any time soon. Perhaps the conflict has even taught them that unionists have a point of view.

If New Jerseyans find themselves less drawn to Irish politics, some have been attracted anew to Irish culture. One consequence of civil unrest has been closer attention to the customs, traditions, and language of so troubled a land. This cultural curiosity runs along familiar lines. Enjoyment of dancing and music, buying *The Irish Echo,* taking a holiday in Dublin, watching the Rose of Tralee beauty pageant: these are still the best indications of a

*The New Jersey Irish community took an often well informed interest in Irish history but concentrated on the grievance of partition rather than on arguments that might be made on behalf of Ulster Unionism.*

❧

certain kind of Irish American identity. Other expressions of ethnic identity are self-consciously modern: the rock of U2, Bono, and the Pogues, part celebration, part condemnation, of the folk and ballad tradition of the Chieftains, the Clancy Brothers, and the great John McCormack. And for those whose tastes fall somewhere in the middle there is Riverdance: perfect vehicle for a wispy, ethereal, ersatz Celticism, New Age meets Diarmuid and Grainne. All were popular in New Jersey in the closing decade of the twentieth century.

Other features of recent years have been the growth of Irish language classes in New Jersey, the effort to incorporate the Irish famine into a Holocaust curriculum for schools, and the establishment in Morristown of the Irish American Cultural Institute, a national organization of high standing with a major journal and support for scholarly research. All suggest that intelligent alternatives are on offer to the hoarier clichés of and about Irish America.[20]

LEFT: *Dr. James McGlone, founder and artistic director of the Celtic Theatre Company.*
RIGHT: *Joseph McGlone and Mark Fallon, veteran members of the Celtic Theatre Company.*

☘

COURTESY: DR. JAMES McGLONE

Perhaps the most impressive of these cultural explorations has been revived interest in Irish drama. The formation in 1978 of the Celtic Theatre Company under Professor James McGlone of Seton Hall University was significant in this regard. Since its debut with John B. Keane's *The Field* the company has staged over fifty shows, many unperformed in America and underperformed in Ireland, among them the linguistically brilliant works of M. J. Molloy, the clever and compact dramas of George Shiels, and the solidly constructed entertainments of Denis Johnston and Lennox Robinson. These attempts to recover an increasingly hidden theatrical tradition have won praise both in America and in Ireland. "It is rewarding to see American players in action," wrote the drama critic of Ireland's *Cork Examiner* in September 1992, "[and to applaud their efforts] to bridge the cultural gap between here and there."[21] That gap remains substantial, but efforts to narrow it deserve high praise.

# Epilogue

**W**HAT TO MAKE of a history that began in the seventeenth century with the scattered settlements of the Irish Tenth and ends four hundred years later with Noraid, Riverdance, and the Friendly Sons of the Shillelagh? It is a remarkable and complex coming of age, recognition, after long experiment, that New Jersey, not Ireland, is home. The standard way to make sense of it—offered every March at a thousand corned beef dinners—is that the Irish assimilated themselves to a place both hostile yet also of limitless promise. Rebuffed at first, they made the New World their own. Nor is this account false. On the contrary, this book has shown instances of integration at every turn, which speak in small and great ways of the best of America. In thousands of stories we glimpse the fulfillment of the dreams that prompted the immigrant journey. It is right to celebrate such success.

Consider the history of one Richard P. Hughes, a nineteenth-century immigrant whose descendants left their stamp on New Jersey history. Hughes arrived in Baltimore from County Clare in 1856. In 1862 he enlisted on the Union side in the Civil War, more anxious for pay than for glory. After the war he married an Irish-born New Jersey widow, Alice Lynch Duffy, and, consummating a union of another sort, became an American citizen in 1876. (His citizenship papers contain no signature, merely his mark.) Hughes became a father the year he became a citizen. His son Richard lived to typify the upward movement of the Irish of the second gen-

*Saint Patrick's Day advertisement from 1965.*

❧

*Richard P. Hughes (1876–1961), warden of Trenton State Prison in 1916 and mayor of Burlington in 1948, was the son of an unlettered Irish immigrant, also named Richard P. Hughes, and father of Governor Richard Hughes who later served as chief justice of the supreme court of New Jersey.*

❦

*Richard Hughes was a master of old-fashioned political campaigning, not unlike Hubert Humphrey, who once considered him a possible running mate in the 1968 presidential election.*

❦

eration, involving himself in Democratic party politics and serving variously as warden of Trenton State Prison, a state civil commissioner, and mayor of Burlington. The family reached an apogee in his own son, also Richard. That child, born in 1909, graduated from New Jersey Law School, served as Mercer County Democratic chairman, ran unsuccessfully for Congress in 1938, was appointed to the Appellate Division of the Superior Court in 1957, and was elected governor of New Jersey in 1961. Hughes was reelected in 1965 and left office in 1970. An astonishing career was not yet over. His successor, William Cahill—another Irish Catholic, although a Republican—appointed Hughes chief justice of New Jersey's supreme court in 1974.

The journey that brought Richard P. Hughes's grandson to a governor's mansion was rich in irony and historical echo. No one was more alive to those echoes than Hughes himself. Shortly after leaving office he spoke to a Saint Patrick's Day dinner in Massachusetts:

In New Jersey, governors live in an executive mansion called Morven, . . . built in 1701 by the grandfather of Richard Stockton, one of the signers of the Declaration of Independence. [A history of Morven recalls that] "in November 1830 work began on a stretch of canal between Rocky Hill and Trenton. Gangs of Irish laborers made the nights hideous with their drunken brawls." Still another history recalls that it was sometimes necessary for one of the Stocktons . . . to discipline the Irish with a whip. The next time there is any record of anything Irish happening in Morven was Saint Patrick's Day, 1962, when the Hughes clan moved in. And now, another governor of Irish lineage is in residence. How does one say "touché" in Gaelic?[1]

It would be hard to argue with such a genial assessment. Not only was Irishness safe enough to be celebrated: for one day a year it was virtually compulsory. As assorted Friendly Sons donned well-tailored tuxedoes, no one disputed their claim to social arrival. In the middle of March in a hundred hotel lobbies, the sign read "Only Irish Need Apply."

Yet if that was the point of assimilation, it was also its paradox. With everyone Irish for a day, Irishness itself lost its distinctiveness. A category that captured everything captured nothing. Besides, as Hughes himself intuited, too much heritage and not enough history meant the victory of self-satisfaction over self-knowledge. The denizens of Morven did well to remind themselves of humbler origins. The balance of celebration and memory that Hughes understood was and remains a cultural ob-

*Governor Richard Hughes's first inauguration was at once exuberant and suitably deferential to ecclesiastical authority.*

❧

*The incomparable Professor John Sweeney of Seton Hall University, drum major of the Essex Shillelagh Pipes and Drums in 1985. In October 2001 the band marked its thirtieth anniversary by sailing around Manhattan and playing "Amazing Grace" at Ground Zero—an appropriate tribute to the many Irish Americans (firefighters, police officers, and workers at the World Trade Center) who died on September 11, 2001.*

❧

ligation of every Irish American. When the balance is wrong, when celebration becomes forgetful of its own past, the result is wearisome wearing of the green, a surfeit of blather and blarney.

Assimilation may be the most attractive telling of the New Jersey story, but other narratives are also compelling. Indeed, assimilation itself must be understood with greater versatility than some bring to its analysis. It is too simple to imagine, as many do, that acculturation means merely the acceptance by a smaller group of the norms of society as a whole. That offers the easy paradox of social arrival by self-dissolution, a seat at the table but with Irishness left at the door. This is a false dichotomy. It forgets that the Irish themselves helped to determine the social understanding of the polity of which they formed a part. Eighteenth-century Ulster Scots did not conform to "America": they were among those who invented it. Nineteenth-century huddled masses did not accommodate themselves to urban politics: by force of numbers they made urban politics accommodate itself to them. Twentieth-century Hibernians did not compromise their Catholicism: they offered it as a gift to a skeptical, then accepting, nation. The Irish, of course, were Americanized: that was the nature of assimilation. But America, too, was Irishized, given new identity by the continued integration of its constituent parts. Everyone *was* Irish for a day; in less conscious ways, Irish all the time. To identify the separate strains of "Americanness," even to speak of "Irish Americanness," is thus to miss a wider point. "Irish America" was not a mixing and matching of cultures, one encountering the other like two strangers at the altar. Without the first, the second had no meaning. In meeting Ireland, America was meeting itself.

Let it be agreed that there is more to Irish America than its annual clichés. A complex human creation deserves better than to be parodied even if, on occasion, it is prone to parody itself. But let it also be agreed that there is more to America than the practice of cultural co-option. To be sure, national identity has always been easily commoditized, turned into something cheap and cheerful. Tradition, the moment it emerges from Ellis Island, seems to be reduced to trinketry. Even so, if cultures have been co-opted, they have also been preserved. They have been given a life they might otherwise have lost. They have been allowed to breathe free in a new time and place. Naturally they have been transformed by the immigrant journey, but it would be crude to argue they have been traduced.

*Irish American apogee in New Jersey: Governors Brendan Byrne, William Cahill, and Richard Hughes.*

❧

Yet in the ocean crossing a peculiar occurrence may be noticed. What is the nature of the renewed cultural life of diverse America? More than a keeping of faith with the homeland, it is a keeping of faith *for* the homeland. It is an act of custodianship on behalf of cultures unaware of themselves as culturally endangered. This is the real paradox. Memories of Irishness are liable to fade—not in America but in Ireland itself. A modern traveler to the latter place may discover precisely that cultural forgetfulness which is supposed to be the American way—every town with its McDonald's, every home piped with MTV. Coming in search of roots, he finds root beer. Looking for another way of life, he finds only a greener version of his own. Even postcard Ireland—land of lakes and castles, cottages and ceilis—sometimes seems a simulacrum of the Disney original.

Too much may be made of this cultural amnesia. Having tramped through country graveyards, the root-searcher hopes his hotel will have a power shower and CNN. Likewise, Ireland's identity can hardly be said to have disappeared beneath an American wave. Still, preservation of shared memory has its peculiarities. As Galway thirty-somethings watch the latest *Seinfeld,* their New Jersey contemporaries are learning Irish. As the Abbey Theatre in Dublin stages Beckett's *Waiting for Godot,* the Celtic Theatre Company in South Orange offers the world premiere of John B. Keane's *Pishogue.* As Bruce Springsteen sings at Slane, three Irish tenors play Ellis Island. The old observation—that outsiders who settle in Ireland become more Irish than the Irish themselves—needs modification. The Americans are more Irish than the Irish themselves, and the place where it is most pronounced is somewhere off the Garden State Parkway.

These oddities of cultural exchange suggest the richness of a shared but malleable Irishness. They hint, too, at a proper sense of mutual indebtedness. "Irish Americanness" is not a compromise culture, a mixing and matching of one and the other. It is distinctive in itself. It is, moreover, distinctively generous, willing to repay debts to Ireland in characteristically inventive ways. In 1992, the Celtic Theatre Company staged a play written by one of their own, James Moore. Called *Acts and Contrition,* it is set in a Roman Catholic parish in industrial New Jersey in the mid-1980s. The play was performed not only in South Orange but also in Waterford, Clonmel, Cork, and Tralee—places that peopled New Jersey decades and centuries before. "We trust you will hear reflected in our American accents and gesture," wrote director James McGlone in the program for the Irish tour, "in our eastern, big city, contemporary manner, the cultural echoes of our Irish heritage." That heritage was not a legacy to be hoarded. It was, rather, a gift to be handed on and, suitably refashioned, handed back. The echo was historical as well as cultural, reminding us of the point from which we began. New Jersey may have a history as curious as its geography, but Benjamin Franklin had the place only half right. "A barrel tapped at both ends," he called it, draining to New York and Philadelphia, leaving only dregs behind. Not so. The barrel stretched across an ocean and, that way, found not depletion but replenishment.

# Notes

## INTRODUCTION

1. Quoted in Peter O. Wacker, *Land and People: A Cultural Geography of Pre-Industrial New Jersey* (New Brunswick: Rutgers University Press, 1975), 39.
2. James J. Powers, ed., "Faith and Fatherland," in *The Pastoral Letters, Addresses, and Other Writings of Rt. Rev. James A. McFaul, Bishop of Trenton* (Trenton: Diocese of Trenton, 1915), 11–13.

## 1. VARIETIES OF IRISHNESS

1. Quoted in Eoin MacNeill, *Phases of Irish History* (Dublin, 1919), 143–144.
2. Ibid., 160, 229.
3. Quoted in Olivia Robertson, *It's an Old Irish Custom* (London: Dobson and Company, 1953), 53.
4. Quoted in A. J. Otway-Ruthven, *A History of Medieval Ireland* (London: Ernest Benn, 1980), 1, 66.
5. Quoted in John P. Harrington, *The English Traveller in Ireland: Accounts of Ireland and the Irish through Five Centuries* (Dublin: Wolfhound Press, 1991), 31.
6. Ibid., 85, 99.
7. Quoted in Robert James Scally, *The End of Hidden Ireland: Rebellion, Famine, and Emigration* (Oxford and New York: Oxford University Press, 1995), 8.
8. E. Estyn Evans, *Ireland and the Atlantic Heritage: Selected Writings* (Dublin: Lilliput Press, 1996), 32.
9. Quoted in ibid.
10. Ibid., 33–34.
11. See, for example, Tom Paulin, "It's a Small Step from Cosy Nationhood to Ugly Racism," *Sunday Times* (London and Dublin), 16 July 2000, 19.
12. Edward O'Meagher Condon, *The Irish Race in America* (New York, 1887; reissued Ogham House, 1976). Seumus MacManus, *The Story of the Irish Race* (New York: Devin-Adair, 1949), dedication. Rev. A. J. Thebaud, S.J., *The Irish Race in the Past and Present* (New York: P. F. Collier and Son, 1902), 4. Sophie Bryant, *The Genius of the Gael* (London: T. F. Unwin, 1913), 18.
13. *Journal of the American Irish Historical Society* 11 (1911–1912): 131.
14. Michael O'Brien, "The Irish in New Jersey Probate Records," *Journal of the American Irish Historical Society* 27 (1928): 91.

15. Theodore Roosevelt, "Episodes from the Winning of the West," quoted in Billy Kennedy, *The Scots-Irish in the Hills of Tennessee* (Londonderry: Causeway Press, 1995), 29.

16. William Strickland, *Observations on the Agriculture of the United States of America* (London, 1801), quoted in Evans, *Ireland and the Atlantic Heritage*, 98.

17. W. H. Mahony, "The Irish Element in Newark, N.J.," *Journal of the American Irish Historical Society* 21 (1922): 144.

18. Which race, Gen. Robert E. Lee was once asked, make the best soldiers? "The Scots who came to this country by way of Ireland. Because they have all the dash of the Irish in taking up a position and all the stubbornness of the Scots in holding it." Quoted in Kennedy, *Scots-Irish in the Hills of Tennessee*, 30.

19. Bryant, *Genius of the Gael*, 18.

20. Mahony, "Irish Element in Newark," 133.

21. Arthur D. Pierce, "A Governor in Skirts," *Proceedings of the New Jersey Historical Society* 83 (1965): 3.

22. Quoted in Kennedy, *Scots-Irish in the Hills of Tennessee*, 31.

## 2. IRELAND AND NEW JERSEY IN THE SEVENTEENTH CENTURY

1. John Elliott, "Colonial Identity in the Atlantic World," in *Colonial Identity in the Atlantic World,* ed. Nicholas Canny and Anthony Pagden (Princeton: Princeton University Press, 1987), 4.

2. K. G. Davies, *The North Atlantic World in the Seventeenth Century* (Minneapolis: University of Minnesota Press, 1974), 15.

3. Ibid., 12.

4. Quoted in Nicholas Canny, "Identity Formation in Ireland: The Emergence of the Anglo-Irish," in Canny and Pagden, *Colonial Identity in the Atlantic World*, 168, 173.

5. Davies, *North Atlantic World*, 36.

6. Ibid., 139.

7. Maxine Lurie, Introduction, in *New Jersey: An Anthology,* ed. Lurie (Newark: New Jersey Historical Society, 1994), 3.

8. Ibid., 4.

9. Davies, *North Atlantic World,* 71.

10. W. H. Mahony, "The Irish Element in Newark, N.J.," *Journal of the American Irish Historical Society* 21 (1922): 133.

11. W. H. Mahony, "Some Seventeenth-Century Irish Colonists in New Jersey," *Journal of the American Irish Historical Society* 26 (1927): 243–247.

12. Cf. Edward MacLysaght, *The Surnames of Ireland* (Dublin: Irish Academic Press, 1997), 306.

13. Mahony, "Some Seventeenth-Century Irish Colonists," 247.

14. See, for example, Norman Vance, "Celts, Carthaginians, and Constitutions: Anglo-Irish Literary Relations, 1780–1820," *Irish Historical Studies* 22, no. 87 (March 1981): 216–238.

15. Davies, *North Atlantic World,* 136.

16. Sharp quoted in "History of Newton, Gloucester County, N.J.," *Journal of the American Irish Historical Society* 8 (1908–1909): 207 ("to a very good degree of living" is his); Joseph John Kelly, *The Irish in Camden County* (Camden: Camden County Historical Society, 1984), 1–2.

17. Philip E. Mackey, ed., *A Gentleman of Much Promise: The Diary of Isaac Mickle, 1837–1845* (Philadelphia: University of Pennsylvania Press, 1977), 1:xiii.

18. See Chapter Four, p. 81.

19. Richard P. McCormick, *New Jersey from Colony to State* (Princeton: Princeton University Press, 1964), 47.

20. Benedict, *History of the Baptists,* quoted in Milton J. Hoffman, "Religion in Colonial New Jersey," in *History of New Jersey,* ed. Irving Kull (New York: American Historical Society, 1930), 1:355.

21. "Cumberland County, N.J.," *Journal of the American Irish Historical Society* 8 (1908–1909): 209.

22. Michael O'Brien, "Some Early Irish Settlers and Schoolmasters in New Jersey," *Journal of the American Irish Historical Society* 11 (1911–1912): 123.

23. Michael O'Brien, "The Irish in New Jersey Probate Records," *Journal of the American Irish Historical Society* 27 (1928): 77, 81, 92, 93.

24. McCormick, *New Jersey from Colony to State,* 25.

25. O'Brien, "Irish in New Jersey Probate Records," 124.


### 3. ULSTER, IRELAND, AND NEW JERSEY IN THE EIGHTEENTH CENTURY

1. Jonathan Bardon, *A Shorter Illustrated History of Ulster* (Belfast: Blackstaff Press, 1996), 94.

2. R. J. Dickson, *Ulster Emigration to Colonial America, 1718–1775* (Belfast: Ulster Historical Foundation, 1966, 1988), 30.

3. Ibid., 28.

4. Jonathan Bardon, *A History of Ulster* (Belfast: Blackstaff Press, 1992), 175, 176.

5. Bardon, *Shorter Illustrated History of Ulster,* 95.

6. Ibid., 93.

7. Dickson, *Ulster Emigration to Colonial America,* 35.

8. Ibid.

9. Bardon, *Shorter Illustrated History of Ulster,* 94.

10. Quoted in E. M. Johnston-Liik, "The Development of the Ulster-Scottish Connection," in *Cultural Traditions in Northern Ireland: Varieties of Scottishness,* ed. John Erskine and Gordon Lucy (Belfast: Institute of Irish Studies, 1997), 30.

11. Dickson, *Ulster Emigration to Colonial America,* 5.

12. Bardon, *Shorter Illustrated History of Ulster,* 94.

13. Dickson, *Ulster Emigration to Colonial America,* 38.

14. Ibid., 47.

15. Quoted in Johnston-Liik, "Development of the Ulster-Scottish Connection," 34.

16. E. Estyn Evans, *Ireland and the Atlantic Heritage* (Dublin: Lilliput Press, 1996), 101.

17. Ibid.

18. Theodore Roosevelt, *Episodes from the Winning of the West,* quoted in Billy Kennedy, *The Scots-Irish in the Hills of Tennessee* (Londonderry: Causeway Press, 1995), 29.

19. W. H. Mahony, "The Irish Element in Newark, N.J.," *Journal of the American Irish Historical Society* 21 (1922): 138.

20. Arnold Toynbee, *A Study of History* (London and New York: Oxford University Press, 1948), 302, 311.

21. Evans, *Ireland and the Atlantic Heritage,* 100.

22. Michael Zuckerman, "Identity in British America: Unease in Eden," in *Colonial Identity in the Atlantic World,* ed. Nicholas Canny and Anthony Pagden (Princeton: Princeton University Press, 1987), 129.

23. John E. Pomfret, *Colonial New Jersey: A History* (New York: Scribner, 1973), 204.

24. Ibid.

25. Theodore Thayer, *Colonial and Revolutionary Morris County* (Morristown: Morris County Heritage Commission, 1975), 87.

26. William Dunlap, "History of the Arts of Design," quoted in *Journal of the American Irish Historical Society* 8 (1908–1909): 203.

27. Carl Magnus Anderson, "Pastor Wrangel's Trip to the Shore," *New Jersey History* 87 (1969): 24.

28. Ibid., 24–25.

29. Zuckerman, "Identity in British America," 129.

30. *New Jersey in the Revolution: Newspaper Extracts*, 1776, 32.

31. Thayer, *Colonial and Revolutionary Morris County*, 107.

32. *New Jersey in the Revolution: Newspaper Extracts*, 1776, 108.

33. Ibid., 85.

34. Ibid., 110.

35. Ibid., 139.

36. Ibid., 539.

37. *New Jersey in the Revolution: Newspaper Extracts*, 1777, 288.

38. Thayer, *Colonial and Revolutionary Morris County*, 107.

39. Michael O'Brien, "Some Early Irish Settlers and Schoolmasters in New Jersey," *Journal of the American Irish Historical Society* 11 (1911–1912): 126–127.

40. Charles E. Baker, " 'The world was all before me': James Hering, Village Schoolmaster of 1810," *Proceedings of the New Jersey Historical Society* 72 (1954): 11.

41. Louise Bird Ralston, "The Old School House in Mount Holly," *Proceedings of the New Jersey Historical Society* 72 (1954): 38.

42. James P. Snell, *History of Sussex and Warren Counties, New Jersey* (Philadelphia, 1881) quoted in O'Brien, "Some Early Irish Settlers and Schoolmasters," 127.

43. O'Brien, "Early Irish Settlers and Schoolmasters," 129.

44. "Teachers named Flannery and Welsh are remembered by the older people [of East Millstone] as being here about the opening of the nineteenth century" (Snell, quoted in O'Brien, "Early Irish Settlers and Schoolmasters," 128). William Dougherty was the first teacher in the Mountain Grove District; Oliver Dunleavy taught in Hunterdon County; a "Master Fitzpatrick" taught at Larison's Corners; Francis Finigan taught at the Bethlehem Presbyterian Church school (O'Brien, "Early Irish Settlers and Schoolmasters," 129).

45. Richard Webster, *A History of the Presbyterian Church in America . . . with biographical sketches of its early ministers* (Philadelphia, 1857), quoted in Broadus Mitchell, "The Man Who Discovered Hamilton," *Proceedings of the New Jersey Historical Society* 69 (1951): 93.

46. Mitchell, "Man Who Discovered Hamilton," 104.

47. See, for example, Howard Harris, " 'The Eagle to Watch and the Harp to Tune the Nation': Irish Immigrants, Politics, and Early Industrialization in Paterson, New Jersey, 1824–1838," *Journal of Social History* 23 (spring 1990): 575–597.

48. W.E.H. Lecky, *A History of Ireland in the Eighteenth Century*, 1:167–168, quoted in John Brady and Patrick Corish, *The Church under the Penal Code* (Dublin: Gill and Macmillan, 1971), 25.

49. See Cathaldus Giblin, O.F.M, *Irish Exiles in Catholic Europe* (Dublin: Gill and Macmillan, 1971), 1.

50. John Joseph Kelly, *The Irish in Camden County* (Camden: Camden County Historical Society, 1984), 5–6.

51. Joseph Mahoney and Peter Wosh, eds., *The Diocesan Journal of Michael Augustine Corrigan, Bishop of Newark, 1872–1880* (Newark: New Jersey Historial Society, 1987), 181.

52. For this paragraph, see Raymond Kupke's excellent *Living Stones: A History of the Diocese of Paterson* (Clifton, NJ: Diocese of Paterson, 1987), 9–24.

53. Ibid., 24.

54. W. H. Mahony, "Irish Footsteps in New Jersey Sands," *Journal of the American Irish Historical Society* 26 (1927): 250–254.

55. E. R. Walker et al., *A History of Trenton, 1679–1929* (Princeton: Princeton University Press, 1929), 2: 923.

56. *New Jersey in the Revolution: Newspaper Extracts*, 1778, 384.

57. *New Jersey in the Revolution: Newspaper Extracts*, 1776, 554.

58. Thomas Purvis, "The European Origins of New Jersey's Eighteenth-Century Population," *New Jersey History* 100 (1982): 24.

59. Reverend William Steel Dickson, quoted in R. B. McDowell, *Irish Public Opinion, 1750–1800* (London: Faber & Faber, 1944), 72.

60. *New Jersey in the Revolution: Newspaper Extracts*, 1780, 237.

61. Thayer, *Colonial and Revolutionary Morris County*, 87.

62. Thatcher, "Military Journal 1779–80," *Journal of the American Irish Historical Society* 8 (1908–1909): 208.

63. Thayer, *Colonial and Revolutionary Morris County*, 244.

64. *New Jersey in the Revolution: Newspaper Extracts*, 1776, 78.

65. *New Jersey in the Revolution: Newspaper Extracts*, 1777, 345.

66. Ibid., 431.

67. A.V.D. Honeyman, "An Unwritten Account of a Spy of Washington," *New Jersey History* 85 (1967): 219.

68. Thayer, *Colonial and Revolutionary Morris County*, 194.

69. *New Jersey in the Revolution: Newspaper Extracts*, 1777, 316.

70. Larry Gerlach, "Loyalist Studies," *New Jersey History* 95 (1977): 69–84.

71. Marianne Elliott, *Wolfe Tone: Prophet of Irish Independence* (New Haven: Yale University Press, 1989), 267, 274.

## 4. THE NINETEENTH-CENTURY EXPERIENCE

1. Walter Cox, *Advice to Emigrants, or Observations Made during a Nine Months' Residence in the Middle States of the American Union* (Dublin, 1802), in MacManus Collection, Seton Hall University, 1, 3, 18–19.

2. Quoted in J. R. Pole, "Suffrage in New Jersey, 1790–1807," *Proceedings of the New Jersey Historical Society* 71 (1953): 50.

3. Howard Harris, " 'Towns-People and Country People': The Acquakanonk Dutch and the Rise of Industry in Paterson, New Jersey, 1793–1831," *New Jersey History* 106 (1988): 35, 37–38.

4. Raymond Kupke, *Living Stones: A History of the Catholic Church in the Diocese of Paterson* (Clifton, NJ: Diocese of Paterson, 1987), 42.

5. Harris, "Towns-People and Country People," 38–39.

6. Howard Harris, " 'The Eagle to Watch and the Harp to Tune': Irish Immigrants, Politics, and Early Industrialization in Paterson, New Jersey," *Journal of Social History* 23 (spring 1990): 590.

7. Quoted in James Roosevelt Bayley Papers, Record Group 1, 1.31, folio 68 (Archdiocese of Newark Archives).

8. *Newark Eagle,* 24 March 1840.

9. *Newark Sentinel,* 21 November 1843.

10. Rev. Thomas Cooke Middleton, "A New Jersey Sea-side Mission," *Records of the American Catholic Historical Society of Philadelphia* 17 (1906): 148; William McMahon, *A History of Our Lady Star of the Sea Parish, Atlantic City* (Egg Harbor: Laureate Press, 1970),17.

11. Quoted in Maxine Lurie, Introduction, in *New Jersey: An Anthology,* ed. Lurie (Newark: New Jersey Historical Society, 1994), 6.

12. Quoted in Robert Kee, *The Green Flag,* vol. 1: *The Most Distressful Country* (New York: Delacourte Press, 1972), 170.

13. Quoted in Robert James Scally, *The End of Hidden Ireland: Rebellion, Famine, and Emigration* (Oxford and New York: Oxford University Press, 1995), 9, 10.

14. Quoted in Kee, *Green Flag,* 170.

15. Quoted in ibid., 172.

16. Quoted in Cecil Woodham Smith, *The Great Hunger: Ireland, 1845–1849* (New York: Harper & Row, 1962), 96.

17. Quoted in ibid., 24.

18. Quoted in ibid., 89

19. Peter Gray, *The Irish Famine* (New York: Harry N. Abrams, 1995), 43.

20. Christine Kinealy, *A Death-Dealing Famine: The Great Hunger in Ireland* (London and Chicago: Pluto Press, 1997), 60.

21. *Northern Whig,* 17 October 1846.

22. Quoted in Smith, *Great Hunger,* 159.

23. Kinealy, *Death-Dealing Famine,* 94.

24. Quoted in ibid., flyleaf.

25. Quoted in ibid., 60.

26. Routh, Clanricarde, and Trevelyan, all quoted ibid., 4.

27. Quoted in Smith, *Great Hunger,* 193.

28. Maire Ni Grianna, quoted in ibid., 155.

29. Two Acts of Congress of February and March 1847 required fourteen feet of deck space per passenger in immigrant ships. Most did not conform, and for a time numbers dropped off.

30. Quoted in Gray, *Irish Famine,* 43.

31. Alien Passengers and Paupers, Commonwealth of Massachusetts, Senate No. 46, 1848, quoted in Terry Coleman, *Passage to America* (London: Pimlico, 1972), 60.

32. Quoted in ibid., 41.

33. Carl D. Hinrichsen, "The History of the Diocese of Newark, 1873–1901" (Ph.D. diss., Catholic University of America, 1962), 421.

34. *Newark Sentinel,* 16 February 1847.

35. *Newark Sentinel,* 2 and 9 March 1847.

36. Other cities contributed as follows: New York $170,150; Boston $45,000; Baltimore $40,000; Philadelphia $50,000; New Orleans $25,000; Albany $25,000; Washington $5,000. See Christine Kinealy, *This Great Calamity: The Irish Famine, 1845–1852* (Dublin: Gill and Macmillan, 1994), 164.

37. Philip E. Mackey, ed., *A Gentleman of Much Promise: The Diary of Isaac Mickle, 1837–1845* (Philadelphia: University of Pennsylvania Press, 1977), 1:39, 132, 207, 2:445.

38. James Roosevelt Bayley Papers, Record Group 1, 1.71, Newark Diocesan Scrap Book, 1855–1872 (Archdiocese of Newark Archives).

39. Edwin V. Sullivan, "An Annotated Copy of the Diary of Bishop James Roosevelt Bayley,

First Bishop of Newark, New Jersey, 1853–1872" (Ph.D. diss., University of Ottawa, 1956), 1:22.

40. Ibid., 2:68, 74.
41. *Newark Sentinel*, 27 October 1846.
42. Bishop James Roosevelt Bayley Papers, Record Group 1, 1.71, Newark Diocesan Scrapbook, 1855–1872 (Archdiocese of Newark Archives).
43. The following discussion relies on Douglas V. Shaw, "Ethnicity, Politics, and Murder: The Hanging of James P. Donnelly," *New Jersey History* 109 (1991): 37–55. Quoted here, 39.
44. Ibid., 47.
45. Ibid., 45.
46. Quoted in ibid., 43.
47. Quoted in ibid., 45.
48. Quoted in ibid., 50.
49. Quoted in ibid., 51.
50. Ibid.
51. Ibid., 52.
52. The discussion of Mehegan and the Sisters of Charity relies on Sister Mary Agnes Sharkey, *The New Jersey Sisters of Charity and Mother Mary Xavier Mehegan: The Story of Seventy-five Years* (New York: Longmans, Green, 1933). Quoted here, 1:24.
53. Ibid., 273.
54. Ibid., 77.
55. Ibid., 89.
56. Ibid., 91.
57. Ibid., 157.
58. Ibid., 162.
59. Ibid., 229.
60. Ibid.
61. Ibid., 236.
62. Ibid., 234.

## 5. A TRICKLE BECOMES A FLOOD

1. Edwin V. Sullivan, "An Annotated Copy of the Diary of Bishop James Roosevelt Bayley, First Bishop of Newark, New Jersey, 1853–1872" (Ph.D. diss., University of Ottawa, 1956), 2:19.
2. Ibid., 1:50.
3. Quoted in Carl D. Hinrichsen, "The History of the Diocese of Newark, 1873–1901" (Ph.D. diss., Catholic University of America, 1962), 189.
4. Rev. Patrick Byrne to Bishop Michael Corrigan, 9 August 1874, Record Group 12, ADN 10–89, Other Bishops, Box 1 of 2 (Archdiocese of Newark Archives).
5. See p. 116.
6. Bishop Bernard McQuaid to Bishop Michael Corrigan, 22 September 1874, Record Group 12, ADN 10–89, Other Bishops, Box 1 of 2 (Archdiocese of Newark Archives).
7. Douglas V. Shaw, "Political Leadership in the Industrial City: Irish Development and Nativist Response in Jersey City," in *Immigrants in Industrial America, 1850–1920*, ed. Richard Ehrlich (Charlottesville: University of Virginia Press, 1977), 89.
8. Quoted in ibid., 89–90.

9. William Gillette, *Jersey Blue: Civil War Politics in New Jersey, 1854–1865* (New Brunswick: Rutgers University Press, 1994), 294.

10. Quoted in ibid., 242.

11. Space precludes an exhaustive account of the Irish contribution to the war. As a flavor of it, however, the example of Trenton is worth recording. By the middle of the century the Irish population of the town had become quite substantial, especially in the Fourth Ward. Notable among the Irish soldiery were Hugh McQuade, captain of the Irish Volunteers, organized in 1852; John Travers, captain of the Sarsfield Guard, organized in 1854; Lawrence Farrell, Robert Johnston; James Tallon, Walter McCormick, John Leary, Edward Mullen, Michael Hurley, John Walsh. See E. R. Walker et al., *A History of Trenton, 1679–1929* (Princeton: Princeton University Press, 1929), 2: 924.

12. Richard A. Hogarty, "The Political Apprenticeship of Leon Abbett," *New Jersey History* 3, nos. 1–2 (1993): 1.

13. Ibid., 6.

14. Ibid.

15. Quoted in Gillette, *Jersey Blue*, 288.

16. Ibid., 288, 294.

17. James Roosevelt Bayley Papers, Record Group 1, 1.71, Newark Diocesan Scrapbook, 1855–1872 (Archdiocese of Newark Archives).

18. Ibid.

19. Sullivan, "Annotated Copy of the Diary of Bishop James Roosevelt Bayley," 1:149, 2:58.

20. Ibid., 2: 19.

21. See Rt. Rev. John J. Dougherty, ed., *The Bishops of Newark, 1853–1978* (South Orange: Seton Hall University Press, 1978), 28.

22. Joseph Mahoney and Peter Wosh, eds., *The Diocesan Journal of Michael Augustine Corrigan, Bishop of Newark, 1872–1880* (Newark: New Jersey Historical Society, 1987), 283.

23. Ibid., 136.

24. Ibid., 15.

25. Ibid.

26. For all Corrigan quotations in this paragraph, see Carl D. Hinrichsen, "The History of the Diocese of Newark, 1873–1901" (Ph.D. diss., Catholic University of America, 1962), 121 ff.

27. Quoted in Mahoney and Wosh, *Diocesan Journal of Michael Augustine Corrigan*, 284.

28. Quoted in ibid., 88.

29. Quoted in ibid., 102.

30. Bishop John J. O'Connor Papers, Record Group 4, 4.34, Minutes of the Annual Meeting of the Archbishops of the United States, 1904 (Archdiocese of Newark Archives).

31. James Roosevelt Bayley Papers, Record Group 1, 1.51 (Archdiocese of Newark Archives).

32. James Roosevelt Bayley Papers, Record Group 1, 1.51/2 (Archdiocese of Newark Archives).

33. Ibid.

34. Winand Wigger Papers, Record Group 3, 3.36, Box 7, General and Clerical Correspondence (Archdiocese of Newark Archives).

35. Winand Wigger Papers, Record Group 3, 3.36, Box 5, General and Clerical Correspondence (Archdiocese of Newark Archives).

36. Winand Wigger Papers, Record Group 3, 3.36, Box 8, General and Clerical Correspondence (Archdiocese of Newark Archives).

37. See, for example, Hinrichsen, "History of the Diocese of Newark," 295.

38. Winand Wigger Papers, Record Group 3, 3.36, Box 10, General and Clerical Correspondence (Archdiocese of Newark Archives).

39. Hinrichsen, "History of the Diocese of Newark," 298.

40. In his impressive *Century of Catholicism: The History of the Church of the Immaculate Conception, Montclair, New Jersey* (Newark: Washington Irving Publishing, 1957), George Reilly offered a generous assessment: Father Mendl's "birthday was March 17, the Feast Day of St. Patrick. . . . His career in Montclair was to demonstrate his understanding [of] the Irish and their veneration of Eire's patron saint" (24–25).

## 6. THE TWENTIETH CENTURY: FROM HISTORY TO HERITAGE

1. Henry R. Schnitzer, "A Glimpse of Bayonne in the 1880s," *Proceedings of the New Jersey Historical Society* 80 (1962): 248.

2. Quoted in Jeffrey L. Patrick, "Becoming a Soldier at Camp Dix: The World War I Letters of Private William Lehman," *New Jersey History* 114, nos. 1–2 (spring/summer 1996): 71.

3. Ransom E. Noble, "Four Wilson Campaign Speeches," *Proceedings of the New Jersey Historical Society* 77, no. 2 (April 1959): 88.

4. David Steven Cohen, ed., *America, the Dream of My Life: Selections from the Federal Writers' Project's New Jersey Ethnic Survey* (New Brunswick: Rutgers University Press, 1990), 35.

5. Ibid., 39.

6. Ibid., 36.

7. Ibid., 38.

8. S. H. Popper, "New Tensions in Old Newark: Germanic Influence and the Sabbath Observance Controversy, 1870–1910," *Proceedings of the New Jersey Historical Society* 70 (1952): 122.

9. Ibid., 123 ff.

10. Ibid., 129.

11. When established in 1853 the diocese covered the entire state. In 1881 a separate Diocese of Trenton was created.

12. For this paragraph, see Carl D. Hinrichsen, "The History of the Diocese of Newark, 1873–1901" (Ph.D. diss., Catholic University of America, 1962), 294, 303.

13. *New York Freeman's Journal and Catholic Register*, 29 October 1892.

14. Edwin V. Sullivan, "An Annotated Copy of the Diary of Bishop James Roosevelt Bayley, First Bishop of Newark, New Jersey, 1853–1872" (Ph.D. diss., University of Ottawa, 1956), 2: 226, 253.

15. *New York Freeman's Journal and Catholic Register*, 29 October 1892.

16. *New York Freeman's Journal and Catholic Register*, 12 November 1892.

17. *New York Freeman's Journal and Catholic Register*, 29 October 1892.

18. Joseph J. Kelly, *The Irish in Camden County* (Camden: Privately printed, 1984), 16.

19. Ibid.

20. George Hills, *The Ku Klux Klan of the Present Day* (New York: Privately printed, 1923), 5.

21. J. L. Cushing to Bishop John J. O'Connor, O'Connor Papers, Record Group 4, 4.33, Clerical and General Correspondence, 1903, A–C (Archdiocese of Newark Archives).

22. Bishop John J. O'Connor Papers, Record Group 4, 4.41, "20th Anniversary of Episcopate: Thoughts on Social Movements," typescript memorandum (Archdiocese of Newark Archives).

23. Cohen, *America, the Dream of My Life,* 43.

24. Ibid.

25. Ibid., 44.

26. Ibid., 40.

27. Ibid., 45.

28. John D. Buenker, "Urban, New-Stock Liberalism, and Progressive Reform in New Jersey," *New Jersey History* 87 (1969): 83.

29. Kelly, *Irish in Camden*, 15.

30. Buenker, "Urban, New-Stock Liberalism, and Progressive Reform," 81.

31. For this paragraph, see Eugene Tobin, "The Progressive as Humanitarian: Jersey City's Struggle for Social Justice, 1890–1917," *New Jersey History* 98 (1975): 79, 88.

32. The efforts of Irish-born nuns to cope with poverty and illiteracy are worth a volume in their own right. We have noticed already the work of Mother Mary Xavier Mehegan and her followers in the world of education. Equally notable was Margaret Anna Cusack ("the Nun of Kenmare"), founder of the Sisters of Saint Joseph of Peace. Born to a respectable Protestant family in Dublin in 1829, she converted to Catholicism in 1858 and entered the Sisters of the Poor Clares in Newry, County Down, the following year. An early agitator for women's voting and property rights, she clashed with English and Irish ecclesiastical authorities to such an extent that she left for the United States in 1884. Receiving a warmer welcome from Bishop Wigger of Newark than from Archbishop Corrigan of New York, she established a principal house for her congregation at 235 Grove Street, Jersey City, and another at 25 Grand Street, Jersey City. Later the congregation purchased property at Englewood Cliffs, New Jersey. The chief mission was the education of poor and, especially, blind children. See Dorothy A. Vidulich, *Peace Pays a Price: A Study of Margaret Anna Cusack, the Nun of Kenmare* (Englewood Cliffs, NJ: Center for Peace and Justice, 1975).

33. Richard P. Connors, *A Cycle of Power* (Metuchen, NJ: Scarecrow Press, 1971), 73.

34. Ibid., 57.

35. See Bishop John J. O'Connor Papers, Record Group 4, 4.41 "20th Anniversary of Episcopate: Thoughts on Social Movements," typescript memorandum (Archdiocese of Newark Archives).

36. Connors, *Cycle of Power*, 94.

37. James P. Moran, "The Jersey City Municipal Election of 1929" (M.A. thesis, Seton Hall University, 1963), 18–19.

38. Ibid., 20.

39. Archbishop Thomas J. Walsh Papers, Record Group 5, ADN 6–89, 1926–1932, Box 2 of 2, File M (Archdiocese of Newark Archives).

40. Connors, *Cycle of Power*, 160.

41. The following discussion relies on LeRoy McWilliams with Jim Bishop, *Parish Priest* (New York: McGraw-Hill, 1953); quoted here, 234, 235.

42. Ibid., 210.

43. Ibid., 2.

44. Ibid., esp. 13, 133, 114.

45. Ibid., esp. 166, 39, 45.

46. Ibid., esp. 60–61, 75.

47. Ibid., 5–6.

48. Ibid., 4.

49. Ibid., 158.

50. Ibid., 149.

51. Ibid., 123.

52. Ibid., 117, 122, 91.

53. Ibid., 83.

54. Ibid., 160.

55. Ibid.

56. Ibid., 153.

57. The information on the Degnans in the following paragraphs comes from the privately printed *Erin to New Jersey—A Family Saga*, an excellent history of the Degnans by Joe Rush, one of their number.

## 7. THE END OF THE JOURNEY

1. Archbishop Thomas J. Walsh Papers, Record Group 5, ADN 1–89, Clerical and General Correspondence, 1931–1952, Box 1 of 3 (Archdiocese of Newark Archives).

2. Archbishop Thomas J. Walsh Papers, Record Group 5, ADN 8–88, Series I: Subject Files N–Z (Archdiocese of Newark Archives).

3. See T. F. McGrath, *History of the Ancient Order of Hibernians: From the Earliest Period to the Joint National Convention at Trenton, New Jersey* (Cleveland, Ohio: Privately printed, 1899). See also Rev. Walter Leahy, *The Diocese of Trenton* (Princeton: Princeton University Press, n.d.), 399.

4. *Hudson County Hibernian*, January 1959, 3, in Record Group 6, Archbishop Thomas Boland Papers, ADN 17–89, Box 1 of 11 (Archdiocese of Newark Archives).

5. *National Hibernian Digest*, May–June 1960, 1, 3.

6. *New Jersey Hibernian*, September–October 1965, 2.

7. Quoted in *New Jersey Hibernian*, April 1960, 2.

8. Andrew J. Wilson, *Irish America and the Ulster Conflict, 1968–1995* (Washington, DC: Catholic University of America Press, 1995), 14.

9. Ibid., 15.

10. The degree to which this discrimination was state sponsored is controversial. See Dermot Quinn, *Understanding Northern Ireland* (Manchester: Baseline Books, 1993).

11. Wilson, *Irish America and the Ulster Conflict*, 33, 35.

12. *New Jersey Hibernian*, October–December 1969.

13. Archbishop Thomas Boland Papers, Record Group 6, ADN 17–89, Box 1 of 11, Inactive Organizations (Archdiocese of Newark Archives).

14. Archbishop Thomas Boland Papers, Record Group 6, ADN 17–89, Box 1 of 11, Inactive Organizations (Archdiocese of Newark Archives).

15. Quoted in Jack Anderson, "Ulster Aid Funds Are Spent on Arms," *Star-Ledger* (Newark), 12 March 1970.

16. Quoted in Wilson, *Irish America and the Ulster Conflict*, 45.

17. See Anderson, "Ulster Aid Funds Are Spent on Arms."

18. Wilson, *Irish America and the Ulster Conflict*, 70.

19. Easily the best account is Andrew Wilson's *Irish America and the Ulster Conflict*.

20. The Holocaust curriculum is controversial. For arguments pro and contra see *New York Times*, 21 March 2001, B7.

21. *Cork Examiner*, 9 September 1992.

## EPILOGUE

1. Typescript of speech supplied to the author by Professor Thomas Hughes (son of Governor Hughes), Kalamazoo Valley Community College, Kalamazoo, MI.

# Index

Farren, Bishop Neil, of Derry, 188
Fedigan, the Reverend John, 65
Fenians and Fenianism, 75, 112, 118–119, 122
Finley, the Reverend Samuel, 42
*Finnigan's Fortune* (play), 131
Fitzgerald, Thomas, 127
Flannery, Michael, 196
Fleming, Thomas, 33
Flemington, 33, 37
Flood, Edward, 57
Flood, Henry, 47
Florio, Governor James, 170
Flynn, Paul, 99
Ford, Jacob, 38
Franklin, Benjamin, 208
Friendly Sons of Saint Patrick of the Oranges, 129
Friends of Brian Boru, 197

Gallagher, the Reverend Michael, 64
Galway (Ireland), 11
Garrigan, Edward, 98
George III, king, 46
Gerald of Wales, 9
Gilliland, William, 38
Gladstone, William Ewart, proposes Home Rule for Ireland, 111
Glendalough (County Wicklow, Ireland), 13
Gloucester County, 22, 25, 45
Golden, William, 26
Gordon, Lord Adam, 14
Gouganbarra (County Cork, Ireland), 84
Gourley, William B., 136
Graham, Sir James, 73
Grattan, Henry, 47
Griffith, William, complains of "swarms" of Irish in 1799, 55–56, 66

Hackett, Samuel, 33
Hackettstown, 33
Hague, Mayor Frank, of Jersey City, 151–160
Hakluyt, Richard, 18
Hamilton, Alexander, 41
Hennessy, James, 79
Hinrichsen, Carl, 126
Hodnett, John Pope, organizes Hibernians in Jersey City, 112
Honeyman, John, 51–52

Hudson County, 88, 105, 108; Irish votes in 1958 in, 156; Saint Patrick's Day in 1865 in, 112
Hughes, Governor Richard J., 184, 188, 198, 204–205, 207
Hughes, Richard P. (father), 203; (son), 203–204
Hughes, William, 135
Hume, John, 191, 193
Hunter, Richard, 22
Hunterdon County, 34, 37
Hyde, Edward, Lord Cornbury, 3, 4, 15

Irish Association of Newark (1843), 63
Irish Immigrant Society of New York, 77
Irish National League, 111
"Irish Road," between Gloucester and Salem, 24
"Irish Tenth," 24–25

Jackson, President Andrew, 60
Jersey City: election of 1864 in, 109–110; ethnic mixture in, 1880–1910, 152; nineteenth-century Irish in, 62, 98; Our Lady of Victories Parish in, 152; political aspects of Saint Patrick's Day in, 113; politics of, in mid-nineteenth century, 104–106; riot in 1857 in, 99; Saint Aedan's Parish in, 153–154; Saint Michael's Parish in, 158, 159–167
Johnson, President Lyndon B., 180
Joyce, James, 127

Kane, Thomas, 45
Keach, the Reverend Elias, 26
Kean, Governor Thomas, 170
Keane, John B., 202, 207
Kearney, Brendan, 97
Kearney, Michael, 45
Kelly, William, 23
Kelsey, the Reverend Robert, 26
Kennedy, President John F., 183, 184
Kenny, John, 158
Kerry (Ireland), 11
Kilkenny, Victor, 198
Killeen, the Reverend Thomas, 100–101; anti-German feeling of, 144–145
King, Archbishop William, of Dublin, 29, 30
Kinkead, Eugene, 174

## ABOUT THE AUTHOR

Dermot Quinn is a professor of history at Seton Hall University. Educated at Trinity College, Dublin, and New College, Oxford, he is author of *Patronage and Piety: English Roman Catholics and Politics, 1850–1900* (1993) and *Understanding Northern Ireland* (1993), as well as many articles and reviews.